Gary MacEoin

REVOLUTION
NEXT DOOR

REVOLUTION NEXT DOOR

Latin America in the 1970s

GARY MacEOIN

HOLT, RINEHART AND WINSTON
New York   Chicago   San Francisco

Library of Congress Catalog Card Number: FO-138891
First Edition

Designer: Berry Eitel
SBN: 03-086002-4
Printed in the United States of America

For my grandchildren,
Mary Kathryn and Gary,
and for all their contemporaries
whose survival hangs on the
success of the revolution
here and next door

CONTENTS

REVOLUTION
NEXT DOOR

1

A DECADE OF
DEVELOPMENT

"If this is what one decade of development does for us, spare us from another," said Joel Gajardo. The speaker was a young Latin American of the new breed, with receding hairline, trimmed beard, penetrating look and revolutionary commitment. Graduate of a Chilean university, he has a doctorate from a leading United States institution. He was referring to the promise the major industrial countries had made at the United Nations ten years earlier to concentrate their efforts in the 1960s on promoting the progress of the world's backward countries, and their recent resolution in favor of a second "decade of development" in the 1970s.

"The 1960s was the most disastrous decade in the entire history of Latin America," Gajardo explained. "Instead of narrowing, the gap between rich and poor countries grew significantly wider. Foreign aid from governments has been used, not to develop us, but to achieve the political purposes of the donors. Repayments of principal and interest will soon exceed new loans, if they don't already do so. In another ten years, the mountain of debt will smother us. As for foreign private investment, the impact is even more negative. The proportion of the working population employed in manufacturing has remained practically stationary at under 15 percent for forty years. Foreign firms are more interested in buying out local competitors than in building new factories. Profits and royalties exported far exceed the importation of new capital. We no longer have a voice in our most basic economic decisions. If there is a silver lining, it is that people are starting to face the facts. By a majority of two to one, the Chilean electorate has rejected capitalism and opted for socialism. Chileans have proclaimed what all Latin Americans believe."

Gajardo is not an isolated crackpot. Pessimism is today the universal mood in Latin America. Life is barely tolerable for 80 percent of its 275 million people, and all the indications are that things will get worse before getting better, if ever. Political and social analysts no longer see their countries at the beginning of a period of progress. Rather, they believe they are victims of affluent nations which are deliberately arresting economic growth with programs ostensibly designed to encourage development.

Some are talking of a total separation and isolation of the poor nations in their backwardness, while the developed surge forward technologically and cybernetically to a new evolutionary plateau, reducing the Latin Americans (and other underdeveloped countries) by the end of the century to the level of primitives, destined to survive only as the apes of a new mankind. Even the optimists foresee more poverty, misery, oppression and inhumanity, more convulsions and cataclysms, for twenty to fifty years. And most believe that Latin America cannot hope to control its destiny unless and until the power monopoly of the rich nations is broken either by their internal decomposition or by civilization-destroying war.

Such are the dominant attitudes I encountered in a three-month survey conducted in thirteen countries of the continent, including all the major ones. During that time I traveled more than 20,000 miles and talked to at least a thousand persons representing every social class and political viewpoint—oligarchs, military, businessmen, intellectuals, teachers, social workers, clergy, slum dwellers, and peasants. There was a surprisingly broad range of agreement—even most members of the oligarchy with whom I talked have ceased to believe in the system they operate. Like their counterparts in eighteenth-century France, what they hope is to postpone the inevitable.

The change of mood has been rapid. In a book on Latin America published in the early 1960s, I shared the universal attitude of the time when I expressed my "belief that what must be done can be done, and confidence that it will be done."[1] Latin America, long neglected, found itself in the spotlight. The United States, fresh from its enlightened, magnanimous and successful rehabilitation of Europe through the Marshall Plan, had committed itself in the Alliance for Progress to a similar continental revolution in prosperity, no strings attached. There was, no doubt, some naïveté to the assumption that the ruling classes would live up to the commitments to land reform and other structural changes which they made in the Alliance. But even those who questioned the sincerity of their professions felt that they had to be given a chance. They also felt that the United States could and would wield enough leverage to force the unwilling to accept significant reform in return for the benefits of a dynamically expanding economy. Whether or not the United States might have done this has never been determined. The assassination of President Kennedy, on whom the Latin Americans had placed fantastic, and possibly illusory hopes, was quickly followed by policy changes which undercut the social objectives of the Alliance. It was decided to concentrate efforts on economic development, on the hypothesis that the expansion of the economy would work automatically to effect social modernization. Many Latin Americans were disappointed, but they had no choice other than to try the alternative. When I again toured the region in 1965 to collect data for another book,[2] the hope was still widespread that the promised results would be achieved.

Actual experience subsequently negated the theoretical projections. The difference in per capita income between the Latin American and the citizen of the United States is, as Joel Gajardo stressed, greater each year. Simultaneously, the gap between the small wealthy groups and the impoverished masses of Latin America has also widened. The widening of the internal gap can easily be overlooked, even by people on the spot. I found this misjudgment particularly prevalent among United States diplomats. "You were here ten years ago," one of them will say. "You saw those perfectly hideous shanty towns as you came from the airport, flimsy shacks with lean-to outhouses, no sewers, no water, nothing. We have changed all that. One is now a Kennedy City, another an Alliance City. You must visit them."

I did. In Santiago, Joel Gajardo was my guide; in Argentina, José Ruiz;[3] in Recife, Sergio de Freitas; in Bogotá, Enrique Cornejo. All of them, and the others who conducted me on similar tours of inspection on the outskirts of many other cities, are either frequent visitors to the slums or live in them, being involved in programs to develop internal leadership among the slum dwellers. Indeed, there is a constant influx to these slums from the countryside; while the population grows, mechanization and chemical weed killers reduce demand for agricultural labor. The departure of surplus workers and their families has cut the rural proportion of Latin America's population from 61 percent in 1950, to 54 percent in 1960, and 44 percent in 1970. The movement, however, is *toward* the city rather than *to* the city. A whole new, little studied and less understood society is forming in the suburbs—a society of tent dwellers, cave dwellers, and squatters, as well as homeowners—a society in constant motion, with an enormous turnover of people who are improving their situation and of others who are falling deeper into misery.

What the United States officials say is perfectly true. The slums of ten years ago, along the highways and close to the edge of town, have in many cases been transformed into modest but respectable lower-class housing developments. But, José Ruiz commented, as he took me on a tour of Lanus Oeste on the outskirts of Buenos Aires, it has been "a cosmetic solution to a systemic problem." Kennedy City has electricity, water faucets at street corners, some paved roads. But behind it, new and worse slums are mushrooming, fed by migration from the stagnant countryside and by expellees from the upgraded areas. The further they are pushed away from the city center, the fewer prospects the inhabitants have to earn a pittance by shining shoes, selling lottery tickets, or similar make-work activities. Even prostitution, the most lucrative and flourishing activity, becomes more difficult. The enormous competition keeps rates low, and much of a woman's earnings are spent on transport to and from the city.

At Lanus Oeste, one can see all stages of the process. You take Bus 132 from the center of Buenos Aires to Plaza Once, cross the plaza to Bus 32P and buy a ticket to La Fábrica de SIAM. It is a dreary, uncomfortable hour's ride along the canal, left, through a very poor district where barefoot children play soccer on the street with a ball made of rags, then winding around, crossing a railroad track and turning right. The SIAM factory is to the right, silent and deserted like many factories around Buenos Aires, and Lanus Oeste is in a short distance on the left. First come the Kennedy City houses, a few dozen of them, well designed and solidly constructed. The United States had provided the plans, materials and technical supervision. The people had done the work. The group who would get houses was first selected, but nobody knew which house would ultimately be his. They all worked together, each double-checking every step in case this should prove to be his property when the lots were drawn. United States know-how overlooks no detail. It is particularly strong on worker motivation.

"That is the façade, a beautiful one," said José, "now for the reality." We pulled on the rubber boots we had brought and started our way on the dirt tracks through water-filled ruts and ankle-deep mud. "In the United States," José said, "you have let the inner city rot. Here, the rich have their mansions in spacious parks on tree-lined avenues within easy reach of work. The poor, like Lazarus, are outside the gates. Each city has a different word for the settlements. The most common names are *barrios*, *barriadas*, *tugurios*, *villas-miseria*, *callampas* or *favelas*. Some cities distinguish the different classes, calling the good neighborhoods *barrios*; the intermediate, *barriadas*; and the worst, *tugurios*. The only name I don't like is *villa-miseria*. Not that they are not misery towns, but that is for us outsiders. The people who come from the country see them as cities of hope. They are the dynamic ones who have the courage to 'conquer' a patch of land. A squatter operation is highly organized by people who have pledged allegiance to death. Come and see this shack. It has no municipal services, no water. You can smell the stench from the dry closet and a worse stench in that open drain where they all dump their garbage, and where the kids get typhoid and enteritis and all the rest of it. But these people have a pride of achievement. It is a start. Even the right to squat is a recognized property value, which a man sells to his successor when he moves on. 'Moving on' for most is unhappily downward, because the man couldn't get enough work in this neighborhood to make out. But sometimes, it is up to a small semi-improved lot which a lucky one can afford to buy. There he has water and electricity. He puts up a shack, then spends years building a home, room by room, as he can afford to buy lumber, corrugated metal and other materials. Homeownership is one of the most important objectives in the life of the poor, constantly pursued, but seldom attained."

Even the lucky few who attain it usually cling to their privilege precariously. The designers of the homes in Kennedy City in Bogotá, after intensive study, came up with basic plans for the ideal home for a Colombian family. It had a living room, a dining room, three bedrooms, a patio, a garage, and two toilets. But the people who got them didn't have incomes to pay the installments. So in six months, the dining room and the three bedrooms were let out to lodgers; the garage had become a small general store; pigs and chickens occupied the patio. The family was together in the living room day and night, as had been its previous practice. Such overcrowding is universal. In Barrio Castilla, a high-class barrio of Medellín, I came across thirty-nine people in one small house, twelve living in a single room.

Poor housing and overcrowding are obviously affected by population growth, more rapid in Latin America than almost anywhere else in the world. The region had 23 million people in 1810, 63 million in 1900, 166 million in 1950. It caught up with the United States and Canada combined in 1955, when the figure was about 183 million. An annual rate increase of almost 3 percent brought the total to 280 million in 1970, and the forecast for thirty years later is an incredible 600 million. Analysis of the statistics reveals additional cause for concern, as will be seen if we return for a moment to the barrios of the poor. The typical Latin

American city is set in a valley surrounded by mountains. In spite of high walls and Kennedy Cities along major approach arteries, the slums can be seen from almost anywhere in the city. They cling to the hillsides, like the tents of a besieging army, or like vultures waiting, sad-eyed and patient, for the wounded animal to cease its struggling. But they are not just waiting. Their presence is perpetually felt. One of the more bizarre expressions occurs each rainy season in various cities, when the accumulated human filth is washed down from the hills into the streets and water systems, sharing with the wealthy the typhoid and enteritis which the poor enjoy all the year round. Some of these para-cities are approaching in size the cities they parasitize, their numbers fed not only by the inflow from the country but by their own population increase. Gross statistics merely show that Latin American population is increasing at close to 3 percent annually, but the reality is far more startling. The upper and middle classes, the city people who contribute to the gross national product, exhibit a modest increase rate of 1 percent or 1.5 percent. The other sector, with minimal productivity and a marginal level of consumption, grows at 5 to 6 percent per annum. As it increases in size, it requires a bigger share of the gross national product simply to survive.

It is obvious that if the population grows without a corresponding growth of the economy, there is less for each. But that is about the extent of agreement among Latin Americans on the population problem. The supporters and beneficiaries of the status quo look to population control to restore a balance between the labor needs of the society and the supply of labor. In this, they have the solid backing of the United States. President Johnson said that $5 spent on population control in poor countries is equal to $100 spent on economic development. Robert McNamara, as head of the World Bank, added that aid priority would be given to countries which develop policies to control population.

Latin Americans outside the ranks of the oligarchy found Johnson's comment particularly offensive. It suggested to them a cheap shortcut to ease pressures for de-

velopment. Opposition to contraceptive programs on religious grounds, while important, is secondary. The major
criticism of progressives, Christian and communist alike, is
that the rich countries seek to substitute birth control for
structural reform in order to maintain the traditional relationship of dependency with the poor. "It is absolutely in-
correct to speak about overpopulation in Latin America, or
even of 'demographic explosion'," according to Leopoldo
J. Niilus, the Argentine lawyer who is now director of the
Commission on International Affairs of the World Council
of Churches in Geneva. "A brief look at statistics will show
that it is one of the world's least populated continents. The
overpopulation already existing in Latin America is not
demographic, but structural. To preach birth control without mentioning change of structures seems to indicate a
desire to perpetuate a predatory status quo."[4]

The economics department of the National University
of Guatemala made another typical criticism in November,
1969, when it charged that women were being sterilized
and fitted with contraceptive devices against their will.
They said that the Agency for International Development
(AID), in contravention of Guatemalan law, was paying
doctors $5 for every intrauterine device (IUD) they fit. So-
cial workers in Huehuetenango, Guatemala, confirmed these
charges for me in April, 1970. They said that Indian women
were rounded up and fitted with IUD's without being told
what was being done or its purpose. There is no follow-up
inspection; and because of the low health levels resulting
from endemic malnutrition, typhoid and hepatitis, the incidence of membrane perforation and hemorrhage is ab-
normally high. The Indians, particularly the men, abhor
the idea of contraception when it is explained to them,
not for religious reasons, but because they regard children
as economic assets and as insurance against illness and old
age. To bear and raise a child involves no money outlay
for people living at a subsistence level. In a few years, the
child is able to help tend domestic animals and perform
light chores on the land. As with migrant labor in the
United States, the entire family often works with the father
when he hires himself out to cut sugarcane or pick cotton.

And a strong family unit ensures survival when, for any reason, parents cannot work.

Aware of the widespread negative reactions to the official United States commitment to birth control as the solution for Latin America's problems, the officials of AID publicly discount their activities in this area. Off the record, nevertheless, they admit that population control is still Washington's top priority. But even they agree that their efforts have so far had no effect, and that there is no indication of a significant impact in the foreseeable future. It seems to be well established, by the experience of India and other countries, that contraceptive techniques require a level of education and motivation which are absent precisely in those sectors of the Latin American population whose birth rates are highest and whose contribution to the economy is lowest. One hears talk of compulsory sterilization or the development of a mass method (such as treatment of drinking water) of involuntary contraception. But even one so totally committed to the urgent need for a rapid and steep cut in the birth rates of underdeveloped countries as Gunnar Myrdal, the Swedish economist, warns that this approach is politically unviable. "It will never be possible to recommend and use a contraceptive technique there which is not accepted and used in the developed countries," he insists. "There will always be nationalistic intellectuals in an underdeveloped country who then would protest against the people being used as guinea pigs. All dreams about, for instance, radically lowering fertility through the spread of chemicals in the drinking water, have to be given up as entirely illusory, besides being inhumane and inconsiderate."[5]

In most countries, educated Latin Americans have easy access to contraceptives, and as a rule, they are willing to use them when they seek to avoid or postpone a pregnancy. Nevertheless, even this group is not deeply motivated to reduce family size. The big family is still socially approved as an indicator of *machismo*, the highly rated prowess of the male. An abundance of cheap domestic help also takes much of the burden of child raising off middle-class parents. In addition, there is the obscure, but possibly significant impact of a tradition of abortion. In his recent major study of abortion, Daniel Callahan points out that "it is not easy either to substitute modern forms of contraception or to maintain careful contraceptive practice" in countries with a tradition of abortion. In many Latin American countries, the abortion rate is far higher than in the United States. One study in Chile found that 23.2 percent of all pregnancies ended in induced abortion. In Uruguay, there are three abortions for one live birth.[6] Until such attitudes change, there is little prospect of significantly cutting the rate of population growth. And Gunnar Myrdal, on the solid ground of his lifelong study of the problems of development, warns that outside pressures can be counterproductive. "The new flourishing interest in the rich countries in reducing the population increase in the poor countries," he writes, "sometimes produces a backlash effect by supporting the inhibitions in the latter countries against undertaking a firm policy at home for that purpose," especially if—as in the case of the United States—foreign aid is concentrated on family planning while health programs have been "quietly downgraded or phased out in most densely populated underdeveloped countries." This is the more deplorable, he says, because "improving health has important effects for raising labor utilization and for making poor people more responsive to development efforts generally," and because "a decline in infant mortality is almost a condition for spreading birth control."[7]

Some Latin Americans have nevertheless conditioned themselves to ignore not only the growing distortions produced by the steady increase in numbers of people with no corresponding growth of the economy, but also all the other defects and distortions of the reality they live. Ignacio Vélez Escobar, mayor of Medellín, Colombia, a medical doctor by profession and former Rector of the University of Antioquia, assured me that everything in Colombia is improving steadily. Since the first figures on unemployment were compiled in 1962, he said, the rate has been declining steadily. Medellín treats 98 percent of all drinking water and its water is far purer than that of Chicago. The number of schools and teachers is growing much faster than the population. Only a trifling percentage of school-age children cannot be accommodated, and in a few years this deficit will be eliminated. Seventy percent of the population is literate. Malaria and intestinal diseases have all been wiped out, and typhoid is down to a marginal level. Hospital services are so extensive that 98 percent of all births in Medellín take place in hospitals under the supervision of doctors. Wages are rising faster than the cost of living.

As will be made abundantly clear in the course of this book, every one of these assertions—with the possible exception of the *obiter dictum* on Chicago's water—is outrageously unrelated to the facts. Dr. Vélez Escobar apparently does not even see the hideously misshapen and emaciated beggars who block one's path on every Medellín street and sidewalk. Many of his fellow Latin American oligarchs seem equally able to tolerate the daily sight of unspeakable human misery and degradation, but I met few as apparently unconcerned with the direction of events. They are particularly frightened by the threat to their own function and privilege offered by the rapid transfer of control of banking, industry, and commerce to United States interests, a development we will see in detail later.

Increased visibility of North Americans and their influence as a result of the take-over of local enterprises is undoubtedly a factor in the intensification of anti-United States sentiment. I have been constantly associated with Latin Americans since living for five years in the Caribbean in the 1940s, and am well aware of the endemic resentment of the Colossus of the North. But until recently, most of that was a stylized, conventional affair. Its main vehicle was a slogan borrowed from post-reconstruction Europe, "Yankee, go home!" It reached a significant level only among students and leftist-leaning intellectuals with political ambitions.

Now, on the contrary, it is a gut matter, spread across the entire spectrum of political and ideological opinion. It is felt by doctors and schoolteachers, by suburban housewives, and urban priests.[8] Organized workers are convinced that twenty years of massive effort by the AFL-CIO and the State Department had no purpose other than to emasculate their trade unions. As mentioned above, a related resentment affects the ruling class who see their monopolistic control of economic and political power being eroded by international conglomerates taking orders from headquarters in the United States. The sentiment is even spelled out in the official documents of the Latin American hierarchy —until yesterday, the bastion of conservatism and stout defender of the status quo.

Ironically, all this has occurred during the years of most intense exposure of Latin America to the viewpoint of the United States culture. Newspapers, magazines, radio, and television, often controlled directly—and always indirectly through advertising allocations—by United States interests, have presented the American Way of Life in the most appealing terms to the entire region, to the effective exclusion of other interests. Countless additional millions have been spent on the Voice of America, the mass translation, production and distribution of books, the libraries and other programs of the United States Information Service, the shipping of thousands of Latin American students and intellectuals to the United States for education and indoctrination, the blanketing of the region with Peace Corpsmen and other emissaries. As with the pacification programs in Indochina, the more total the penetration, the more negative the result. Political scientists must, in the future, cite this experience as no less significant than that of the Vietnam war when they discuss the limits of power of the great.

Combined with, and a major element in this anti-American sentiment, is the conviction that a CIA agent lurks behind every bush. Not only do people not trust North Americans, they don't trust each other. "The absorption of power by the North Americans introduced a more general phenomenon," explains Bolivian writer Sergio Almaraz Paz. "Bolivians began to feel unhappy in each other's presence. If a stranger inserts himself as a permanent intermediary; if he has the final say on plans as diverse as electrification, roads, and schools; if he has to tell us how we should live and how we should think; if our officials don't know how to deal with their colleagues in another office because they do not know what is their status with the foreigner; if, in a word, what is done or left undone depends on the interests of another nation, the result is that the citizens are separated from one another and unable to communicate."[9]

The fact was demonstrated for me early in my trip when an overzealous friend, anxious to ease the pressures imposed on me by a tight schedule, brought together about twenty people, many of whom didn't know each other, for an open discussion of what they thought about the United States. The result was two hours of utter boredom and frustration. They mouthed empty platitudes about the good-neighbor policy and John F. Kennedy. One or two of the more daring ventured into historical analyses of the Monroe Doctrine and the Platt Amendment. My friend was overwhelmingly apologetic for wasting my time. "You must remember," he said, "that they have to live here. They are all sincere and dedicated people, but they couldn't be sure of each other on such short notice. At every level there are more people than jobs. Once you get on the CIA card index with a question mark, you've had it as far as the establishment is concerned."

My friend knows. Held two days for questioning in another country because he was carrying some books regarded there as subversive, he discovered when he returned home, that the local security people had a full report on the incident. He is perfectly satisfied that the information was transmitted through United States Southern Command headquarters in the Panama Canal Zone, which coordinates intercept and counterinsurgency activities, and which is on the public record as having "a voice communication net . . . with the ministers of defense" of the region.

I had a similar experience in another city where I was invited to meet a group of artists and hippies. They had no hesitation about smoking pot in my presence—apparently that is not a CIA concern. But my friend had overlooked the need to exchange references all around, and once more the discussion was a fiasco.

I quickly came to the realization that this process of identification could not be short-circuited. First of all, I had to come from somebody who was known and trusted. That was essential, but it was not enough. Particularly since Operation Camelot in Chile, which had been presented as a purely scientific study, but turned out to be an immense espionage operation, all North Americans are suspect of being subsidized by the CIA, or at least their unwitting accomplices. People started from the assumption that if I was not a paid spy collecting information about subversives, I was inevitably a part of the United States establishment, and anything I might write was simply to benefit that establishment. I had to persuade them that my interest was to establish the facts, that long study and experience had convinced me that relations between the rich and the poor countries are unjust, and that the biggest contribution I could make to correcting that injustice was to publicize the issues. I had to be constantly on guard to protect my image of friendly neutrality. On one occasion, a friend said to me: "While you were talking with Joaquin, you mentioned that you were once associated with the National Federation of Coffee Growers of Colombia. That's all right while you're talking to the mayor. But not with anyone outside the establishment. It immediately types you as a member of the oligarchy." In the end I found the magic formula, one which had the added value of being true. "I was born and educated in Ireland," I would say. "For the past twenty-six years I have lived in America, for eighteen of them in the United States." The delicate touch was the distinction between America and the United States. A small, but chronic complaint of Latin Americans is that one part of the continent has arrogated to itself the name of the whole, as though the rest was of no importance. The sense of emotional identification effected by this phrase almost invariably started a conversation. After that, emotion gradually led the way to truth.

I stress this for two reasons. One is to place the atmosphere of fear on the record as a significant factor in the current Latin American situation. It is most obvious in the countries in which terror stalks openly, with official approval—Brazil and Guatemala, and to a lesser extent Argentina. But it is present everywhere. The rule of law simply does not exist, only a rule of persons. The poor man on the scene of a crime is not interested in getting witnesses to confirm that he was not involved. His concern is to get away before the police come. If they suspect him, they will throw him in jail indefinitely, perhaps torture him. I remember the story of a store clerk in Brazil called to headquarters to identify a man who had passed a bad check. "While I was waiting," he said, "the cops brought in a man, his hands tied behind his back, stark naked. They propped him against the wall, and one pulled down a cord running through a pulley in the ceiling, and put a slip knot on his genitals. Then they began to drag on the other end of the rope. I couldn't stand it. I sneaked out and got back to the store as fast as I could. We wrote off the bad check."

My second reason for stressing the difficulty of communicating with Latin Americans is that it helps to explain many of the contradictory reports that we get from the region. The Latin American culture is much less direct than ours. An evasion is more acceptable than downright refusal, an attitude which is also a prudent one for the weak in their dealings with the strong. What kind of answer can one expect to be given to a Washington official, with a minimal grasp of Spanish, who suns himself on the beach while a conference is in progress? At the end of the meeting in April, 1970, of the Inter-American Development Bank at Punta del Este, Uruguay, Charles A. Meyer, Assistant Secretary for Inter-American Affairs and Coordinator for the Alliance of Progress, met the press while he was having breakfast. Between bites, he assured the newsmen that everything was just beautiful. There had been a lot of heady words for the record, but the Latin Americans had explicitly assured him that no substantive differences existed. James Goodsell of the *Christian Science Monitor,* a man who knows Spanish and for whom Latin Americans are human beings, finally exploded: "Mr. Secretary," he interrupted, "I just want to ask you one question. How is it that what Latin Americans tell me is always the exact opposite of what they tell you?"

The pessimism and the anti-Americanism of the Latin Americans as they start the 1970s are balanced by yet another emotion. Wherever I went, I found a widespread conviction that the moment had come to assume a leadership role in the worldwide war against imperialism and economic exploitation; to play a part in the struggle of men to be free. "We have passed beyond such concepts as de-velopment or integration," says Gustavo Gutiérrez of Peru, a progressive Roman Catholic theologian and sociologist. "What is now at issue is liberation and the processes by which we free ourselves."[10] Latin Americans reject the term *development*, Dr. Gutiérrez says, because it was used by the international agencies who were careful not to attack "the powerful international economic interests and those of their natural allies, the national oligarchies," and because many of the changes they proposed "were only new and con-cealed ways to increase the power of the mighty economic groups." *Liberation* better expresses the need of countries "oppressed and dominated by their own internal human and nonrational conditions, as well as by external forces," and also the determination of the man who sees himself as "a creative subject," who "seizes the reins of his own destiny" in order to create "a society which will be free of every kind of slavery." There is a sense of urgency to this move-ment. "Everything indicates that the decision must be made within the next ten years," according to Helio Jaguaribe of Brazil. "If it is not, the internal dynamism of the process will irreversibly determine the outcome."[11]

Such Latin Americans no longer think of themselves as acting alone. They identify with the revolt of the young against the shallowness of formulas for living offered by the generation which made man, for the first time, master of his fate. They feel a solidarity with the black, Puerto Rican and Chicano minorities in the United States. They are elated by the successful resistance of the people of Vietnam to the most powerful military machine in history. Most of all, they derive confidence from the ten years of the survival of Cuba, one of their own smallest and most vulnerable countries in its open challenge of the imperialist domination from which all of them seek to escape.

Freedom now, they say. Ideas today fly electronically at the speed of light, hastened by artificial satellites, around the world. Roman Catholics march in Northern Ireland to the strains of "We Shall Overcome." Wall artists in all parts of Latin America honor Martin Luther King, Jr. alongside Che Guevara and Camilo Torres. "Get the Yankee assassins out of the University of Antioquia" was scrawled by one who felt no need to detail the Mylai or Songmy massacres.

Those who want freedom now, however, are not so naïve as to think they will get their wish this year, or even soon. They feel the depressing weight of their historical experience. They remember that independence from Spain also brought an intensification of colonial dependency. Democratic constitutions have for 150 years buttressed oligarchs and dictators. The total failure of the Alliance for Progress in the 1960s to reach any of its limited goals has confirmed the negative judgment of the many who insist that progress is impossible without first restructuring the society. Many talk and dream of violence. With Noel Olaya of Colombia, a member of the Golconda Movement (named for a farm where fifty priests met in July, 1968, to study *Populorum progressio,* the papal encyclical on development), they see today's guerrilla as "the beginning of a popular army to defend the people." But they also recognize, as does Olaya, that in the present world situation the countervailing power of the status quo reduces the practical function of the guerrilla to being a prophetic sign. Hence they form ambiguous groups within the framework of the limited freedom they enjoy, establishing national and international contacts, living on the hope that Karl Marx was right when he said that the structures of capitalism carry within them the seeds of their destruction.

Who are these Latin Americans who today consciously see their homelands as involved in a worldwide historical process? Obviously, they do not include every adult among the 270 million people who live on this continent to the south of the United States. One can estimate that in the United States approximately 20 percent of the people are so economically and culturally deprived that they lack the capacity to change or influence their environment. It is the other way around in Latin America.[12] More than 80 percent of the people are not incorporated in any meaningful way into the national economies of their countries. Formerly, they lived and died in the remote countryside. In this century, drawn by the worldwide suction of urban life and the

other factors already noted, they have established themselves in vast and growing numbers in the slums and squatter settlements that ring every Latin American city. The racial
and cultural background of most is preponderantly Indian,
especially in Mexico, most of Central America, Ecuador,
Peru, and Bolivia. In the northeast of Brazil, the Caribbean
islands and around some of the mainland seaports, an
African heritage is uppermost. This economically marginal
and culturally deprived lower class, in one or another of a
mixture of races physically distinguishable from the upper
classes, is present everywhere, even in such countries as
Argentina and Chile, which used to pride themselves on
their cultural unity, their purity of blood and their differences from their neighbors, but which today are beginning
to suspect that the similarities of their problems outweigh
the differences.

The dispossessed do not share a single culture, Neither
are they members of the politically dominant culture, and
the level of their participation in its superficial elements
varies widely. They do not share an outlook or program
in common, except at the very rudimentary level of all being
aware—increasingly aware—that they are hungry in the
presence of food, poor in the presence of ostentatious wealth,
slaves in the presence of freedom. Their cultural deprivation
limits their ability to think in abstract terms or to put the
knowledge they possess into a logical frame of meaning.
Many do not know the name of the president either of the
United States or of the country in which they live. Even if
they have transistor radios, as they do in increasing numbers, the information received from that and other sources
is inserted into a mythical framework. It concerns "the
world of the robbers" which is their enemy, always threatening, always pressing, envying them the little they have left.
They do not regard themselves as Brazilians or Peruvians
sharing a common heritage and enjoying equal rights by
reason of citizenship. What they have known traditionally
in the countryside is the *hacienda* or *finca* (estate) to which
they belonged, where the only law was the word of the
owner, and which they left at the peril of their lives. Jean-
Loup Herbert describes the situation in Guatemala,[13] where

no distinction is made between public and private life, as anyone can testify who has seen the estate manager walk into the shack of one of his workmen. There continues to exist on the part of the colonizer, say Herbert, "a pathological tendency to invent *barriers,* illogical frontiers, artificial divisions whether administrative, linguistic, cultural, or ethnic, all with the sole purpose of keeping the colonial from acquiring a consciousness of his unity."

If there is one thing on which those who best know the dispossessed agree,[14] it is that the top priority among their ambitions is to give their children something better, even a little better, than they themselves have enjoyed. For this they work incredibly long hours and with heroic dedication. But, statistically, they never achieve their object. On the contrary, deep in their bones most of them realize that their children are going to be worse off than they were. A Nicaraguan poet, Leonel Rugama,[15] recently told their story.

> The great-grandparents of the Acahualinca
>   people
> were less hungry than their grandparents.
> The great-grandparents died of hunger.
>
> The grandparents of the Acahualinca people
> were less hungry than their parents.
> The grandparents died of hunger.
>
> The parents of the Acahualinca people
> were less hungry than the people are today.
> The parents died of hunger.
>
> The people who live today in Acahualinca
> are less hungry than their children.
>
> The children of the Acahualinca people
> are not born because of hunger
> and they hunger to be born
> so they can die of hunger.

Perhaps the most profound change in Latin America in the past decade is the transfer to center stage of this amorphous proletarianized mass, about which so little is known beyond its hunger and its concern for its children. Joel Gajardo, José Ruiz, Sergio de Freitas, and Enrique Cornejo, mentioned previously as my guides on tours of city slums, are but four of thousands who have turned to the people, as the Russian intelligentsia did at the turn of the century, as the source of national regeneration. They cover the entire spectrum of opposition to the status quo, from middle-of-the-road Christians to Maoist communists. Although at first there was bitter competition among these various groups, they have steadily come closer together in outlook and operations, thanks in large part to the adoption by all of them of the Freire method for stimulating internal leadership and community action among illiterate peasants.

Paulo Freire is a Brazilian educator, now in exile and working with the World Council of Churches in Geneva. From a middle-class background, he experienced deprivation as a youth in the depression. "I know what it is not to eat, not only qualitatively but quantitatively," he recalled recently. "I fished in the rivers. I broke into orchards to steal fruit. I was a go-between for the youngsters of my own group and those of the day laborers." Later, he learned the language of scientists. He can speak and write about "the historic development of the dominated consciousness and its dialectic relationship with the dominating consciousness in the structures of domination." But he has not forgotten how the poor think and speak. His method for reaching them is called *conscientização* in Portuguese, a word that was quickly adopted in Spanish and is being used more frequently in English. It is an adaptation of the Socratic method of forcing a man to reflect on the reality he is living. It starts by asking him what certain ordinary words mean to him, words like poor, hungry, barefoot, land, sick. The discussion leader guides the reflection to the point where it becomes obvious to the group that their relationships to the realities expressed by these and similar words is not merely a fact, still less the disposition of a wise providence, but the result of a man-devised system maintained for the benefit of a few. Development of an awareness of a situation of injustice and of a realization that the unjust situation is not inevitable quickly arouse the desire for action for change.

The effectiveness of the technique is widely recognized and is confirmed by its rapid adoption throughout Latin America. Ivan Illich of the Cuernavaca Institute, and one of today's most illustrious educators, asserts that Paulo Freire proved in Brazil that "about 15 percent of the illiterate adult population of any village can be taught to read and write in six weeks, and at a cost comparable to a fraction of one school year for a child. An additional 15 percent can learn the same but more slowly."[16] Illich believes that those who succeed are the ones with a political potential, and that they become involved because they recognize that literacy is a tool to facilitate greater political participation. "I will never forget an evening with Freire's pupils, hungry peasants in Sergipe, in early 1964," Illich recalls. "One man got up, struggled for words and finally put into one utterance the argument I want to make . . . : 'I could not sleep last night . . . because last evening I wrote my name . . . and I understood that I am I . . . this means that *we* are responsible'."

A number of concrete, if limited, changes effected by the application of the Freire method are presented in the course of this book, the most dramatic of which is the militant organization of slum dwellers and squatters in Santiago, Chile, described in Chapter 3. The reason why success has been limited is also explained by Illich. "The program teaching such reading and writing skills, of course, must be built around the emotion-loaded key words of their political vocabulary. Understandably, this fact has gotten it into trouble."

As will be seen later, the ruling classes have always thought of the common people as animals. The privileged minority lives with the subliminal fear that "they" will come down one day out of the mountains "and kill us all." Nothing is more terrifying for the wealthy than the idea that the urban and rural poor, totally proletarianized for centuries, are acquiring a class consciousness. One of the first things the right-wing military dictatorship did when it seized power in Brazil in 1964, was to proscribe the Freire method and exile its author. How the Pentagon and the CIA have participated with the local armed forces in repression of movements sparked by the propagators of Freire's method in Brazil, Guatemala and elsewhere will be recounted shortly. An instance of the extremes to which the repression has gone is found in Chapter 8, which describes the fate of some students charged before a military court in Brazil with "disguising themselves as workers . . . to stir dissension, promote class war, overthrow the government, destroy Brazil."

People who arouse such hopes and fears merit exploration in greater depth. This will be done in the next chapter.

2

THE PEOPLE

In mid-1970, an unprecedented natural disaster lifted briefly to the world headlines the bleak, cold Andean highlands of northern Peru. The entire western slope of 22,000-foot high Huascarán trembled, crushing to rubble the work of hundreds of years. Huarás, a city of 40,000 people, was a mass of ruins. The tower of the ruined cathedral survived, the stopped hands of the clock marking the fatal hour, 3:27 in the afternoon of May 31. Three cities were almost totally destroyed. Huge blocks of ice detached from glaciers hurtled down the mountain, followed by millions of tons of rocks and earth, wiping out villages in their path. The dead, believed to exceed 50,000 and including seven-eighths of Yungay's 20,000 inhabitants, will probably never be counted or buried. Seen from the air, that beautiful town was a river of mud from which protruded the tops of four royal palms marking the corners of the main square, and a monumental statue of Christ, a copy of the one which dominates Rio de Janeiro.

A disaster brings out the best in people and dramatizes human unity. Help poured in from nations big and small, capitalist and communist, rich and poor. It included a pint of blood from Fidel Castro. Volunteers vied with newsmen in fighting their way into the devastated regions. It was a heartwarming overflow of solidarity. Churches in the United States held special collections, and supermarkets set out boxes to collect used clothing.

Very soon, however, the news introduced jarring overtones. The first helicopters sent for those needing emergency hospitalization returned with the wives and families of government officials, pants-suited and nail-polished, requiring no medication other than an aspirin for an elegant hangover. The reports failed to make clear the reason why none of the Indians, who constituted 99 percent of the inhabitants of the ravaged areas, needed medical attention. One was left with the impression that the Indians of the highlands were so primitive as not to realize that something could be done for the injured and maimed. Such an interpretation, however, was quickly proved inadequate by a report brought back by another helicopter crew. They had landed with food and medical supplies near a partly devastated village, and were immediately impressed by the high level of social organization and the excellent community spirit. The surviving villagers had already organized themselves into first-aid and clean-up teams to bury the dead, help the injured, and provide emergency shelter for the homeless. With astonishing efficiency they formed a work party to unload the helicopter, giving appropriate indications of their appreciation for the sorely needed supplies. Then they doubly astonished the helicopter crew by their equal cooperation in reloading the supplies, when it was discovered by a radio message that shipment had been intended for a different village. Their attitude gave no indication of disappointment. "With Indians you never know what they are thinking or if they are thinking," was all the enlightenment a long-time observer could offer.

Some explanation of such unusual behavior began, nevertheless, to emerge within a short time. Spokesmen for the government of Peru dropped hints that there was no real shortage of food, clothing or medical supplies. "The government wants cash, and our requests for lists of needed supplies appear to irritate them," a European diplomat told the *New York Times*. "They had no emergency planning despite their past history of earthquakes, and many of my colleagues have the impression that the only plans the government has concern projects for Lima and other large cities." Lima, far to the south, had not been damaged. What had happened was that thousands of Indians were pouring out of their Andean settlements and moving toward valley and coastal communities. As Irenée Guimarães, correspondent of *Le Monde* of Paris, put it, "One thing seems perfectly clear: most of the destroyed villages will not be rebuilt.

The people today live in terror. They are afraid of the earth, of the mountain, of the water. They are definitely going to move elsewhere." The announcement on the radio of the accumulation of food and medical supplies would tend to encourage migration. The government was quick to cut off this inducement, because improvement of the lot of the Indians is not one of its priorities. It fears them, as they fear it. When an earthquake devastates their homes, its concern is not to feed the survivors or tend the injured, but to keep the refugees out of the capital.

However anxious to move en masse, the Indians resisted the efforts to evacuate those needing emergency medical attention. Weeks later, the injured and the orphaned were still being hidden. "Their distrust of outsiders is based in part on the fact that it is still common here to obtain Indian children in rural areas by ruse and to raise them as servants," according to H. J. Maidenberg of the *New York Times*. "Only in recent years, indeed, has the practice of using Indians as beasts of burden been dying out on some plantations. The Indian is considered to be less than human by many people of European stock, who have thus justified their exploitation." Indeed, the practice of using Indians as beasts of burden is far from dead in Peru and other countries.

The contradictions thrown to the surface by the earthquake are probably the most basic of all that afflict Latin America. Their roots are so deep in the subconscious that most non-Indians simply refuse to reflect rationally on them. A policy decision was made nearly five hundred years ago that the inhabitants of the continent were barbaric and pagan and had no future until they became civilized and Christian. So much blood has been spilt on that proposition that for those whom it favors it has become a dogma. The military regime that came to power in Peru in 1968 boasts that it is a defender of the ordinary people against the oligarchy, and the entire thrust of its reforms has in fact been in the direction of broader sharing in the national wealth. But its idea of the people does not include the "unassimilated" Indians who constitute more than half the country's population.

The North American must resist the temptation to

identify the Indian by race. In race terms, most Latin Americans are Indians, including many who claim exclusively European ancestry. The proportion is higher than usually admitted even in such countries as Chile, Argentina and Brazil, as a tour of the slums of Santiago, Buenos Aires and Rio will confirm. But even among those Latin Americans of predominantly Indian ancestry, a majority do not think of themselves, and are not thought of by others, as Indians. They are the ones who, in the course of the centuries, have adopted a certain number of non-Indian practices. They speak Spanish, wear some European clothes, in principle send their children for a year or two to school. Many, especially in Brazil and in coastal lowlands, have substantial African admixture. Many also have some European ancestry.

The overlapping between the groups is geographical as well as racial. In a city like Cuzco, nearly 12,000 feet up in the Peruvian Andes, one can see the dynamic interplay of cultures, both in historic depth and in day-to-day living. Indians from the country climb the steep streets with short plodding steps to the main square, the woman with a broadbrimmed bowler hat perched on her jet black hair and a baby strung on her back enshrouded in a multicolored shawl, the man doubled under a load almost as big as that of the llama the woman is leading. In the square they may leave their burdens and the animal to pray before the silver-covered altar of the seventeenth-century cathedral. Or it may also be a prayer to Viracocha, "maker of the earth, lord of the universe," on the cyclopean foundations of whose temple the Spanish raised the monument to their God. As they continue on their way, they may express their reverence when passing the church and cloister of St. Dominic; or is it a tribute to the Sun God, father of the Incas, whose sanctuary once rested on those same cut stones? At the corner, they cannot fail to notice the scores of brightly colored comic books and girlie magazines spread on the outdoor rack. Further down, if they can make out a few words of Spanish, they will learn that the current offering at the Inca Palace is *Mata, Bebé, Mata*, which was originally called by Hollywood *Burn, Baby, Burn*. But their stolid faces will express no gleam of emotion as they pass the "Gran strip tease Parisien" or the "Kiss Club: Dancing and Music" which after midnight will rock to the revelry of their sophisticated city cousins and longhaired tourists.

Nobody knows exactly how many fit into this category described as Indian, nor is there really much pressure to find out, because the others do not even think of them as fellow citizens of their respective countries. It is estimated that they number between twenty-five and thirty million in the Andean heartland of Peru, Bolivia and Ecuador, and in the northern continuation of the same mountain chain in Guatemala and Mexico. These are precisely the inhospitable regions in which the ancestors of today's Indians created great civilizations—the Incan empire stretching from Argentina to Colombia, bordered by the Chibchas to the north, the Mayan, Quiché, Aztec, and other cultures in the Mexico-Guatemala area. Current indications are that these numbers will be maintained for the indefinite future and may even increase. The projection is different for lowland areas like the Amazonian basin, a region half the size of the United States. Indians there are steadily declining in numbers and there are now probably no more than half a million. The reasons are much the same as those which earlier caused their virtual elimination from Chile and Argentina. Their social organization and economic structures have been disrupted by the advance of the white man's civilization. They lack resistance to diseases they had not previously known. And not infrequently they are the victims of genocidal practices on the part of unscrupulous settlers.

Two qualities characterize the Indians in the minds of the others: they are something less than human, and they have never accepted the role accorded them by civilized society. The less-than-human attitude goes back to the Conquest. Some of the missionaries tried to protect the Indians from the start, Bartolomé de las Casas early in the sixteenth century, and the Jesuits who founded the settlements known as *reducciones* in Paraguay a century later. But it took many years to get the theologians to agree that the Indians had immortal souls and were proper subjects for conversion to Christianity. And even that ruling was, in practice, applied restrictively. It made the Indian capable of becoming a human by accepting baptism and its cultural accompaniments. As an Indian, he was still less than a man, certainly not the possessor of human rights.

How this view persists is recounted by H. J. Maidenberg in a dispatch to *The New York Times* which dealt with the moves to prevent migration of the Indians after the earthquake. "Less than twenty years ago," he quotes an upper-class Peruvian as telling him, "one could sit in Plaza San Martín (Lima) and have a drink in the evening and not see one dark face. You could walk around downtown Lima and not see any of the scum of either sex perform natural functions in the street. Lima was an elegant city. Today the animals have taken everything over."

Historians are providing new information about the process by which the Indians were converted into animals. Carlos Guzmán Böckler and Jean-Loup Herbert, for example, Guatemalan and French sociologists respectively, have cooperated to piece together the Guatemalan experience. What the Spaniards found was a highly developed society, with economic, social, cultural, legal and political institutions that compared very favorably with their own. According to Bartolomé de las Casas, "they believed in one God creator of all." Their ascetic practices compared with those of the Christians. This religion, said Las Casas, "was approved and preached by their prophets, priests and diviners, and it was practiced by their priests with great and admirable devotion and penance and with examples of honesty."[1]

What the Spaniards had, and what the Indians lacked because they never needed it, was a war mentality and the hardware to impose it, both acquired largely from the Arabs with whom they had been disputing the possession of the Spanish Peninsula for the previous seven centuries. The first step was to scorch the earth. The Indian cities were systematically pillaged and demolished, and new cities were built for the exclusive use of the conquerors, often using the same foundations and the same cut stone. All the best agricultural land was transferred to the conquerors, starting the process of concentration of ownership and power which have characterized the entire subsequent period. These rich lands were reserved for export crops, while the Indians had to learn to live with what they could produce for themselves on the marginal slopes of the mountains. In this respect, also, the Indians were treated like animals, turned out to graze with the secure knowledge that there would always be enough of them to round up as needed. For the master, while he despised the Indian, could not survive without him. He was a necessary animal. His labor made possible the production of the export crops on which the cycle depended. Gradually a system was worked out under which some Indians were domesticated and assimilated to function as the lower class in civilized society, while behind them, in the mountains, the others reproduced in sufficient numbers to maintain such inflow into the domesticated group as fluctuating labor needs required.

Division of the people into Indians and *mestizos* requires the maintenance of an emotional gap between the two. The *mestizo* understandably seeks to stress his difference from the Indian, his superiority. But it is an ambivalent attitude. He recognizes his closeness each time he denies it. Guzmán Böckler describes his mixed emotions beautifully, referring specifically to Guatemala where the *mestizo* is called a *ladino*. Etymologically, the word means *Latin,* but in modern Spanish it describes a trickster or con man. "One of the collective attitudes of *ladinos* in all parts of Guatemala is expressed in the foreboding that 'one of these days, the Indians are going to come down out of the mountains and kill us all.' This reflects a history that goes back into the distant past in the villages of the interior, and it is revealingly different from the derogatory phrases that float around all the time when an Indian is mentioned in relation to the ordinary happenings of the day (phrases which dismiss him as of no account). The real fact is that the Indian is always and inescapably present in the depths of the *ladino* conscience. But he is there in the form of a collective shadow, accusing and threatening. This situation helps to keep constant the identity crisis of the *ladino*. His contradiction is, thus, the stability of his instability."[2]

This fear of the Indian coming down out of the mountains and killing us all is what the Peruvians felt after the earthquake. It has grown steadily during the present century as a result of the disturbance of the earlier ecological balance, in part by population growth resulting from improved public health, in part by a decrease in labor needs because of mechanization. Added to that is a growing sense of power and identity among the Indians. The Peruvians were made to feel it in 1964 and 1965 when Indian squatters took possession of farms in the southern highlands. The army was sent, as usual, to drive them out and punish them. But the news it brought back was that the land-hungry had grown in numbers almost beyond the point of control, and that the level of organization of the discontented was alarming. The Indians now number probably more than half of the 13.5 million population of Peru, and they form part of the same cultural groups as 4 million Indians in Bolivia and an equal number in Ecuador.

An integral element in the uneasy political balance within Latin American countries has been the success of the ruling classes in maintaining hostility between the Indian and the *mestizo*. One of the most significant new factors in the life of the hemisphere is a broadbased effort to unite these groups. The first to start the movement were the communists, applying the Marxist analysis of the colonial society. But it has spread now to many elements, including intellectuals, students, and missionaries.

Concern for the people began to assume previously unknown characteristics after World War II. The stress on education by UNESCO and by the world climate of opinion, combined with the first serious efforts to compile statistics, made governments conscious of the major population elements totally unreached. It became a matter of national pride to match the educational performance of advanced nations. A belief that education and development were correlatives also helped. Simultaneously, the communists began to realize that organized labor and the small middle classes offered an inadequate power base. The church, similarly, was coming to see that its former support in the upper and middle classes had been gravely eroded, and that its monopoly of control of a nonthinking mass, baptised but unevangelized, could not survive the transformation from a rural to an urban society.

By 1960, all these elements had established their contacts among the people, both in the new urban slums and deep in the countryside. Already, in fact, a decisive split was becoming visible. While the agents of the various groups were all generally in some kind of pedagogical relationship to the masses and buried out of sight as far as the larger society was concerned, there were differences of approach. Governments, with the approval and help of foreign technical assistance agencies, were copying the experience of developed countries. They tried to create grammar, trade, and high schools open to all, a bridge to social acceptance and economic success. These schools would perform the conventional functions. They would provide child care, leading to ritual certification of membership in society, within a framework of paternalistic control that would ensure a total emotional integration into that society. Two fatal defects quickly showed in this approach. There is not enough money in Latin America to implement it. And since society as constituted needs and can absorb no more than 1 percent of the marginalized people who become available each year, the 99 percent of underachievers are left with the blame and inferiority complex of being themselves responsible for their publicly certified marginality.

Other groups interested in the people concentrated on the adult population, and they were more realistic to the extent that they encouraged informal classes in existing community buildings with volunteer teachers and radio aids, thereby reducing to a manageable level the problem of cost. The communists specialized in projects that promoted class consciousness while bringing identifiable benefits—communes, peasant unions, planned invasion and occupation of land, development of slum settlements. Church movements tended at first to be paternalistic, but when religiously motivated young people came into contact with the poor through social service and literacy projects, they were quickly shocked by sudden recognition of the incred-

ible misery they found everywhere, and also by the inertia
and lack of hope which dominated the lives of the masses.
By the early 1960s, the church projects had split into two
categories. Some, like the highly touted Radio Sutatenza
programs of adult education in Colombia, had effectively
become a part of the state system—subsidized, institutionalized and bureaucratized. Others had thrown themselves
into the class struggle, making common cause with the
communists, at first along parallel lines but gradually with
a union of forces on the ground and even at policy levels.
By this time, governments almost everywhere had come to
regard the independent efforts at creating internal dynamism among the people as dangerous and subversive,
certain to generate demands they could not satisfy and unleash forces they could not control. Official persecution
forced both communist and noncommunist movements
underground, hastening radicalization and unification.

A case history was given me in Bogotá by one who was
in at the start of a major operation. Antulio Segundo is in
his early twenties, from a professional family, a slight, almost fragile figure, of medium height, with an open smile.
"So we started on a five-year course in sociology in the
National University. While I was in the first semester, the
Galán experiment began and I went to work there." Galán,
started in the mid-1960s, was the first of the MEI (*Modelo
Educacional Integrado,* integrated educational model)
schools opened in the barrios of Bogotá by progressive
priests who were then working as pastors. They included
René García, Luis Currea and Noel Olaya, all subsequently
founders of the Golconda Movement and relieved of their
pastoral duties by their superiors. (Marymount nuns, originally from the United States, but also including Colombian
members, participated in the Galán experiment and were
later ejected from Bogotá.) The MEI schools provided day
and evening instruction, serving children and adults with
strong emphasis on the Paulo Freire method. To avoid the
stigma of paternalism, the parents were made to pay all costs
of the schooling but these costs were nominal. The buildings
belonged to the parishes and were provided free. The
teachers took no salaries and lived on the school premises,

needing only food and clothing. Although the schools were not recognized by the state, and the diplomas in consequence lacked commercial utility, the people quickly appreciated their intrinsic value. When the progressive pastors were suspended by the bishop after the government had jailed several of them as subversives, the parents got together and constructed new buildings to keep the schools in existence.

Although Antulio and some of the other university students who came with him were known for their Marxist views, they were welcomed to cooperate without strings attached. "My experience at Galán," he said, "quickly showed that the sociology taught in the university had no meaning in the barrio. The joke is that all of us who want to become revolutionaries in Latin America start with sociology. We think it is the way to find new forms, when in fact it is the worst road. It offers no solution, because it is the continuation of a tradition that has no relation to our reality. Take the approach to new social values—that is to say, countervalues. The sociological literature, unconsciously identifying the status quo with the ideal, equates countervalues with delinquents and dropouts. Similarly, it presents counternorms as those of prostitutes, prisoners and subversives. Such suppositions may suit Europe and North America, but they are hopelessly misleading for a society in search of values—countervalues—on which to build a revolutionary order in dignity and justice."[3]

Many of the students shared Antulio's reservations about their studies, and about 150 of them indicated an interested in taking part in the Galán experience. "So I simply canceled my registration," Antulio recalled, "not because I lost interest in sociology, but because I realized that this kind of sociology was a waste of time. It formulated problems in isolation from the general context of our structures. Those who apply it think they are establishing communication with the people, when actually they don't know the people's language. So they speak one language and the people speak another, with a totally false analysis of the situation as the end result."

Antulio and his companions realized that there was no economic base for what they were proposing. About half of the original 150 dropped out while they were still in the planning stages. Nobody was paid, and they went to their parents' homes for meals and sleep. "The first month of teaching, the number dropped to thirty-five and the second to fifteen, most still part-time, some more, some less. The miraculous part was that the economic problem solved itself for the four or five who finally remained and who became completely involved. It was the people themselves who insisted on this total involvement. They said we should stay with them permanently, so we got a house and went to live there. The money the school provided was minimal. We lived like the people around us, and they always gave us enough to keep going. These people produce their own clothing and shoes, and they were always anxious to shower more on us than we needed, especially with regard to food."

They gradually spread out into different educational experiments. "We worked in four or five places. Each was trying his own way and promoting his own ideas. Some of us had a background in communist youth, some in the Christian Democrats. Some were of liberal tendencies and others were from the associations of Christian youth. We were all trying and none of us was getting very far. Then Camilo Torres came on the scene. He worked quite a bit in our barrio, and we began to see that Camilo was getting to the people because he was a priest. The people, however, do not see the priest in terms of religion but in terms of magic. It is a fetishistic approach. Camilo developed leadership like those magicians or wizards who gave themselves totally to the service of the people in order to achieve a quick mobilization of forces.

"The utilization of this mystique is perhaps the only remaining hope that the revolution will be less bloody. What I mean is that it can be a revolution *for* and not *against;* that it will move in a predetermined direction and not simply be a catastrophic explosion of frustration. The dynamism produced by the religious approach permits a start from the logic of our people, not from a European or North American logic. A central difference is that the people are motivated less by competition than by the social security of the group. They do not individualize themselves as persons but as a group. They have a deep community sense, the characteristic which the logic imported from abroad tries to destroy. We seek a popular revolution to enable us to have, not to enable us to be. We already are a community. For you in the United States, it is the very opposite. What you need is to be, because you have. Ours is already a human society with close bonds of solidarity. What we lack is the material base—food, clothing, shelter."

The popular response to Camilo brought a quick reaction from all the vested interests it threatened. "We started with these ideas," Antulio continued, "and we began to spread the MEI system. It brought on an avalanche, from the church on one side and from the left-wing groups on the other. They both came after us on a purely opportunistic basis. They realized that the method we used was reaching and channeling the deepest dynamic forces of the people. The church people offered to let us run some high schools if we would put ourselves on the record as non-Marxist. We said that those of us who were Marxists could not deny what we were, but that this was beside the point, that the revolution was neither Marxist nor Christian but a revolution of the people. Similar offers from the other side were rejected in similar terms. Some of our own group went away because we were too far left and others because we were not far enough. And the end result was a further strengthening of the movement, the strength that results from purification. It enabled us to spread out to many parts of the country, especially to Cali, Medellín and the coastal cities. It also took us into new barrios of Bogotá, including La Florida and Florencia.

"The expansion created the need for a medium or vehicle of contact, and we found it in the newspaper *Frente Unido* (united front) which Camilo founded in 1965 and which we continue. We have broken many of the traditional forms. Formerly, for example, three or four people drew up a political platform and looked for others who would accept it. We do the opposite. We ask the people to develop their own political program, and we have no idea what it is going to be. That is why we call ourselves a movement, though we believe that the movement is now reaching a new stage, becoming a political organ with a certain extension in the ideological field in the sense of accepting various currents in the process of self-definition."

Antulio was very enthusiastic about the innovative aspect of *Frente Unido*. "It is quite different from the usual revolutionary newspaper," he explained proudly. "It is designed for illiterates and for people who have little practice in reading. The type is big and we use as many drawings and cartoons as possible. In addition, we are developing the popular verse form known as the *copla,* which is derived from the Spanish *romance*. The people improvise *coplas* to express and record their everyday experiences, and we encourage them to develop revolutionary themes. In addition to promoting the cause, it stimulates their creativity." As with the MEI schools, the newspaper runs on a low budget. "Friends chipped in at the start, but now the circulation pays the production costs. Some of our helpers have other jobs and turn over what they can. People in the country make traditional garments, blouses, embroidered skirts, and *ruanas,* which we sell. The full-time workers live where they can find a bed—in a high school, the rectory of a sympathetic priest, the printing plant. That includes those of us who coordinate national activities or who are engaged in a theoretic systematization of our programs."

Asked what kind of relationship they maintained with their tradition-oriented parents and relatives, Antulio smiled. "You'd be surprised," he said. "Most of us are from Catholic families. Our parents are churchgoers. They rate highly the virtue of filial duty and the obligation to carry on the family business or profession. It has been hard for them. We provoke a crisis of identification. They see us giving up all the comforts, the security, our future in their terms, but that we are doing it to further the objectives which they know they should, as Christians, be furthering. It creates a problem of conscience for them. Some fight us, but I suspect that most feel some pride and satisfaction deep down because their son has what it takes to risk himself for a better world."

Antulio's involvement with the people started in a city

slum, and that is the usual first contact for university students. Dr. Hernán Mejía is one who has graduated to the countryside. A medical doctor, he has cut himself off completely from his wealthy relatives and rejected the lucrative city practice which could have been his when he finished medical school. The Andean village still lives under the shadow of a *patrón* who exercises his authority with the arbitrariness of a feudal lord. The *patrón* of the first village in which Dr. Mejía tried to establish himself preferred to see the people with no doctor rather than permit one who dealt with them as fellow humans. Hounded from there, he has succeeded in blending into the landscape in another location. His home is a little cottage built by a *campesino* for himself on a small plot he had hacked out of the mountain, but which he had to sell in order to educate one of his nine children.

Dr. Mejía was extremely reluctant to talk in specific terms about his work. "It is not that I distrust you personally," he assured me. "But we are at war. Our local oligarchs and the United States will do everything in their power to maintain the unjust system which benefits them. We are weak, and our most powerful weapon is the secrecy with which we build our strength." One thing of which he is convinced, and which he did not hesitate to say, is that the wealthy Latin Americans can save themselves only by cutting themselves off from the United States and learning to live at the level they can afford with their own resources. "The *campesino* knows he can survive no matter what, and that is the basis of his self-respect." Dr. Mejía's own life style shows that many of the assumed necessities of the city are in fact superfluities.

One point on which he spoke with some frankness was the need to politicize the work of the professional in a poor country. "Take the doctor," he said. "He cannot be a doctor unless he is also a politician, or at most he is a truncated doctor. The doctor has an ambivalent relationship to disease. It is in his interest that there should be sick people. He makes his living from them. But his interest is that there should be no sick people, and that forces him to seek conditions in which they can be well. The endemic tuberculosis in this village is an environmental disease. So are typhoid, hepatitis, parasitic diseases, malaria, and malnutrition. They come from a combination of poverty, ignorance and the lack of hygienic facilities. The doctor here spends 90 percent of his office time treating children for parasites and undernourishment. He is plowing the sea because the cures are not in his office. All he does is deal with symptoms. The hospital in the next town has twenty cots in the children's ward, eighteen occupied by children receiving no medical treatment. They are simply being fed a balanced diet. That is all they need. It is pure tokenism, and also a waste of our limited technical services. But that will continue until doctors become politicized and stop the sham."

I asked if his colleagues agreed. "Many think in the same terms, especially at first, when they are more idealistic, or perhaps when they are better related to the truth. But most adjust. Today, I can't talk to my colleagues without wounding them. They are very touchy, very defensive. So I search in the village for people I can talk to."

"And you find them?"

"Yes, I find plenty. The people feel their need, and they are forced to have a political awareness. I am not talking about the middle-class types, the only ones the Peace Corps members get to know even when they live in a village. I am talking about the really poor. It is they who develop a political awareness, even when they do not express it clearly. They are hesitant about expressing it, very hesitant. When they try, it is a word at a time, little more than a hint.

"What do they feel? Well, they feel a tremendous sense of frustration. Most of those with whom I live have a religious sense which helps them to sublimate their environmental problem, namely, that they have always been pushed down. This is what most frustrates them. Outsiders think the people are ignorant, but they themselves know that they are more capable than the man with a collar and tie who is always on top. The *campesino* knows that he gets up at three or four o'clock in the morning, that he is capable. He is a very self-assured man. He knows how far he can go with his work, and how far his body is able to endure work. And he knows that he can work all morning and all afternoon without tiring. When he takes a spade in his hand, he knows he can dig a hole, and he knows how deep he can dig it, and that makes him self-assured. It is only in the city that he is regarded as a backwoodsman, poor and ignorant, and he plays the part, giving himself the last place. You will notice he is always last through the door, and even then he waits to be invited."

"But who does the *campesino* judge to be his main enemy, the one who keeps him from getting his fair share? How does the United States come into his picture?"

"He sees everything very concretely in his down-to-earth framework. In the foreground is the man wearing the collar and tie who is just above him. As for the United States, it is something vague, away out there—but most definitely hostile. 'They are stealing our petroleum and our gold,' he will say. In this respect, the middle class is more specific in its views while more ambiguous in expressing them. It secretly agrees with the students who paint anti-Yankee slogans on the walls, while loudly denouncing their actions through fear of losing the little it has."

"And what are the concrete desires of the *campesino?* What does he want to get out of life? Is food his overwhelming concern?"

"The *campesino*'s interest is not in himself but in others. Where I live, he has enough to satisfy his hunger. What he concretely seeks is to educate his children. That is the strength the Chinese people have discovered under Mao Tse-tung: the strength of the poor. There is nothing the poor will not do for their children. They have no thought for themselves. They want their children to get an education, and it is an enormous frustration when they realize this goal eludes them. The *campesino* has to strip himself of everything, to the depth of misery, to educate his child. The man I bought my cottage from had devoted his life to moving the earth, to clearing the rocks, to creating a fertile patch here on the mountainside, to building a home; and he sacrificed it all to educate just one of his nine children. The boy became a priest, a member of a religious

order, so that he never had five cents to pay back. But the
father is perfectly satisfied. You can see his pride in his
achievement, photographs all over the place. Today he is
almost blind, but he is a happy man."

A friend of Dr. Mejía shared his negative evaluation
of the Peace Corps. "When I lived in the United States,"
he said, "I was an instructor for a group in training, and
what most impressed me was the apparatus that had been
developed to weed out the applicants who might stray from
the State Department line. They had psychologists and
security interrogators and all kinds of specialists. What got
through wasn't worth having." When I asked him if he had
met any Peace Corps workers in the field, he confessed he
hadn't. "I don't know what they are doing with them," he
said. "There are none around here." Further inquiries established that the numbers are down and that those who
remain are generally less visible than before. The operations
staff in Venezuela has dropped from 250 to 150 (with nearly
fifty administrators and other service people to look after
them). Colombia used to have between 700 and 800, now
has 270. Ninety percent of the Peace Corps volunteers were
at first involved in education or community development
in Colombia, activities in which they dealt directly with
the public. Now they come to a job in a government or
para-government agency, as members of a team with Colombians and often at an office desk.

"The original idea of free-lance catalysts who would
stimulate the Indians to dig wells and build schools just
didn't work," a Peace Corps executive told me. "You had
somebody with progressive ideas who brought the wrath
of the local landlords down on him by preaching independence to the peasants. Or you got somebody who simply
wanted to transplant his New England or Texas experience
and was denounced as a destroyer of the national culture."
This executive did not, however, accept the view that all
critics of the status quo had been weeded out in the selec-
tion process, and I found many to agree with him. "You
get all kinds," was the way one expressed a common view,
"draft dodgers, freaks, you name it. But the proportion
of committed people is high. And when you get down to

the level of the village and see the real conditions, they become radical. That's the good part of it. When they go home, they know the facts of life in Latin America."

Most of the Peace Corps people I met fitted this evaluation. A husband and wife team in Venezuela told me that they had "pretty well given up on the United States." Two young men I met in a restaurant in Bolivia spoke even more strongly. They said they had been deeply at odds with the system in the United States before they joined the Peace Corps and that their experience in Latin America "had strengthened their negative convictions that the United States system represents not the common good but the good of big business." One of them, on leave from Harvard Law School, plans to specialize in constitutional law and use his specialized knowledge "to fight the system." The other, a Midwesterner who worked for Eugene Mc-Carthy in the 1968 primary campaign, will do graduate study on his return with the same general objective in mind.

Antulio Segundo stressed the "deep community sense" of the slum dwellers of Bogotá, just as Dr. Mejía stressed the *campesino*'s interest as "not in himself, but in others." Antulio had contrasted this attitude with that of the United States, and Dr. Mejía made a parallel contrast with the attitudes of middle-class Colombians. "The *campesino* values his work as such while the other does not. He is unconcerned whether he can accumulate capital, being content to satisfy his needs and those of his family. The other seeks to accumulate capital by his work, and the more capital he has, the less he works. For him, work has no value in itself, and he works simply to be able not to work. It is an immense difference."

I met many who share Dr. Mejía's belief in the basic dignity and nobility of the people, but fewer who had tested their romantic notions on the touchstone of reality to the extent he has. But the obsession with "the people" is a continental movement. It is significantly influenced by Marxist literature and shares some of the characteristics of the similar movement among the Russian intelligentsia at the end of the nineteenth century. It is particularly strong among university students. Some just sit and talk about the people, but I met others who are actively involved in a concrete project in a slum or village, a project which always seeks to develop a class consciousness and awaken a realization of the power of the people. Most work part-time at it, but some live for extended periods with the poor in their shacks.

Thomas Melville, expelled from Guatemala in 1968 for suspected guerrilla sympathies after eleven years of work as a missionary to the highland Indians, tells a story which illustrates the response of the peasants to this approach. "Father," an Indian said to him one day, "what would the Samaritan have done if his donkey had run faster?" "The Samaritan? His donkey? What are you talking about, man?" "Yes, Father, the good Samaritan. You know the story in the Gospel. If he got there before the bandits had smashed the man up—while they were still beating him—what would he have done? Would he have stood by, with folded arms, waiting for them to finish, so he could then take out his oil and bind the wounds? Or would he have challenged them? And in that case, would he have let them kill him too, or would he have used whatever weapon he had to hand?" When he recovered from the shock, Melville replied: "Well, I'm sure he'd have fought. Or at least, I would." "I agree with you, Father. That's what we all have to do here. They are killing our brothers, and instead of burying them, we ought to be protecting them. You can't protect them unless you are prepared to fight."[4]

Those who, like Dr. Mejía, dedicate themselves to encouraging political awareness and organization among the peasants often function as a liaison between the rural guerrillas and the sympathizers in the cities who keep them supplied. I found everywhere a great sympathy and respect for the guerrilla movements, even among people who considered them as militarily absurd. "A lot of people, including students, join the guerrillas, knowing they have nothing to gain by it," Dr. Mejía said. "The testimony they give carries enormous weight. The *campesino* recognizes that the guerrilla is a man who is doing something worthwhile. If he comes to his house, he can have whatever he wants."

Turning to the people as the source of salvation implies a whole series of political judgments. It implies, for example, an acceptance of the thesis that underdevelopment is not a purely economic phenomenon, and that it cannot be solved without taking structural and ideological factors into account. This in turn involves rejection of the theory that underdevelopment means the absence of development or a time lag in development because of shortage of capital, technology and technical skills; or that the society can be modernized simply by creating a dynamic entrepreneurial sector. What is visualized instead is an organized relationship with several levels of dependency. There is the external dependence on the developed capitalist countries (neo-imperialism), causing progressive deterioration of the terms of trade, technological backwardness and capital outflow. Its internal counterpart is the oligarchy which has accepted the culture and serves the economic needs of the external overlords.

Official policy both of the oligarchs and of their external associates since World War II has rested on the assumption that the programs of import substitution and internal development started in the 1930s would rapidly reduce the structural distortions. Instead, external dependency has grown. The land structure has failed to meet the demand for more food—caused by rising populations—with corresponding pressure on prices and on the balance of payments. The new industry designed to replace the previously imported consumer goods still requires imports of machinery and semi-processed materials. Installation and modernization involves the piling up of public and private external debt. Technology has to be imported and constantly renewed, at prices fixed by the suppliers. Ownership and control of the new industries has shifted in large part to the international companies with access to credit and technology. The end result is a greater dependence than previously on the foreign exchange generated by the export of the traditional raw materials, and a consequent growth in resistance to social change that would threaten the export economy.

Proponents of change in the 1940s and the 1950s had counted on the electoral process to bring it about. They looked forward to education, labor organization, and the growth of the middle classes to spread the benefits of democracy rapidly to the entire community. The new concentration on "the people" marks the end of that hope.

It does not, of course, follow that this new approach will succeed simply because every other has failed; quite the contrary. But it is a fact that pilot projects in different countries have shown impressive results. The credit unions introduced to the highlands of Peru and Bolivia by Daniel McLellan and other Maryknoll priests from the United States were immediately successful. The first, established at Puno in 1955, soon brought interest rates for its members down to 1 percent from the previous levels of between 20 and 50 percent. Many people built good homes or opened a workshop. Within ten years, the town got its first bus and doubled the number of cars. Most people were able to buy bicycles and sewing machines, and even refrigerators became common. The peasant leagues, both Marxist and Christian, became a power in Brazil's Northeast in the 1950s, dramatizing the misery of that depressed region and helping to win for it national recognition as a disaster area. The Veraguas Plan in rural Panama has significantly improved peasant incomes by starting cooperatives both to buy their produce and sell them the supplies they need. And, as noted earlier, the Paulo Freire instructional method can stimulate adults to learn to read in a few weeks, something previously believed impossible. But, as also noted, it must first stir them to a political awareness that they are victims of a situation of injustice, and this has understandably gotten the method into trouble.

It is not only Freire's program that got into trouble, but every initiative seeking to develop the people into a dynamic social force and create an economic base for independent political action. Brazil is where the process is most clearly observable, because it allowed the movement to develop farther than anywhere else before being forcibly repressed.

The first major success was that of the peasant leagues organized during the 1950's in Brazil's hungry Northeast by Francisco Julião, himself the son of a big landowner, a lawyer and a socialist deputy. The leagues combined elements of trade unions and political movement. Their doctrine was frankly Marxist. As Julião himself explained: "Alive to the sufferings of the poor, seeing in the capitalist structures and concentration of the land in the ownership of a few the source of all the injustice suffered by the poor, it was easy for us to tell the peasants that their freedom was in their own hands."[5] They listened eagerly and they followed his advice, using force when necessary. Invasion and occupation of estates by the landless became common. The government tried to maintain an uneasy equilibrium, as can be seen from an incident in Cabo, Recife, in 1961, as told by one of the principals. "This property belonged to the railways, its only inhabitants being some crickets. And here we were, dying of hunger. So we got hoes and machetes and took possession, with Julião's backing. We spent a month dodging the police, hiding as best we could, eating roots and green plantain. They said we were communists, but the only communism here was hunger. Finally, the government of Pernambuco accepted the *fait accompli*. They sent us agricultural technicians and started two schools, one for the children, the other, based on the Freire method, for the adults. They also gave us a small health clinic, installed electricity and helped us buy five tractors. So we organized a cooperative with 380 members. The arrangement was that all would work in the morning on the land of the cooperative, sharing the profits, and that each was free in the afternoon to take care of the five-acre plot he received for his personal use." Elsewhere, things sometimes evolved less smoothly. Landlords with private armies did not give in as easily as the government. Nevertheless, the leagues grew, if not to the claimed level of half a million members, certainly to a hundred thousand and probably half as many again.

Even more important in historical perspective was the impact they had on the Catholic Church. Alarmed at the communist overtones of the Julião movement, the bishops decided to coordinate and expand their various social works. Peasant leagues of Christian inspiration were formed. At first they were in open competition with those of Julião but gradually forced by the evolution of the situation into more cooperative relations with them. SUDENE, a state entity for the development of the Northeast, grew out of a meeting of the bishops with the heads of the various government departments involved in the affairs of the Northeast, in May, 1959. The meeting was attended by President Kubitschek himself. Celso Furtado, a brilliant young economist, was named head of SUDENE. The agency was given vast authority and located in Recife, where it would be removed from the interference of the Rio bureaucrats. It proposed a vast economic program of road building, water supply, electricity, modernization of agriculture and development of industry. It also stressed social reform, payment of minimum salaries and division of big estates, working closely with Julião's movement as well as with the Christian peasant leagues.

As part of the same process, a church-sponsored program of education by radio was initiated in Natal in the Northeast and expanded to a national level by the bishops in 1961. This was the Movement of Basic Education (MEB) which would arouse one of the most stirring disputes in the cultural history of Brazil. The mechanics of the operation were similar to those of Radio Sutatenza in Colombia. The programs were transmitted from a network of radio stations blanketing the entire country. Volunteer class leaders manned 7,500 receiving posts which were soon bringing together for organized instruction, a total of 200,000 pupils of all ages, most of them dispersed in the countryside, the rest in city slums. As in Colombia, the state paid the cost.

There was, nevertheless, a major difference from Colombia, and this was what caused the conflict. MEB used the Freire method of political conscientization, the method that can make a peasant literate in six weeks of evening classes. Its first reader was entitled *To Live is to Struggle,* words taken from a popular song. The five bishops responsible for MEB had read the text and approved. But Carlos Lacerda, then governor of Rio de Janeiro, an ambitious right-wing politician, saw it, ruled it subversive, and had the edition seized at the printery. Eugenio Gudin, a prominent economist and former finance minister, explained why in the conservative *O Globo*. *"To Live is to Struggle;* how is that for a loaded title? Even more loaded are the illustrations on every page—scenes of violence, undernourished children, backbreaking work. And what about the text? 'He works to support his family. But Peter's family is hungry. The people work and they are hungry. Is it just that Peter's family should be hungry? Is it just that the people should be hungry?' " It was more than Professor Gudin could stand. "To say that every man has a right to a decent life is a proposition worthy of a donkey."

The bishops stood behind the text. Bishop José Vicente Tavora of Aracajú, president of MEB, explained their position to the chief of police. "If I had made a collection of the expressions which I have found by the hundred in the papal documents, from Leo XIII to Paul VI, condemning a historic situation in which man is crushed by an unjust economic and political system, and if I published the results in a pamphlet, this would, on the same grounds, run the risk of being ruled subversive. . . ." Governor Lacerda, for his part, refused to budge. The papal encyclicals didn't worry him, but it was different when they were reformulated in terms meaningful to the peasants of the Northeast. Besides, he was confident that the counterrevolution to overthrow President Goulart which he was industriously organizing would support his notion of subversion, as in fact it did when it came to power two weeks later.

While Julião was dialectically arousing the consciences of Christians by means of his peasant leagues in the Northeast, a similar process was affecting the students in the universities. The Catholic Action movement, given formal status in the Roman Catholic Church as the preferred form of "the lay apostolate" by Pope Pius XI in the 1920s was organized on a large scale in Brazil in the 1930s. In the beginning, its activities were mainly devotional and institutional, sponsoring mass rallies and pilgrimages. But the impact was superficial and the organization languished through the 1940s until it concentrated on specialized branches for youth, including the Christian University Youth (JUC). There was a new start with much enthusiasm, followed by a sense of frustration when high-sounding resolutions of annual conventions produced no impact on the life of the students or on their society. It took nearly ten years to chart a course out of the impasse and embark on significant direct action; there was considerable direct borrowing from such progressive European Catholic thinkers as Lebret and Mounier, and an increased sociological output from several major Brazilian universities. There was also direct contact with the depressed masses and consequent indignation as a result of educational and organizational projects developed by university students in urban slums. Two events particularly electrified the students. One was a paper read in 1959 by Almery Bezerra, a young chaplain; the other, an article published in a student newspaper the following year by Thomas Cardonnel, a French Dominican friar. Almery Bezerra criticized the inadequacy of programs derived from theoretical principles, arguing instead for a marriage of Christian principles with social analysis based on the empirical data of history and society. Cardonnel rejected the former ideal of social harmony in favor of a recognition of the fact of class conflict. "We can never insist enough on the need to denounce natural harmony, class collaboration. God is not so dishonest, so false, as a certain kind of social peace consisting in the acquiescence of all in an unnatural justice. Violence is not only a fact of revolutions. It also characterizes the maintenance of a false order."[6]

When five hundred delegates assembled in July, 1960, for JUC's tenth national congress, the Belo Horizonte group presented an analysis of the social reality of Brazil in terms that showed they had taken Almery Bezerra seriously. Brazil, they said, has to do three things. It has to overcome underdevelopment. It has to free itself from the "gravitational field" of capitalism, because the country's capitalist structures are an impediment to development. Finally, it must break the international equilibrium generated by capitalism, one shamefully based on the complementarity of the metropolitan and the colonial nations. Negatively, this meant disengagement from the control of the international market dominated by the rich countries and the "egoistical policies of the monopolies." Positively, the economy must be planned to establish priorities based on the needs of the people. That requires a solid infrastructure of basic industry, proper transport, the elimination of regional disparities, and a broad internal market to be achieved by land reform and other social adjustments.

Two months earlier, a seminar on university reform, in which most of the participants were Marxists, began a demand for the democratization of education as a preliminary to true democracy in the society. JUC decided to join the National Union of Students (UNE) in this program, and the combined forces devoted the next two years to strikes, demonstrations and other forms of militancy, but with minimal success. The experience convinced them that they were putting the cart before the horse. As a 1963 JUC bulletin expressed it, "the student movement, and particularly its leadership is becoming conscious of the fact that university reform is part of the Brazilian process, intrinsically articulated with the socioeconomic and political structures. This being so, we could not simply start with university reform; . . . university reform has to become part of the Brazilian revolution."

The growing involvement of JUC in political action, the growing radicalism of its statements and the close working relations with Marxist student movements, alarmed the bishops. In December, 1961, they issued a strong directive to the national and regional directorates of JUC and their chaplains, forbidding further radical pronouncements or political activities judged undesirable by the bishops. Meanwhile, many in the movement were questioning the appropriateness of a formal involvement of the institutional church in the rough-and-tumble of political struggle. The result was the creation of a new and independent organization, Popular Action, officially launched in June, 1962, as a political movement but not a political party. It immediately attracted the most active JUC members as well as many other non-Marxist radicals, gathering much support in smaller universities and colleges not reached by JUC, as well as among young intellectuals, professionals, and senior students in high schools.

Popular Action's platform owed much to Pope John

XXIII, Teilhard de Chardin's evolutionary concepts, and Hegel's notion of the dialectic, with a dash of Marx. "Our only obligation is toward man. Toward Brazilian man, first and foremost—he who is born with the shadow of premature death over his cradle; who lives with the specter of hunger under his wretched roof, his inseparable companion as he stumbles along the path of those who travel through life without hope or direction; who grows up stupid and illiterate, an outcast far from the blessings of culture, of creative opportunities, and of truly human roads of real freedom; who dies a beast's anonymous death, cast down on the hard ground of his misery. Thus we struggle for man with man. Our struggle is the struggle for all."

Emanuel de Kadt, whose book *Catholic Radicals in Brazil*[7] describes at length the student involvement with the people, lays major stress on another factor in the thought of Popular Action. This is the "personalist" Christian existentialism of Emmanuel Mounier. Mounier stressed the paramount importance of person-to-person relations, of openness to "the other," somewhat as Martin Buber and others also did. He denied that Sartre's description of human relations, as of subject to object, of tyrant to slave, exhausted the possibilities. All too often, it fitted the facts but he insisted that man could really make himself "available" to others, put himself in their position, understand them. Popular Action applied this concept to its own function vis-à-vis the people. It rejected any action curtailing the freedom of choice of the people or forcing them in directions not genuinely their own. Even if outside help was needed to enable the people to come to know their own thoughts, the contribution of the people themselves was the most basic element. This excluded paternalism on the one hand, and on the other the techniques of mobilization and manipulation of the masses developed by European totalitarians of both right and left—techniques which they also accused the Goulart government of using. Here they were touching on a major unresolved dilemma of the entire movement to politicize the people in Latin America. All the practitioners insist that their purpose is to make actual only those concepts and desires already latent in the minds of the people. Yet the very formulation of the issues gives a direction to the answers.

Popular Action developed almost immediately into a major force. It became the general vehicle for the expression of leftist ideas. At times it was used by its partners, especially by the Moscow-oriented communists who were legally prevented from openly participating in politics; but it learned quickly from its mistakes and began to formulate ground rules for cooperation which would force each member of the coalition to openly state its areas of agreement and disagreement with the others, thus preventing unfair manipulation. Its members also became prominent in the movement to achieve mass literacy, the bishops' MEB in particular, and the Centers of Popular Culture which were autonomous organizations financed with public funds.

The response of the oligarchs to all these convergent movements to bring the people into the decision-making process was the coup d'état of April, 1964. Landowners and businessmen had become terrified at the mounting demands for land, jobs, living wages, education, and adequate housing—demands which the inept politicians did not know how to handle and which the system, in any case, was incapable of satisfying. The military regime was relatively restrained during its first period. In addition, it enjoyed broad support from ordinary citizens who were pressed by galloping inflation and could only see that the Goulart government had lost control of the situation. This view was shared by the vast majority of churchmen, who were either conservative or, at most, cautiously reformist, and many of whom had been outraged by the efforts to invoke Christian principles as authority for restructuring Brazilian society. In fact, two months after the coup, the Catholic bishops hailed the military as the saviors of the country.

On one issue, however, the new regime was adamant from the outset. The whole process of stirring up the people had to stop. Francisco Julião was jailed and his peasant leagues were wiped out. The parallel Christian trade unions were emasculated. Celso Furtado and Paulo Freire were stripped of their rights as citizens and exiled, soon to be joined by Almery Bezerra, Helio Jaguaribe and most of the country's intellectual leaders. The Basic Education Movement was seriously hit. Many schools were closed immediately and leaders arrested. But progressive Catholic bishops fought hard for the Basic Education Movement and they achieved a compromise. Its activities were limited mainly to the Amazon region and some other areas which were socially and politically less explosive. In addition, the "subversive" content of its teaching was thoroughly filtered out. What Ivan Illich calls "the emotion-loaded key words" of Freire's political vocabulary have disappeared, and with them the motivation that spurred peasants to become literate with six weeks of evening classes.

All the student movements were banned, and the work they did through autonomous organizations like the Centers of Popular Culture ended. By late 1966, the military regime seemed to be in complete control of the situation and able to start a relaxation of controls. It did not take long, however, to reveal that a major and perhaps irreversible change had been effected in the Brazilian society by the people-oriented activities of the years preceding the coup. Popular Action and the other student movements became increasingly active underground, and they also became increasingly radicalized, dominated by the various currents of Marxism, Stalinist, Castroite and Maoist. Simultaneously, the church showed a significant move to the left and a new willingness to throw in its lot with the people, even if that meant the loss of its traditional support among the wealthy. The regime reacted by restoring curbs and entering on a new spiral of violence and terror.

Other countries have shown the same instinctive resistance to the creation of people power. Lip service is paid to programs of community development, and controlled experiments at a pilot level are encouraged. But reaction is swift when they threaten to alter the balance of power— that is, when they show the start of a counterforce against the existing monopoly of power. In Colombia, church and state came together to isolate and defuse the Golconda movement. In Panama, the Veraguas Plan finds itself blocked as it threatens the power structure of landlords, merchants and moneylenders. The military regime in Peru, for all its populist tendencies, cannot accept the notion that the Indians are equal citizens. Neither can the reactionary government of Guatemala, committed by its pathological fear to a policy of terrorism and assassination. Yet the underground infiltration of the masses continues, fed by malcontents, by idealists, and by the important elements in both Catholic and Protestant churches committed to a social gospel. The conflicting forces spiral dangerously, driven inexorably toward a confrontation that threatens to be more apocalyptic the longer it is postponed.

3

NEOCOLONIALISM

Latin America, says Josué de Castro, the Brazilian statesman who heads the International Center for Development in Paris, "has to accomplish a revolution and a synthesis. First, it must cast off the feudal yoke, destructive monopolies, acquire economic independence, and allay the hunger of stomachs and hearts. Then, it must reconcile the requirements of revolution with human respect and refrain from sullying the present in the name of a bright future."

"I think it is obvious that the United States capitalist system, by its control of world markets, has succeeded in developing a vast imperialist system," says Jaime Ponce, Bolivian sociologist. "The main features of the system are the control of the extraction of raw material in the countries conventionally called underdeveloped, and the control of the prices of these materials in the world markets."

"Latin America's economics ministers," adds Joel Gajardo, a Chilean theologian specialized in social and political studies, "said in 1969 that we are tired of paying for the economic progress of the United States and other advanced nations. Those countries are developing at our expense. Our subdevelopment is a direct cause of their continuing advance, and their development requires the maintenance of our underdevelopment."

"When our cheap raw materials cannot pay for the expensive machinery we must import, the United States lends to us at high interest rates," says Vicente Mejía, a Colombian priest. "The center of decision for these loans is the United States. The ruling classes allied to the North American capitalists grow stronger, while the real Colombians of the middle and lower classes experience a progressive lowering of their living standards."

The above comments, typical of scores recorded by me in Latin America in 1970, have one common factor—a belief that Latin America is the victim of a system of inequality and injustice. The existence of such a belief is itself a fact of enormous significance. It means that the assumptions on which world policy was formulated a quarter of a century ago, at the end of World War II, assumptions still proclaimed to be valid by the United States, are no longer shared by Latin Americans.

In 1945, the newly created United Nations agreed that the great unfinished business of mankind was to end the colonial period. In pursuance of that policy, more than fifty new nations came into being in the course of the following ten or twelve years, each accepted into the family of nations as fully sovereign and entitled to equal rights, duties and privileges with those who welcomed them to membership. The Latin Americans actively promoted this process through which they themselves had passed a century and a half earlier. They were conscious of the advantages they already possessed: an average per capita income of $200, twice that of most countries of Asia and Africa, experience in self-government, universities with long traditions, a relatively developed system of education. They were confident that they would share the benefits of programs designed to start the former colonies on their way to a better life, maintaining the lead in the economic, cultural and political areas which their earlier emancipation had given them.

At that time it was generally agreed, even if for obvious reasons the socialist states would not admit it, that the goal toward which the new nations aspired was the condition of well-being already achieved in all spheres by the United States and enjoyed in large part by many of its allies. And, as the United States constantly insisted, this was a dynamic condition. It would continue to spiral onward and upward without end.

The world's foremost economists, engineers, and social scientists were put to work developing programs to speed the process. Older theories about the division of labor, the

superiority of certain human types and the impact of
tropical climates on incentive were discarded. For them were
substituted models showing the inputs of capital, technology, labor, and time which a country at a stated level of
backwardness would need in order to "take off" and continue to advance by its own efforts. The countries of Latin
America were enthusiastic. Being farther ahead to start, they
would be the first beneficiaries. Indeed, some of them ob-
jected to the description of "underdeveloped," and the term
was eliminated from official documents. They were, they
insisted, already on the way, in "the process of development."

Such were the assumptions on which policy for the
development of the world's backward countries was established after World War II. While avoiding the politically
disfavored language of spheres of influence, it was agreed
that the various countries of Western Europe would take
the lead in bringing their respective colonies to the point of
takeoff, and that for historical and geographic reasons, the
United States would perform the same role for the Latin
Americans. That situation still prevails officially, both for
the countries involved and for such international agencies
as the United Nations, the World Bank, and the Inter-
American Development Bank. It was accepted from the
outset and continues to be supported verbally by the ruling
classes in the poor countries, groups whose privilege derives
from their key position in the production and export of raw
materials, and who control the communications media in
their respective countries.

While the ruling classes still give lip service to this
approach and grasp at foreign aid from whatever source and
under whatever conditions, neither they nor anyone else in
Latin America thinks it is achieving the stated objectives.
As the 1960s progressed, it became increasingly obvious that
the entire model had been oversimplified. The same economists who had written the birth announcement were forced
to draft the obituary. One of them, Felipe Herrera, president
of the Inter-American Development Bank, wrote in 1967
that "although we are more than halfway through the
development decade, the gap between the one world and the
other is widening instead of closing as we had hoped. If

current tendencies continue until 1970, the developed nations of the Organization of Cooperation and Economic Development (western Europe, United States, Canada, and Japan) will have increased their wealth by $600 billion over 1960. That means an average growth of 5 percent yearly, and it also means that the per capita annual income will be $2,200. During the same period, the world in process of development will have achieved a gross increase of only 4 percent; and when we allow for its much higher rate of demographic growth, we end up with the fact that the developed nations will have increased their wealth by 50 percent (in ten years), while the other two-thirds of the world population will continue to struggle in a sea of misery and frustration. We have not moved toward the international distribution of income which we had discussed, neither by means of commerce nor through financial aid."

In the same year, the Economic Commission for Latin America of the United Nations specifically applied to the region what Herrera had formulated on a worldwide basis. "In the evolution of the Latin American economy in 1966," it said, "we recognize again two characteristics which were evident in previous years: the slow rate of economic development and its irregularity. The gross production per inhabitant remained practically stationary for the region as a whole, after two years of relatively satisfactory progress, two years that had been preceded by an equal period of depression." The negative trend has grown still more marked in subsequent years.

What stationary gross production and negative trends mean was translated for me into concrete human terms by Joel Gajardo, the Chilean theologian mentioned earlier. He is a graduate of Princeton Theological Seminary, where he came under the influence of Richard Shaull, a Presbyterian clergyman and a scholar widely known for his support of revolutionary movements seeking a more human society. Dr. Shaull worked nearly twenty years with young people in Latin America, and his views on revolution grew out of that experience. "A type of realism that cannot conceive of peace and stability independently of justice," he has said, "recognizes that in certain situations conflict must not only be permitted but also encouraged."[1] This is a sentiment that Joel Gajardo shares.

"The average Latin American is between 5 feet 2½ inches and 5 feet 4½ inches in height," Gajardo said. "But if you go into a university in Chile, you will find that the average student is a good inch taller than the average man in the United States. In other Latin American countries, you have the same disparity in size between the average man on the street and the member of the privileged classes. It is not a matter of genes but of food. Thirty percent of Chileans are undernourished in their first year of life. By the age of seven, the percentage has risen to 60 and it stays at that level during the following critical years of physical development. If you or I are careless enough to let the number of red corpuscles in our blood drop below a scientifically determined level, we fall down right away in a faint. There are places in my country where through generations of deprivation the peasants have learned to keep going with blood that has only half that number of red corpuscles per unit. And when one of them is brought into a hospital, if an inexperienced doctor gives a transfusion of normal blood, it can send him into shock right away. As you can imagine, the impact of this kind of undernourishment is not merely physical. Studies have demonstrated a clear correlationship with intellectual capacity as well. And that stands to reason. If you starve the brain, what can you expect? This means that a high proportion of the population has limited ability to incorporate into a technical society, even when the opportunity occurs."

Gajardo agrees with the large and growing number of economists, sociologists and other students of current trends in the relations of rich and poor nations who reject the developmental thesis. "The rich countries, both of the so-called Free World and of the Soviet bloc, continue to claim that they are trying to help us catch up with them," he says. "But their actions belie their words. We now know that our underdevelopment is an integral factor in their progress. They moved ahead in the first instance at our expense, and the continuance of their growth requires the maintenance of our backwardness. Naturally, they prefer that we should cooperate, but they have demonstrated—as in Brazil—that they will also use whatever force is necessary. Even the conventional economists have finally come to recognize the facts. The economic ministers of Latin America declared in a joint statement in 1969 that the poor countries are tired of carrying the weight of the development of the rich countries, especially those of North America."

The implications of the "dependence model," as this evaluation of the relations between rich and poor countries is called, are profound. The developmental model assumed a partnership that would gradually narrow the gap and spread equitably the fruits of progress. The dependence model implies a conflict, a projection into international relations of the class war concept which Marx developed to explain exploitation of the poor by the rich within capitalist societies. And while at the level of theory, the process is projected as one operating equally in the relations of all rich states (including the Soviet bloc) and all poor states; in practice the Latin American thinks of the United States as the enemy, not only because it is the richest of the rich states but because it is the one whose activities are most visible from his perspective. "You are rich," he says, "because you are unjustly using your power to get the lion's share of our common effort, and consequently you are deliberately keeping us poor."

Many Latin Americans believe that they are the victims of a conscious and calculated conspiracy. More emotionally involved than informed about the facts of international life, they project secret meetings of the White House, the CIA, the Pentagon, the State Department, and Wall Street, to determine roles and share the benefits. The dependency theory does not, however, demand such conscious conspiracy. What is at issue is a type of structure. A Brazilian political scientist, Helio Jaguaribe, now in exile and teaching at M.I.T., has put it very well. "The United States today," he said, "is an objectively imperialist system. However, the majority of North Americans are not yet conscious of the imperialist condition of their country, and they are not willing to pay the price demanded by the role this condition has assigned them in the world."[2]

In round figures, thirty of the world's nations, with a quarter of the world population are classed by the United Nations as developed. They include not only the United States and her capitalist associates but also Soviet Russia and most of her partners. Below the development line are more than a hundred sovereign nations, as well as many nonsovereign territories. They account for nearly three-quarters of the world's inhabitants, and in general their population is growing at a faster rate than that of developed countries. This world of poverty has begun to call itself the Third World, thereby stressing its self-identification as distinct from the two developed worlds of capitalism and communism.

A characteristic shared by all the poor countries is that they produce a single product or a few products for sale outside their own borders—tin, copper, coffee, bananas, sugar, and so on. They have an externally-directed economy based on the export of raw materials and the import of manufactured goods. Land ownership is highly concentrated. The land is exploited inefficiently, with high inputs of unskilled labor, and a minimum of capital and technology. The benefits are concentrated within the class of landowners. Workers are allotted small plots of the poorest land to grow subsistence crops for their families and themselves. Employment is largely seasonal, and unemployment levels are high. A high rate of unemployment is in fact an integral element in the system, protecting the landlord against demands for better labor conditions. Most of the people, in consequence, live in poverty, hunger, illness and ignorance. At the same time, the external direction of the economy maintains the country in industrial, technological and industrial backwardness. It creates a psychological atmosphere in which the export sector is regarded as the sole contributor to the national well-being, entitled to monopolize capital and technology, and to determine political and social policy. But the external direction of the economy is simultaneously the basic reason for the country's failure to progress. It means that outsiders call the shots. Rapid fluctuations in the world prices of raw materials prevent any long-term planning. In addition, and particularly since

World War II, the growth of science and technology in the rich countries has steadily eroded the base of the export market for raw materials. The plastics and other man-made materials, first introduced as strategic substitutes for materials unavailable in wartime, are steadily improving in quality and falling in cost. In consequence, while factors within the rich countries cause the prices of their manufactures to continue upwards, the price they pay for imported raw materials goes inexorably down.

Price instability of raw materials on the world market has been studied in a United Nations survey of the first half of the present century. Annual fluctuation reaches 14 percent. That means that if the volume of exports remains constant from one year to the next, the income may nevertheless increase or decrease by 14 percent. In addition, because of weather and other factors outside the control of the producing countries, the export volume fluctuates to the average extent of 19 percent. The total fluctuations in export revenue dependent on volumes and prices averaged about 23 percent from one year to the next, but they can reach 37 percent from a falling cycle to a rising cycle, the average cycle being about four years. Such uncontrollable variations in national income prevent a developing country from making the medium-term forecasts essential for a program of development. All efforts to create an international system to cushion these shocks have been successfully resisted by the rich nations, with the United States always the one most inflexibly opposed. Nor is foreign aid utilized as a cushion, this in spite of the fact that in one recent year, Latin America lost ten times as much through a sharp drop in prices of raw materials as the credits received from the United States and the international agencies.[3]

Other studies give an idea of the additional negative multiplier factor introduced by the rising prices of the manufactured products which the underdeveloped countries import. During a recent ten-year period, the ratio between the prices of raw materials and those of manufactures changed by 26 percent, due for the most part to the increased cost of the manufactures. The drop in the purchasing power for all exports from developing countries as a result of this deterioration in the terms of exchange amounted to more than $13 billion.[4]

The developmental model espoused by the rich countries after World War II as the solution to the ills left behind by nineteenth-century colonialism, recognized the weakness of an economy dependent on the vicissitudes of the export of raw materials. To correct the imbalance, it proposed help from the rich nations and the international agencies to create an internally-directed economy as a counterweight to—and ultimately a substitute for—the existing externally-directed one. This was to be done in the first instance by encouraging the creation of light industry. Actually, some of the bigger Latin American countries started in that direction during World War I with the limited purpose of replacing the manufactured goods previously imported, but not available from the traditional sources in wartime, and the process had developed further when the import flow dwindled to a trickle during World War II. From light manufacturing, it was projected that the countries would move to heavy industry, while the state would take care of the infrastructure, transport, power, water, and so on.

All of this, it was believed, would free the poor countries of their dependence on the export of raw materials and leave them free to make their own economic decisions. It would simultaneously weaken the power of the traditional oligarchies and permit a broadly based participation of the middle classes and workers in the political process. Simultaneously, by integrating the masses into production as factory workers, it would give them the money to enable them to consume the fruits of their production. The end result would be a modern, independent state.

Progress was in fact registered during the 1950s and 1960s. With the expansion of industry came a decline in the importance of the landowning oligarchies. The industrialists now participate with them everywhere in the exercise of power, and in the more highly industrialized countries they not only participate, but dominate. The change is sometimes obscured by the fact that many of the industrialists have come from the ranks of the traditional landowning aristocracy and continue to think that the land is the source of their power. But in objective terms, this is progressively less true. We have entered a phase dominated by a professional management class, less traditional, more pragmatic, little interested in politics.

Simultaneously, the prospect of work in the new industries accentuated the migration from the countryside to the cities. The growth of industry did indeed increase significantly the number of people in the market economy, with a corresponding expansion of the potential base for political participation. But it proved impossible everywhere to reach a level of industrial activity capable of absorbing the labor supply. Instead, the newcomers from the country crowded into slums and squatted on both public and private land around the cities, creating enormous social problems. A low level of labor skills combined with the labor surplus to keep wages low, preventing the development of mass markets for the products of industry. The total result was to create a condition of progressively greater social and political instability.

Under pressure from the governments of the poor countries, who recognized that they were heading for chaos, the United Nations voted unanimously in 1960 to commit itself to a total effort during the next ten years, to be known as the development decade. The goal set was a real increase in economic growth in all countries of 5 percent each year. As part of their contribution, the rich nations were asked to allocate the equivalent of at least 1 percent of their gross national product as aid to the underdeveloped countries.

Figures for the first eight years of the decade show that none of the goals were reached. The average increase per person in the poor countries was only 2.5 percent. In some countries of Latin America, it was considerably less. Meanwhile, the rich countries of the West had an annual rate of increase of 5.2 percent, while the socialist countries of eastern Europe registered an increase of 6.6 percent. And while the average increase in income per person in a group of twenty-two western European countries was $110 yearly over this period, that of the average inhabitant of the poor countries was only $2.20. The overall conclusion is clear. The gap between rich and poor has steadily grown wider.

The United Nations has proclaimed a second decade of development for the 1970s, but hope is slight that it will be more successful than the first. The industrialized countries of both West and East now treat development as a problem of minimal importance or urgency. The rich on both sides of the Iron Curtain are equally offended by the importunity of the poor.

What the efforts at industrialization within the existing economic and social framework proved was, in the words of Professor Rodolfo Stavenhagen of the University of Mexico, that "the progress of the modern, urban, and industrial areas of Latin America has taken place at the expense of the backward, archaic and traditional zones. . . . The trade relations between the urban and the backward areas is unfavorable to the latter in the same way that the trade relations between underdeveloped and developed countries on a world scale are unfavorable to the underdeveloped countries."[5]

One of the most disconcerting effects of industrialization was that it always increased external dependence instead of reducing it as promised. The capital cost of the machines and other equipment which had to be imported in order to set up a new industry always proved more than the traditional exports could pay for, with the result that the level of external debt was raised. Nor did the outflow end there. The industries required a continuing inflow of petroleum, chemicals, specialized equipment, replacements and technology in order to stay in business. The earlier imports had mainly been luxuries for the wealthy. It was easy to regulate their inflow as the prices of exports moved up and down. But the mass demand created by domestic production of textiles, soap, cigarettes and similar products showed no similar elasticity. Once created, it was inexorable. Besides, the industrialists found that they had to keep their machines running and the products flowing in order to survive and prosper. This called for the importation and application of the sophisticated services, running all the way from advertising to credit cards, which facilitate distribution and encourage consumption in the rich countries.

It was all costing money—vastly more money than was realized by the sale of coffee, copper, tin, bananas, sugar, and the other primary products which Latin America has to offer and which the rich countries to the north need. As for the new industries, their products proved disappointingly unwanted in the great outside world. What the rich countries were willing to do was provide money, some in the form of loans, more as risk capital in the new industries. Here the United States played a dominant role. Its government and its financiers vied with each other to outbid all competitors and persuade them that they should look elsewhere for objects of their philanthropy. At first, the United States gave a significant part of its aid in the form of grants, but each year the proportion of loans increased and the interest rates rose. United States private enterprise, for its part, was quite happy to fit in with the high profit margins traditional in the monopolistic commerce of the region. They settled for returns of 15 to 25 percent annually on their investment, sending half the profits back to their parent companies, while utilizing the rest to increase their share of local industry. By the end of the 1960s, they were returning to the United States each year far more than they were sending to the area in new investment. The United Nations Economic Commission for Latin America made a study in 1965 which showed that net private capital flow (including both direct and portfolio transactions) to Latin America amounted to $6.9 billion from 1951 to 1963. Net income transfers from Latin America to the United States in that same period were $11.9 billion, of which 95 percent was interest and dividend payments. United States government aid of $3.3 billion during the same period fell short of closing the gap; and two-thirds of that aid was in the form of loans creating future interest and principal repayments. The long-term external public debt of Latin American nations rose from $4 billion to $16.4 billion between 1955 and 1969. Service on this debt was $2.2 billion in 1969.

As the man who pays the piper calls the tune, the economic, cultural and political influence of the United

States government and business over the lives of Latin Americans rose steadily during this period. Often the limited market and the low level of technology raised production costs so high that the new industries could not compete internationally. But even when they could, a combination of quotas and tariffs prevented them from securing any sizable share of the lucrative metropolitan markets. In order to repay public and private loans and to enable local branches of international firms to remit their profits and the fees for patents and management technology to their parent companies, it became necessary to make new borrowings or to sell existing industry to foreign interests. This process of decapitalization of Latin America has been going on for four hundred years, but never at as rapid a rate as during the quarter century since the end of World War II.

Such are the characteristics of this "objectively imperialist system," as seen by the Latin Americans. The three-tier arrangement that emerges has striking similarities to the colonialisms of the European powers during the nineteenth century and the first half of the twentieth. What distinguishes it and has given it the name of neocolonialism is that it avoids direct political annexation, relying instead on a method of indirect control not unknown to the British and widely practiced by imperial Rome. Historians call it Herodianism, after Herod the Great, who was Rome's satellite ruler in Palestine at the time of Christ. Many Latin Americans accept this concept of Herodianism as accurately describing the lines of power in their countries.[6] At the same time, they point out that it worked for the Romans only up to a point. They were forced by the inefficiency of their Herodian groups to transform their satellites into provinces ruled directly by Roman proconsuls. As they see the growing direct intervention of the United States in their political life, as well as in their economic and cultural affairs, they are asking if a similar process has not begun here.

"Needless to say," as Joel Gajardo analyses the situation, "you have a variety of concerns on the part of the various interests in the United States, and each of these is reflected

in the application of its policy toward Latin America. But
the differences affect details. The nature of the policy
remains always true to the imperialistic purpose. In government circles, what comes through is the concern of the
Pentagon and the CIA to nip in the bud every activity
that could possibly help 'the international conspiracy.' The
State Department retains some concern for the fitness of
things, for the assumption of equality in the international
relations of sovereign states. But it has become the minor
partner in this relationship. More and more we see other
interests subordinated to the security of the United States
as conceived by the Pentagon in Cold War terms. Within
big business itself, tensions are also to be seen. What is good
for the traders is not necessarily good for the manufacturers,
and vice versa. The traders represent the traditional colonial
economy geared to the export of raw materials. Their
objective is a society with an abundant supply of unskilled labor which keeps itself alive at a subsistence level
by its own efforts. The manufacturers, on the contrary,
require labor with some skills and consequently a higher
level of education. They are also willing to pay higher
wages because they are interested in having consumers as
well as producers. But there is not yet any sign of a serious
clash between these two groups. The surplus of labor is
such that agriculture and mining can get all they need at
minimal wage rates after industry has been satisfied. And
both groups live comfortably with the Pentagon and its
objectives. They are happy with a policy based on maintaining order without altering the system."

The origins of the Herodian class go back to the
Spanish and Portuguese immigration of the sixteenth century. While those immigrants intermarried extensively with
the original inhabitants and with the descendants of slaves
from Africa, they have always remained not only a separate
class and caste, but a separate culture. In their own minds,
they are the nation. The people have rights only to the
extent that they abandon their ancestral ways and languages
and incorporate themselves by dress, speech, comportment
and religion into this other civilization. Through the centuries, the Herodians have constantly sought to renew their

identity and their separateness by immigration from Europe and North America. Two categories exist today; the landowners who grow plantation crops for export, and the newer group of manufacturers. While compelled for survival to maintain a united front against the world, these two groups have significantly different interests. The landowners are steadily losing ground, as world prices move against them and as manufacturing comes to occupy a bigger place in the national economy. Whereas formerly they had a monopoly of political power and could manipulate government fiscal policy to their own benefit, they must now compete with the manufacturers and find themselves increasingly in the second place. The manufacturers, for their part, are being given little time to enjoy their victory over the landowners. With startling suddenness, they have experienced the movement into their territory of the international companies headquartered in the United States, and they have no weapons to fight the technology and endless credit enjoyed by the newcomers.

The people at the bottom constitute 90 percent of the 280 million inhabitants of Latin America, and will constitute at least as big a proportion of the 600 million projected for the start of the new century thirty years from now. Perhaps a quarter of them have been integrated more or less precariously into the national cultures as factory and service workers. But even they have no basic allegiance to a system which scarcely permits them to live, adjusting income not to human needs but to the endless labor supply. Approximately an equal number of others are huddled in shacks on the edges of the cities, driven by hunger from the countryside, waiting only for the one in front to collapse to step into his coarse rope sandals.

Back in the countryside the pattern of frustration and underemployment is repeated. Wages on the plantations, as low as fifteen cents a day in places, maintain the worker and his family and provide something for the neighbor who has no job. The system has always depended on an excess of labor. The rich fence off their holdings, holding idle enormous quantities of land above their own needs. They know that the people would not work for them if they had land of their own. Vast quantities of excellent land lie idle while men and children starve. Human labor comes cheap. As the saying goes, a mule costs more than a man. But concern is growing that there may be too much of a good thing. Technology reduces the need for workers both in agriculture and industry, while preventive medicine increases the number of mouths to fill and the number of hands to swing clubs and throw rocks. As violence and banditry grow in city and country, the rich convert their homes into fortresses. In the midst of stagnation, one activity flourishes and expands—the network of repression designed to ensure the indefinite perpetuation of the system of injustice.

As already indicated, while there is a broad consensus among Latin Americans that the program for development of the poor nations established by international agreement after World War II is not working, not everybody has given up hope that it could work. Jaime Ponce of Bolivia, for example, is still trying to persuade the rich and powerful that they owe it to themselves to change their ways. Young, highly educated, committed and frustrated, Dr. Ponce continues to work within the system. A graduate of sociology from the University of Louvain, Belgium, he is a top executive in a nonprofit research institute in La Paz.

"Sentiment here is Bolivia is not against the people of the United States as such," he said, "but against the imperialism of the capitalist system of which your country is the world leader. It is the imperialism, the manipulation of our societies for profit, to which we object. We are not against investment. Some foreign investments are necessary, but we must be able to control them. I am convinced that this requires, in a country like mine, a high level of state participation, and I am also convinced that this is possible without going to the extreme of the socialist states and eliminating private enterprise. Here I appeal to my experience in Europe. Belgium, for example, has very strict controls, and still United States companies are anxious to invest there, because they can make reasonable profits. In Bolivia, the same companies reject all controls and insist on totally unreasonable profits. That was the situation with

the Gulf Oil Company, so that we were forced to expro-
priate its holdings here in 1969."

That, of course, brings us to the vicious circle, one
which Dr. Ponce readily recognizes but from which he
thinks it is possible to escape. In this respect, he is more
optimistic than most of those with whom I talked. "The
foreign companies insist on higher profits here than in
Europe," he says, "because the economic and political instability creates a situation of higher risk. In my opinion,
nevertheless, they themselves are mainly responsible for the
greater instability. The most upsetting event in the history
of Bolivia, the one to which all of our subsequent internal
conflicts can be traced, was the Chaco War of 1932 to 1935
with Paraguay. It was the Standard Oil Company, which
needed access to the Paraguay River in order to ship its
petroleum to the sea, that provoked that war, using diplomatic channels to exercise absolutely unacceptable pressures
on a sovereign government. Both Paraguay and Bolivia are
still paying for that incident in which, between us, we lost
more than a hundred thousand lives.

"That was no isolated occurrence. On the contrary, we
have here a typical example of the pattern of our relationships with the United States—a pattern that must be
changed if we are to achieve normality. The United States
business interests, with the full cooperation of your government, assert and exercise a right of judgment over us. The
perfect example is the Solidarity Act, the so-called Hickenlooper Amendment. On the surface, it seems reasonable.
You stop aid to a country which expropriates United States
assets without prompt and adequate compensation. But in
practice you set yourselves above the law courts of the
country in question as the arbiters of what is prompt and
adequate, a right of intervention which I'm sure you would
never claim over France or any other European country.

"I think, therefore, that there is a whole mentality that
has to be changed. I am too realistic to think that the
change can or should be made for moral or idealistic
reasons. I prefer to present it strictly within the framework
of sound business and economics. There is a good and
potentially stable market in Latin America. All that is

needed to develop it to everybody's advantage is a change
of mentality and a change of methods on the part of the
United States and the other developed nations."

One aspect of the United States mentality urgently
needing change in the view of many with whom I talked
is the double standard concerning free enterprise. "Take
the case of cotton," said Daniel Velasco, who harvests several
hundred acres of that commodity in Mexico. "What an
outcry you have had from the farm bloc in the United
States this year because of proposed legislation to limit the
subsidy to any one cotton farmer to $50,000. So you subsi-
dize the growing of the crop. Then you dump it overseas
under your laws governing the disposal of surplus agricultural commodities. And who is hurt? People like me.
And still you have the gall to represent your system as a
model of free enterprise."

The theory or belief that a change of mentality and
methods on the part of the United States and the other
developed nations can resolve the problems of the world
without a revolutionary change of structures is known as
desarrollismo (developmentism). Its most eloquent, talented
and persuasive proponent for more than twenty years has
been Raúl Prebisch, an Argentine economist. He was, for
many years, head of the Economic Commission for Latin
America of the United Nations. Later, he was the principal
theoretician and strategist of the poor countries in their
efforts to establish a code of ethical principles for world
trade at the highly touted, but supremely disillusioning
meetings in 1964 and 1968 of UNCTAD, the United
Nations Conference on Trade and Development. He is cur-
rently director general of the Latin American Institute of
Economic and Social Planning, also a UN dependency.

I was in Urguay in April, 1970, when the Inter-American Development Bank held its meeting there. The sixty-
nine-year-old Prebisch, gentle-mannered, balding, bright-eyed
and persuasive, was a central figure, as he has long been
wherever the economy of Latin America is under discussion.
This time his contribution was a 75,000-word report entitled
"Transformation and Development: Latin America's Great
Task." It is a typical Prebisch document, a combination of

prophetic commitment and down-to-earth economics. "After six years of absence from Latin America, though without ceasing to search at the international level for the solution of some of its most important problems," he writes in a foreword, "I come back with a deep sense of foreboding, but at the same time with a more intense conviction than ever of the great possibilities of development which the region enjoys."

My reading between the lines of this major study leaves me with more of Prebisch's sense of foreboding than with his intense conviction. It is obvious that he has to express himself within the dialogic framework provided by his position. He is a spokesman for progress, but he is a spokesman for those whose interests make them seek progress within the existing political, social and economic structures of Latin America. He is consequently limited to solutions which are or can be made viable within that system.

It can be done, he repeats in this new report. But it is not being done, and in order to do it, a totally different rhythm of movement must be introduced. Without mentioning the Rockefeller Report or showing that he has it in mind, he demolishes its basic claim that free enterprise can do the job. Instead, as he clearly demonstrates, a full-employment economy for Latin America will require a level of savings for investment which has never been achieved within a liberal capitalist system.

"In Latin America as a whole," he sums up, "it will be necessary to reach an overall rhythm of development of 8 percent within ten years, if we are to prevent an aggravation of the existing deformation in the occupational structure of the work force, and then gradually to correct it.

"In the last two decades, the development rhythm has averaged 5.2 percent annually. To get a better understanding of the effort involved in raising this to 8 percent, it may be noted that it means in practice to move from the 2.3 percent increase in per capita productivity achieved between 1950 and 1965 to 3.6 percent in the next decade, and to 5 percent in the following one. To put it another way, this would mean to raise the annual income per person by 42 percent between 1970 and 1980 (from about $400 in 1960 prices to $570). Between 1980 and 1990, the increase would be 62 percent, thus reaching a product of a little more than $900 per inhabitant in the final year for Latin America as a whole. . . .

"Such a rhythm of development requires a significant effort of capital accumulation. It is estimated that the rate of investment, which is now 18.3 percent, would have to rise to about 26.5 percent by the end of the first decade and remain at that level throughout the second."

What Prebisch does not add, although I am convinced that he expected the reader to feed it into the calculation, is that the model he offers calls for total planning of the economy and a level of control of individual freedom that is possible only under the system of state capitalism found in Soviet Russia and other countries which describe themselves as socialist states.

A basic assumption of the theory of *desarrollismo* is that it is possible for an underdeveloped country to break the stranglehold of its internal Herodian class and channel its energies and resources into a type of economic production that will benefit all the citizens. The one concrete political movement in Latin America which has shown some promise of achieving this kind of objective is Christian Democracy. The success of this movement in Europe after World War II as an alternative to communism resulted in the formation of parties in most countries of Latin America committed to the goal of what they called the communitarian society. "That presupposes," as a spokesman has expressed it, "the elimination of private control over the means of production, an economy in which the state does the planning, determines the goals and allocates the priorities."

After a long uphill struggle against the traditional oligarchic parties, the Christian Democrats won their first big victory when they elected Eduardo Frei as president of Chile in 1964. This was followed in 1968 by the victory of Rafael Caldera in Venezuela's presidential elections. Both candidates promised a major transformation of the economy to end the power monopoly of the oligarchy and ensure a fairer distribution of the national income. In neither case, however, has any decisive change occurred. Frei's greatest success was the conclusion of a series of agreements for the gradual transfer of the copper industry, the main source of external revenue, from United States companies to national ownership. This step certainly lessens the external dependency. As Bolivia had learned earlier, however, when it nationalized tin in the 1950s, you cannot be independent at home while you remain dependent on a foreign buyer for your product. And Chile's increased control over its copper was balanced at least in part by a growth in the control of foreign interests over other areas of its economy.

Another major test failed by the Frei regime was its program of land reform. At the end of five years, only 15,000 new farm units had been created, and the process had ground to a halt as the government struggled to keep peace between peasants frustrated by the delays and landowners organized to hold on to all their productive land. Most of the new units consisted of land that had been abandoned or badly worked, and the state was forced to invest heavily to make it productive. Agriculture in Chile has been growing less rapidly than the population for several decades. The point was reached in the 1940s where total production no longer sufficed for domestic needs, and the continuing decline now requires an annual importation of foodstuffs to the value of $150 million. The reforms introduced by the Christian Democrats were not able to change the direction significantly.

The Frei government was officially committed to carry out its land and other reforms "within a regime of freedom, an authentically democratic framework and the rule of law." Younger elements within the Christian Democratic party, however, irked by the slow rate of progress, grew extremely restive with the president's interpretation of this policy. In 1967, they drafted a new party program calling for "a noncapitalist way of development." Even though the draft was never formally approved, it frightened foreign and domestic investors and contributed to the slowdown in the economy which occurred that year. What became clear was that there existed an insoluble contradiction between the structural changes needed for socioeconomic progress and the climate of confidence for foreign investment to which President Frei gave first priority.

Congressional elections in 1965, the year after Frei became president, were a smashing victory for the Christian Democrats. When election time came around again in March, 1969, on the contrary, the enthusiasm had gone. The traditional right parties made progress and some of the far left also improved their position, all at the expense of the Christian Democrats. It was a far cry from the predictions made in 1965 that the Christian Democrats would repeat the performance of the Institutional Revolutionary Party (PRI) in Mexico and stay in power thirty years until they completed their "revolution in peace." It was also a bad omen for Christian Democrats everywhere. A dramatic breakthrough in Chile might have started a continental trend while the timing was right. But even in Europe, where its gradualism answered to both emotional and political needs in the recovery period after World War II, Christian Democracy has lost much of its appeal. The experience of the 1960s has driven Latin Americans in the same direction. As John Gerassi has put it, "there are few reformers in Latin America anymore. They have become either pro-Americans, whatever they call themselves, who will do America's bidding, or they are revolutionaries."[7] The September, 1970, presidential elections confirmed that Chile was not to remain an exception to this trend. The vote was remarkably high—3 million of the 3.5 million registered voters in a population of 10 million going to the polls. Radomiro Tomic, the Christian Democrat candidate, had correctly sensed the leftward trend of national sentiment. His program promised a dismantling of the country's capitalistic system at a much more rapid pace than his predecessor's; and in fact, 65 percent of the voters agreed in rejecting capitalism. But the majority of these voted for Salvador Allende, the candidate of the Marxist coalition including socialists and communists. He came first with 36 percent, followed by right-wing candidate Jorge Alessandri, who received just under 35. Tomic had to be content with last place and 29 percent.

An important by-product of the Chilean experience was the light it threw on the thoughts and aspirations of the traditionally voiceless masses. The promise of land and a more liberal labor law promulgated in 1967 combined to increase the number of unionized rural workers by 60 percent to 83,259 in a space of twelve months. Statements of complaints submitted to the authorities by farm workers grew from 10 in 1963 and 31 in 1964, to 395, 526, 1,167 and 1,852 in the following four years. Strikes by these workers went up from 5 in 1963 to 693 in 1967 and 647 in 1968. A new phenomenon appeared in 1965, when workers on seven occasions took possession of a farm to speed up contract negotiations or protest a contract violation. The same technique was used 14 times in 1966, 7 in 1967, and 24 in 1968. An important aspect of this movement is that its leadership is internal, according to Gonzalo Arroyo and Sergio Gómez, two students of rural trade unions in Chile. "The same workers who participate in the strike or other action are the ones who decide which political or trade union groups are their friends, and what are the terms on which they will make an alliance. In addition, one sees in this new style a trend to making the conflict general, in the sense that it is no longer a question of action by the workers on one farm or the union members in one locality, but instead a broad swathe embracing a district, department or province. Finally, when the peasants protest, they can count on the help of city workers and students. In other words, the rural struggle is no longer conducted in isolation but has joined up with important urban groups and can count on their aid."[8]

The urban poor have also acquired a new belligerency. In March, 1970, for example, delegates from thirty-two committees of Santiago's slum dwellers and squatters held a three-day congress at the "January 26 Squatter Camp." This camp, situated in the La Granja district of Santiago, houses 575 families, a total of 3,000 persons. To reach it requires an hour's ride on a decrepit and bulging bus. The houses are primitive, largely made of cardboard and scraps of tin. As it seldom rains in Santiago, the bare earth is dried to a fine powder which swirls in the wind and clogs the lungs.

The squatters, however, have a highly developed internal organization. They have formed their own volunteer police force, or militia as they prefer to call it. Camp leaders administer justice. Fighting, wife-beating, drunkenness, games of chance and stealing are prohibited. The penalty for the first offence is a public warning at a general assembly of the group; for a second offence, expulsion from the camp.

The conservative *El Mercurio* newspaper called on the government to wipe out "this seed of a vast revolutionary movement based on the formation of irregular military units." The reaction was one of defiance. Victor Toro, head of the camp, told the squatters' congress that they were involved in the same struggle as "the peasants who seize the land, the miners who nationalize the copper, and the workers who take over the factories. . . . The workers are always the ones who know hunger, exploitation and massacres. With the copper they take out of Chile, they make bullets in the United States to kill the poor in Puerto Montt and the workers in the streets of Santiago. . . . We are ready to meet the enemy face to face in armed conflict. We know who our enemies are. They are our ruling class here at home and Yankee imperialism."

Such rhetoric is becoming widespread, but it is an expression of frustration, not a program of action. The disaffected know the strength of the domestic oligarchies and their external allies, and their reading of the signs convinces them that these groups are not going to change the system either from good will or enlightened self-interest. Since the student-worker uprisings paralyzed France in 1968 and induced waves of sympathetic reaction around the world, however, they see another possible escape from their dilemma. Now they talk about the possibility of cataclysmic change within the rich countries, either through a catastrophic breakdown of the system or the peaceful emergence of new values. Joel Gajardo and many others expressed themselves almost in the same words.

"The profound alienation of the young people," Gajardo said, "makes us look at the United States in a completely new light. Now we can see grounds for long-term hope. We Latin Americans used to see the United States in somewhat the same perspective as Protestants saw Roman Catholics. Only the monolith was visible, strong and firmly united. To attack it was to beat your head against a stone wall. It created an enormous inferiority complex. The United States had a similar monolithic front. All we could see was the economic power, the overwhelming imperialism, something unchallengeable and certainly unbeatable. But this monolith of ten or fifteen years ago begins to reveal evidence of internal decomposition. It has its blackouts, its system breakdowns. The youth protests against the war in Vietnam and against the diversion of the universities from teaching to war-oriented research, the growth and radicalization of the black movements, the organization of Puerto Rican protest and the emergence of the Chicanos as a power in the Southwest, all of this gives us hope. We have allies within as well as without. The United States now has to maintain not only its imperialistic attitudes toward other countries, especially Latin America, it has to build a system of internal controls. Each step provokes a counterstep from those against whom it is directed, placing the United States on a treadmill. A progressively bigger part of its effort will have to be devoted to repression."

Until there is some such external development challenging the neocolonial system, Latin Americans see little hope of progress by their own efforts. At the same time, they believe that they must be ready when the opportunity occurs, and that they must plan on the assumption that it will occur. "What we have to concentrate on most of all," says Joel Gajardo, "is an analysis of our society as it actually exists. In our countries, everything has been for the exclusive benefit of an elite and of foreigners. That is true even of the media of public opinion, or rather particularly, of the media. We have absolutely no freedom of the press and never had. What we have is a press in which one small group has freedom for itself. If you read our newspapers, you find a lot of talk of justice, but it is class justice. You find a lot of talk about property rights, but see how it works out in the courts. The man who steals a chicken is sent to jail for three years. The man who defaults on his taxes or fails to pay the social security contributions for his employees goes scot-free.

"The solution requires that the public have access to the decision-making process. And that brings me to a word people don't like to hear but that has no satisfactory synonym. The word is *revolution*. It is a historical fact, as Martin Luther King, Jr. pointed out more than once, that the powerful never yield power of their own accord. It has to be taken from them. And that is revolution, the forceful transfer of power. Revolution always implies violence, even if it does not inevitably include bloodshed."

Gajardo readily admits the Marxist contribution to this analysis of the continental reality; indeed, most of the Latin Americans with whom I talked admitted the impact of Marxism on their thinking. Jaime Ponce put it very well. "We mustn't be naïve," he said. "There has been a long-term and effective propaganda campaign conducted by the Marxists, principally through the universities and the trade unions. They have created a mentality which is reflected in our views of capitalism. It reaches many on whom they have exercised no political influence." Revolutions need a philosophy just as much as they need a power base, and Marxism is the only revolutionary philosophy with a strong appeal to contemporary man. Even if a rival should develop, it would need to be just as violent in its challenges to the status quo, and it would, in all probability, be just as hostile to the principles proclaimed by the developed Western nations. Their great achievements: political freedom, economic freedom and constitutional law, appear to the world's poor—as in fact they have frequently functioned—to be imperialist tricks to protect privilege. Accordingly, in Latin America today, one finds almost no emotional resistance to communism outside the narrow segment of right-wing reactionaries and traditional Roman Catholics. The only significant exception is Argentina. The neo-Peronists, although they have moved to the extreme left, remain emotionally anti-communist as a hang-up from their days of power.

"The Marxist model is a good instrument for interpreting the Latin American reality," according to Gajardo. "It helps us to understand and integrate many elements which would otherwise escape us. As a Christian, I regard Marxism as an excellent interpretative instrument. It also allows us to assemble and coordinate the various forces and efforts calculated to achieve the more just and more human society that will permit the integration of all people into the social process.

"I do not accept the postulates of Marxism unquestioningly. At the same time, I do not think that Marxism can be concretized in only one form to the exclusion of others. We in Latin America do not have to copy slavishly what was done elsewhere. We can use the model, but in a way that allows more freedom and a more human society."

Contributing to the growth of communism in Latin America is the refusal of the United States to allow any alternative to survive. "A noncommunist but aggressively anti-*yanqui* Cuba might expect to share the fate Nicaragua or Panama suffered in this century and the last, the fate Cuba itself experienced in 1898, 1906 and 1917, the fate of Guatemala and the Dominican Republic in recent years and months when they proclaimed, or ostensibly threatened to proclaim, a leftism that was distinct from communism. When Cuba was a radical state standing against the United States, it had to deal with the Bay of Pigs invasion; but since its open alignment with the Soviet Union, and its acceptance by Soviet Russia and China, it is in the unique position in the Americas of both defying the United States and remaining safe."[9]

Christians no longer hesitate to speak in openly Marxist terms. Luis Currea, a member of the already mentioned Golconda Movement, says that the revolution for which they are working cannot be achieved by a mere change in individual attitudes. "I do not deny the possibility of conversion, but not all the individuals who form the ruling group can simultaneously come of their own accord to recognize the need for change now, nor that all individuals in the working class can similarly assume a consciousness of their class problem. They must be brought to a kind of confrontation, out of which, by the dialectic method, will come a new synthesis; and this must occur on the local, the national, and the international level."

Vicente Mejía, another of the Golconda priests, says that the North American capitalists and their local allies will always seek to keep for themselves the principal benefits of development, "so that the real Colombians of the middle and lower classes experience a continuing fall in their living levels. But the people are coming to see that the only solution is to make ourselves independent of the United States. We are moving toward a Colombian socialism, a socialism adjusted to scientific socialism. Our model is not China or Russia or Cuba, but Colombia, with the means of production in the hands of the people, with a true agrarian reform and a true urban revolution. All of this will have to be part of a broader Latin American revolution in order to provide a unit that can carry its own weight in international trade, without external help. Obviously, there will be difficulties in the first days, but the Colombian people, like the Cuban, will be ready to overcome every difficulty. We think that here Colombia has the experience of China, which was able to lift itself up by its own efforts and using its own resources.

"The United States will not want to permit this. It will never allow the Latin American countries to become independent, if it can stop the movement. But history and our own conviction ensure us that we will free ourselves from this United States yoke. We have the example of Cuba and Vietnam, not to speak of the new problem just arising for the United States in Cambodia. With Che Guevara, I am convinced that all this will so aggravate the problems of the United States that it will finally have to withdraw from Latin America."

Some Protestants are equally explicit. In Latin America, Protestantism has experienced in recent years a polarization even more acute than that of Roman Catholicism. For some considerable time, many of its theologians and other intellectuals had been discussing among themselves the need for institutional change in society as a preliminary to any meaningful Christianization of the masses. They were immensely encouraged by the rapid development of similar ideas among progressive Roman Catholics from the time of Pope John XXIII and the Vatican Council, and in the new ecumenical atmosphere the two movements have established a firm liaison. But when they reached the point of identifying not only the local oligarchs but also the United States as the class enemy of the masses, the progressive Protestants found themselves in open conflict with the governing bodies of their own churches, bodies composed largely of men identified by education and business interest with the United States.

The main expression of this progressive movement among Protestants is found in and through an organization called ISAL, acronym for *Iglesia y Sociedad en América Latina* (Church and Society in Latin America). "From an early reformist stage," when founded in 1962, "ISAL moved rapidly and definitely to a revolutionary option," explained Julio de Santa Ana, its executive secretary. A quotation from Julio Barreiro, another of its top officials, will illustrate what this means: "The Marxist model of the class struggle seems to retain all its efficacy as an instrument for dissecting underdeveloped societies. It seems similarly to be an indispensable hermeneutic tool for understanding the socioeconomic setup in which a highly developed minority of those who both own the land and monopolize industrial and financial activities exploit for their exclusive benefit the work force and the mass of the people. Equally, the Marxist model, as corrected by Lenin, remains valid for interpreting the modern forms of economic imperialism, the most outstanding aspect of the sociopolitical reality of Latin America."[10]

Joel Gajardo developed this point further for me. "I now recognize that the class war is fundamental. We who have come to know Marxism after a long militancy within a Christian framework have been ignorant of this dimension. We have stressed reconciliation, insisting that Christianity—and especially Christ—has already overcome every difference; that for the Christian there is neither Jew, nor Greek, nor barbarian. Yet I think that class opposition is something evident in Latin America. The privileged classes have created for themselves a situation in which they will continue to enjoy privilege until the dispossessed classes acquire an awareness of their own strength. This still creates problems for most Christians, because they have not reflected enough on it to develop a clear theology. When I say this, I am thinking not only of Latin America, but of the total world situation. Even the peace movements among Christians in eastern Europe have not thought it through. I have had many discussions with representatives of these movements, and they always seem to minimize the enormous opposition that exists between classes.

"If the situation in Latin America has delayed so long in ripening and bringing us to a total transformation of structures, I believe the biggest reason is that we have never had a clear class concept. The peasants have been amorphous, without organization or class consciousness. Today, finally, they are being incorporated into the movement of ideas and beginning to recognize that they are members of the working class. Another thing that has confused us is the mistaken notion that a middle class exists in Latin America. At best, we have a middle sector, and an ill-defined one at that. In Chile, for example, they always boasted that they were politically stable because they had a strong middle class, a class with its own identity and characteristics. Now they are coming to see that their belief was a myth. What they were talking about has proved to be a mere appendage of the upper class. When a moment of decision comes in Latin America, the upper stratum of the middle sector identifies with the upper class. The lower stratum of semiprofessionals and white-collar workers has nowhere to go except to the working class. What emerges is a dominant class and a dominated class, an oppressor and a mass of oppressed."

What Joel Gajardo is discussing here is internal colonialism, the exploitation of the poor by the ruling groups in each country. But that is only a subordinate element in underdevelopment. The primary and conditioning factor— what Julio Barreiro called the most outstanding aspect of the sociopolitical reality of Latin America—is the part the rich nations play in maintaining and increasing the gap between themselves and the Third World of poverty.[11] Such, at least, is what Barreiro and people like him claim. A more detailed examination of the effect of government aid and private investment from the United States in recent years may help to determine the validity of the claim.

4

INDIAN GIVERS

The visitor to La Paz, Bolivia, is exposed immediately to some of the benefits of the foreign aid programs of the United States. They built the airport on a plateau above the city, at an elevation of more than 14,000 feet. They built the modern terminal with its cold marble floors. If its severe architecture seems a trifle bleak to the newcomer, perhaps the mood is subjective as his body reacts to the unaccustomed oxygen deficiency. But his subjective condition does not explain what he sees as he speeds down the highway, similarly funded by AID, to the sunbathed city that fills and overflows the valley 2,000 feet below. Lacking bus fare, the barefooted Indians, bent double under huge loads as they plod stolidly along, still struggle on foot back to their homes in the mountains. While efforts have been made to clean up shacks by the highway, it is easy to recognize, as one studies the approaching city, that the reality is unchanged. Bolivia, once the home of one of the world's great cultures and an integral part of the mighty Inca empire, has not begun to reverse the tragic history of its recent past. It continues to stagger from bankruptcy to bankruptcy, conditioned by decisions over which it has minimal control.

In other cities I had asked United States officials why the end results of our aid remained so meager. They were always willing to talk about specific benefits, a housing project here, a dam there, community development programs all over the place. But they resisted efforts at general evaluations. My first success in this area occurred here in La Paz, through a process of cross-checking materials from the United States embassy with those of the Bolivian government's planning office. What emerged was the very definite possibility that the cost to Bolivia of the foreign aid programs was quite out of line with the benefits obtained.

In Bolivia, in 1969, apart from transactions under Public Law 480, which regulates grants and sales of surplus agricultural commodities, the aid transactions consisted of $2.8 million in grants for technical assistance, and $13 million in development loans.

Of this total amount of approximately $16 million, however, a third or less reached Bolivia in the form of dollars. The rest remained in the United States or in United States hands. It represented the cost of studies conducted in the United States, the cost of machinery and supplies bought there and transported in American ships, the profits of United States contractors hired to carry out work in Bolivia and the earnings of their employees retained in, or returned to, the United States. Almost all of the development loans in Bolivia go for roads and airports. Undoubtedly, these benefit the country in the long run, but their dollar-earning usefulness is slight. Airports in particular involve a continuing dollar drain for maintenance, aircraft replacements, crew training, and through the encouragement of foreign travel. The total result is that Bolivia ends the year with its dollar balances enriched by some $5 million (the proportion of aid actually transferred as dollars), but with an obligation to repay $13 million plus interest, or a total of about $20 million. It has increased the mortgage on its tin and other traditional exports by $15 million. Sooner or later, it will have to send abroad products to that amount without getting anything for them in return.

The actual mix will vary from country to country, depending on the purposes for which the borrowed money is spent and the extent to which the borrower is dependent on the United States to provide services. But the end result is not greatly different. Josué de Castro, the already mentioned Brazilian statesman and expert on nutrition, explains what happens under these loan agreements: "American goods are supplied at a price higher than the current United States price; the loans are made for the benefit of the trusts (i.e., affiliates of United States conglomerates) established in the assisted countries; the goods arrive on American ships, are insured by American firms, and banking transactions are carried out by American banks."[1]

In Bolivia, the practice of the aid officials has been to insist on United States contractors, on the ground that local contractors do not have the required expertise. This condition does not always apply in countries with a more highly developed construction industry. A new dollar-easing factor was introduced in 1969 when President Nixon ruled, in deference to long-expressed Latin American complaints, that aid money can be spent on equipment manufactured anywhere in Latin America. The reaction to this relaxation, however, has generally been quite negative. The criticism had been that borrowers had to buy United States manufactures even though Japan or Europe could provide machines more suited to Latin America conditions and at lower cost. Latin America countries, it is claimed, either do not produce what is needed, or they produce under tariff protections which make their products noncompetitive outside their borders. What few exceptions occur are likely to be affiliates of United States companies, so that the end result will be to further increase their share of the market. Most of the aid officials with whom I talked agreed with this analysis. The only dissenter referred to a loan recently approved for the modernization of industrial plants in Uruguay. He claimed that in many cases equipment more suited to local needs than what the United States has to offer will be obtained in neighboring Argentina and Brazil.

"No matter how sympathetically you try to interpret your aid program in our country," a Bolivian economist commented, "you have to admit that it is not doing very much for us. It is simple tokenism, to the point that Senators Fulbright and Church, as well as other congressmen who started out as enthusiastic supporters of what purported to be an altruistic program of world development, are today its harshest critics. But it will continue, because it serves the policy of a strong nation seeking political and economic hegemony over weaker neighbors without reducing them to the legal status of colonies. Bolivia is a particularly good example, but the process is evident in all parts of the hemisphere."

Jordan Bishop was also thinking of Bolivia, but his remarks are of general application. "Bolivia therefore is now free to use her United States credits to buy the capital goods she needs from such well-developed industrial countries as Paraguay and Ecuador! The fact is that there is no competitor to United States industry in Latin America (Mexico comes closest, but falls short by several light-years), and where purchases of capital goods are involved, the alternative is in fact not an alternative. Motor vehicles, rolling stock, etc., made in Latin America tend, owing to lack of economies of scale, to cost much more than identical products imported from the United States. In Bolivia, a Volkswagen made in Germany costs less than one made in Brazil."[2]

The average United States taxpayer, convinced that foreign aid comes straight out of his pocket and totally unaware of any compensating benefits, finds this hard to take. He knows that the Spaniards, English, French, and Dutch all got their cut out of the American continent away in the past, and he is prepared to admit that the United States, in the freewheeling days of the robber barons, may have imitated some of their questionable practices. But he has been told over and over that our foreign aid programs, modeled on the Marshall Plan rehabilitation of war-devastated Europe, ushered in an era of unselfish generosity. Latin Americans in increasing numbers, however, see the situation in the terms expressed by my Bolivian friend. They interpret our aid programs as one of the final steps in a long process of direct intervention, a process designed and calculated to centralize the entire decision-making process for the hemisphere in New York and Washington.

The first point they challenge is our assumption that United States aid to Latin America is an historical prolongation of that provided to Europe to speed its recovery after World War II, and that we have provided it within a similarly scientific framework and on comparable terms. In this, at least, they are correct. Aid to Europe was given in pursuance of clearly established objectives formulated by the Europeans themselves, and at a level capable of achieving those objectives within the specified times. Whereas our aid to Latin America is mostly in the form of loans repayable with interest, some 80 percent of that to western Europe consisted of grants. Its total effect was to create a series of industries, such as automobiles and chemicals, for which a ready market existed in the United States. The export to the United States of these products provided foreign exchange to pay the interest and repay the principal on the small proportion of the aid given in the form of loans. There was not the critical loss of foreign exchange which now plagues Bolivia and her neighbors.

Latin Americans back in the 1940s were quick to recognize the potential of the new program. Proposals for a Marshall Plan for this hemisphere began to come as early as 1948, for example, from the World Trade and Employment Conference at Havana and the Inter-American Conference at Bogotá. By 1954, the UN's Economic Commission for Latin America had worked out fairly specific principles. The United States, however, would have no part of it. The modest proposal for an Inter-American Development Bank presented that year to the Conference of Finance Ministers was adopted without the vote of the United States. Five more years passed before Washington would even agree to discuss the idea. When, in 1958, the president of Brazil proposed an Operation Pan-America as a regional attack on underdevelopment, Secretary of State Dulles said that what was needed was self-discipline, hard work and frugality.

It took the defection of Cuba to bring into being the Inter-American Bank and the related Social Progress Trust Fund. Not until 1961 did the United States agree, at Punta del Este, to a coordinated program, the Alliance for Progress. But the coordination and the commitment to social reform did not survive the man who pledged the word of the United States. President Johnson quickly got rid of Teodoro Moscoso, a man with a record of achievement as engineer of Operation Bootstrap in Puerto Rico and one who really worked with Latin Americans as an equal partner, and the Alliance was returned to the old, time-tested channels of Washington policy for the Americas. From that time on, goals were set without serious study of the economic realities and with little concern for the social impact. When goals were not met, no realistic reformulation occurred with a view to correcting the errors. What Latin Americans saw was not just complacency or thoughtlessness, but a policy of active opposition to reform. The United States was determined to retain its historic practice of deciding unilaterally. At the 1964 United Nations Conference on Trade and Development, our delegate voted against or abstained on eleven of the fifteen proposed principles, the only country to cast a negative vote on four of them. One such negative vote was on the first principle, which won 133 favorable votes—a principle in total conformity with everything the United States claims to stand for: "Economic relations between countries, including trade relations, shall be based on respect for the principle of sovereign equality of states, self-determination of peoples, and non-intervention in the internal affairs of other countries." We similarly sabotaged the 1966 Cocoa Conference, being the sole participant to refuse to accept a compromise worked out by consumer and producer interests. Such is our undeviating role at international conferences. We work consistently to weaken or scuttle proposals for preferential tariffs for the poor countries, international money reform to benefit the poor countries, and aid programs at a level to make a real impact on underdevelopment.

This policy since 1964 has produced a greater stress on military aid, shipment of surplus food, and other political objectives of the United States, than on development. In inverse proportion to the Marshall Plan, grants have accounted for only about 20 percent of the total, the rest being provided as loans repayable in dollars, with interest. Many of the loans are short-term, and the trend each year is to a higher proportion of loans and harsher interest terms. Even most of the shipments of surplus food under Public Law 480 must, in the future, be repaid in dollars. No significant additional wealth capable of being exported to the United States and converted into dollars to pay the debts has been created. The net effect, in consequence, has been to accentuate the dollar shortage of the recipient countries and to force them to devote a steadily greater proportion of their traditional exports of raw materials to debt service.

Nowhere has the disillusionment been so great as in Colombia, the country that was given top priority in the Alliance for Progress program because United States officials wanted a showcase and persuaded themselves that significant results could be obtained rapidly in Colombia by a vigorous injection of aid funds. Over a period of five years it received loans from the United States to a total amount of $732 million, repayable in periods of twenty to forty years.

"What we actually did was to mortgage the country in order to save a ruling class that was headed for disaster," explained Orlando Fals Borda. One of Colombia's most distinguished and respected intellectuals, Dr. Fals Borda once served as his country's Director General of Agriculture. He is Dean of the Faculty of Sociology of the National University of Colombia, a faculty founded in 1959 by him, together with Father Camilo Torres, the priest who later joined a guerrilla unit and was killed in a skirmish in 1966. "It was already tottering when this stimulation came along to enable it to gasp out a few more breaths, the same kind of artificial breathing as that of a dying man who is fed oxygen, and equally expensive. The sad part is that this ruling class will not have to pay the mortgage it incurred. It will be paid, perhaps with the blood, and certainly with the sweat of our children and the working classes, the innocent people who always in the last analysis pay for the broken plates."[3]

Dr. Fals Borda based his conclusions on a report of the Foreign Relations Committee of the United States Senate which surveyed the first five years of the program from 1962 to 1967 and came to the conclusion that it had fallen "far short of the economic and social goals of the Charter of Punta del Este."[4] That charter, signed in 1961 by the United States and nineteen Latin American republics, had committed the signatories "to enlist the full energies of the peoples and governments of the American republics in a great cooperative effort to accelerate the economic and social development of the participating countries of Latin America, so that they may achieve maximum levels of well-being, with equal opportunity for all, in democratic societies adapted to their own needs and desires, . . . levels of income capable of assuring self-sustaining development, . . . economic growth (of) not less than 2½ percent per capita per year, . . . comprehensive agrarian reform, . . . cooperative programs designed to prevent the harmful effects of excessive fluctuations in the foreign exchange earnings derived from exports of primary products."

The aid programs achieved none of these results in Colombia. Land reform and other social changes are still in the future, and the Senate Committee expressed its fear that the United States aid had actually made it possible for successive Colombian governments "to postpone making more basic reforms in such fields as public administration, taxation, local government, education, and agriculture." Industry failed to expand at anything near the projected rate, but in many cases grew more rapidly than demand, creating new distortions. Savings, projected at 23 percent of gross national product, failed to reach 16 percent annually. Inflation was to be kept below 10 percent, but exceeded 15 percent annually. The annual increase in average income should have been 2.5 percent but reached only half that level. Instead of the promised 250,000 new jobs each year, only 50,000 were created. The capital flight should have been held to less than $25 million a year but actually exceeded $80 million. Only 224,000 of the promised 360,000 houses were built. At the end of the program, there remained a deficit of 375,000 houses in the country. The land reform law, enacted in 1961, provided land titles to only 54,000 of more than 400,000 landless families in its first six years. Most of the titles merely recognized existing de facto rights of squatters. No significant expropriation of big estates occurred, and there was no change in the rural power structures. Rather, the reform ground to a halt when it came up against them. Meanwhile, the number of landless families was increasing by 40,000 each year.

To add to the shock, the progress in many important sectors was less than in the previous period. An increase occurred in the level of illiteracy, in the incidence of unemployment, in capital flight. The social structures remained "essentially unchanged" with two-thirds of the population not participating "in the economic and political decision-making" process.

"Perhaps the most significant and most sinister aspect of all of this," according to Enrique Cornejo, a young Colombian political scientist, "is the difference between the final judgment of Dr. Fals Borda and that of the Senate Committee. What Dr. Fals Borda rightly stresses is the mortgage which we Colombians will have to pay with our sweat, if not with our blood. The Senate Committee, while regretting the failure to measure up to the economic and social goals of the Charter of Punta del Este, asserts that 'the United States foreign assistance program in Colombia has achieved a basic political objective.' From the first, states the report, 'a primary objective has been political stability and maintenance of Colombia's democratic political institutions through support of the succession of National Front governments. This has been accomplished.' Even if one does not agree with Dr. Fals Borda's view that it would have been kinder to let the patient die a natural death, the conclusion is inescapable that the United States Senate, like the rest of the United States administration, has repudiated the commitments made at Punta del Este. So long as aid helps to maintain the political stability which has become the obsession of United States policy makers, you are willing to ignore all the other conditions. I know the argument that the United States is committed not to interfere in the internal affairs of our countries and is consequently unable to bring pressure to bear on the oligarchies to mend their ways. It would be a strong argument if you were consistent. But the fact is that you continue to interfere unilaterally when you feel your interests threatened—not only the open invasion of the Dominican Republic, but CIA plots discovered in one country after another, and the shameless manipulation of aid funds to prevent nationalization of firms which threaten our economy. You committed yourselves not to recognize or help military regimes which had overthrown constitutional governments, and you have violated that word at least half a dozen times. In Brazil, aid was suspended to help oust the president, and your cable of congratulations arrived before the army had officially announced the successor."

Latin Americans everywhere agree with the conclusion expressed by Cornejo and share his bitterness. However naïvely, they really believed the Kennedy rhetoric in the early 1960s. He succeeded in persuading them that he thought of them as human beings, that he was serious when he proposed a partnership in which the continent would share equitably the knowledge, the technology and the resources of the whole. The casual and cynical withdrawal from those commitments immediately after his death, and their neglect by subsequent administrations, have done more to harm our image than any other event in the history of the hemisphere. Many remain convinced that Kennedy was conspiratorially eliminated by forces opposed to his idealistic policies. They point to the suddenness and totality of the reversal, the diversion of aid from social reform to the strengthening of reactionary groups who would ensure the continuance of the economic and political hegemony of the United States.

The actual utilization of the loans to Colombia support the policy-reversal analysis. The Senate report shows that the United States approved allocation of $102 million for imports of food; $30 million for salaries of teachers and other government employees who were threatening to strike during the 1962 electoral campaign; $15 million for the same purposes during the 1964 electoral campaign; $15 million to pay delinquent dollar accounts (trade debts due to United States firms). A considerable part of the balance was devoted to maintaining the balance of payments on the country's foreign trade, to refinancing earlier loans, and "to increasing exports from the United States." Only 4 percent of the counterpart funds in pesos were devoted to concrete projects of socioeconomic development. On the other hand, $93 million were given to the Fund for Private Investment, controlled by the country's wealthiest businessmen, and credits and other assistance were concentrated on the large commercial farmers "at the expense of rural social progress." Finally, the military budget was almost doubled between 1958 and 1966 to combat the guerrilla movements and keep workers and students under control.

For Latin Americans, all this fits into a clear pattern. The United States is not interested in modernizing Colombia. Its only concern is to keep in power the regime on which it can depend because the regime depends on it. Even with this assumption, however, one wonders what future there is for such a policy. The mortgage falls due in the 1970s, and Colombia has not developed new sources of dollars to repay it. The Senate report recognizes that fact. It anticipates that unemployment is going to rise at a "catastrophic" rate, with a consequent increase in social unrest. The acuteness of the situation became briefly visible in 1970 when former dictator Gustavo Rojas Pinilla challenged the candidate backed by both liberal and conservative wings of the oligarchy. Contrary to subsequent rationalizations by spokesmen for the oligarchs, the peasants and unemployed slum dwellers were not at all deceived by the demagogic promises of Rojas Pinilla. What they expressed was simply their protest. And the ironic part is that the protest vote would have been much bigger were it not for the efforts of influential elements of opinion which had reached the conclusion that the proper way to express disapproval was to boycott the elections entirely. These included not only many groups of Marxist inspiration, but also such progressive Catholics as the Golconda priests. All of these have considerable influence in the slums and certainly cut down the support for Rojas Pinilla. In spite of their efforts, the protest vote came out in the first count as bigger than that of the official candidate. Whether the subsequent rectifications were legitimate or rigged will probably never be known. Even if they were legitimate, the man elected can hardly see himself as the people's choice.

The pattern of aid used to further the political interests of the United States rather than to promote a coordinated program of economic development and social reform is everywhere visible. When the military in Brazil in 1964 overthrew the constitutional government with the blessing of Washington, the level of aid was immediately raised and has subsequently been kept at a very high level, at a time when the total contribution to Latin America has diminished sharply. The fact that the military government reversed the previous programs of social reform has been overlooked. Nor is the money even concentrated in economic development. Much of it has gone to the underwriting of budget surpluses, to building up the armed forces and raising their salaries, and to the creation of a sophisticated network of repression. The priority previously accorded, at the request of successive constitutional presidents, to the depressed Northeast has been withdrawn at the insistence of the military planners. Now they concentrate the aid funds on programs that serve the armed forces and the wealthy.

Another political manipulation of foreign aid was put on the record in 1969, during the frantic efforts of Standard Oil interests to have the Hickenlooper Amendment invoked against Peru after it had nationalized a Canadian-based subsidiary, the International Petroleum Company. Richard Goodwin, a former member of the Kennedy administration, revealed that all aid to the Peruvian government of Belaunde Terry had been suspended for two years in an effort to encourage it "to moderation" in the negotiations in which it was then engaged with the International Petroleum Company. The person who made the decision was Thomas Mann, Assistant Secretary of State for Latin American affairs, and the decision was never officially communicated to the government of Peru. They were simply kept dangling on a string from month to month, the victims of psychological pressure which cost the country some $150 million.[5]

An acknowledgment of this attitude is found, surprisingly, in the 1969 Rockefeller Report. "The United States has all too often demonstrated, at least subconsciously, a paternalistic attitude toward the other nations of the hemisphere. It has tried to direct the internal affairs of other nations to an unseemly degree, thinking, perhaps arrogantly, that it knew what was best for them. It has underestimated the capacities of these nations and their willingness to assume responsibility for the course of future de-

velopments. The United States has talked about partnership, but it has not truly practiced it."[6]

The most widespread criticisms of the aid programs I
heard from social workers, missionaries, and others directly
involved with the poor, were that the overwhelming beneficiaries are those who least need to be helped. Consequently,
the end result strengthens those forces most opposed to
structural change. The already mentioned contribution of
$93 million to Colombia's Fund for Private Investment
illustrates this effect. The distribution of agricultural credit
in Guatemala follows the same pattern.

Landownership in Guatemala is typical of Latin America. Most of the good agricultural land is held in large
units by a small group of landlords. In the Guatemalan case,
2 percent of the landowners hold 60 percent of the cul-
tivable land. There are few family-sized farms, only about
10 percent of the total. At the lower end come vast numbers
of plots too small to provide a living for those who work
them. Here nearly 90 percent of all farm operators are
crowded on 18.5 percent of the land, much of it marginally
productive land on mountain slopes.

In June, 1952, a Guatemalan government headed by a
young colonel, Jacobo Arbenz Guzmán, decided to do something about this situation. It signed a decree providing for
transfer to the peasants of agricultural land being held idle
by its owners. That act was its own death sentence since it
threatened not only the local oligarchs, but 400,000 acres
belonging to the United Fruit Company. Sponsored by the
United Fruit Company and the CIA, an army of Guatemalan exiles and mercenaries moved into the country from
Honduras in June, 1954. President Dwight Eisenhower
subsequently explained why he had approved of the armed
intervention. "The communists busied themselves with
agitation, and with infiltrating labor unions, peasant organizations, and the press and radio. . . . Ambassador John E.
Peurifoy reported that President Jacobo Arbenz thought
like a communist and talked like a communist, and if not
actually one, would do until one came along."[7] The Arbenz
government, which incidentally had been democratically
elected in 1951, proved no match for United States arms.

It capitulated within ten days. One of the first actions of Colonel Carlos Castillo Armas, the invasion leader, after he had proclaimed himself president, was to return the expropriated properties to their former owners.

Thomas Melville, the United States priest already mentioned as having been expelled from Guatemala in 1968, subsequently testified under oath in a United States court on what happened next. He was shocked, he said, when he read the Eisenhower memoirs, because the former president therein admitted an intervention which his government had denied when it occurred. Melville then made his own inquiries and established that Castillo Armas had slaughtered 3,000 peasants in the process of removing them from 230,000 acres returned to the United Fruit Company. By this time, Castillo Armas had himself been assassinated, and Melville went to his successor, President Ydígoras Fuentes to ask restitution. "He was very nice and courteous, but he said there was not any land for these peasants, because they did not have capital, and they did not know how to work the land."[8]

Not only has United States influence and armed might been utilized to maintain the inequitable distribution of land in Guatemala, but foreign aid has been so arranged as to benefit the wealthy to the detriment of the poor. In Guatemala, as everywhere, one of the principal needs of the farmer is credit. But in Guatemala credit is reserved almost exclusively for the big commercial farms on and near the coast, which grow products for export. This region has 82 percent of the agricultural capital of the country, and commercial agriculture receives 90 percent of agricultural credit. Taking the country as a whole, the big landowners enjoy 95 percent of agricultural credit, while the family farms get 4 percent, leaving a mere 1 percent for the 90 percent of the farm operators whose parcels are too small to support them. In spite of all these advantages, the big operators do not use the land as efficiently as the small. The official statistics for Guatemala show that the smaller the land unit, the greater the value of the produce per acre. Each acre of the smallest units produces about eight times as much as each acre of the biggest units. Part of the reason is that the land of the microfarms is fully utilized, whereas the big landowners leave more than half of their productive land idle.

I met several officials in the aid program who were unhappy about this maldistribution of the benefits, but all ultimately agreed that the United States lost control when it agreed to drop programs of social reform and concentrate on economic development. What that meant was that the local ruling classes could channel all benefits to their own sector. The programs still include projects that seem good for the entire population, but in practice they don't work out like that. The paved roads, running water and sewers are concentrated in the part of town in which the wealthy and the upper middle class live. Slum clearance projects are manipulated so that most of those living in shacks within easy reach of the city are forcibly relocated at a distance. Typical is the case of Pedro Mineiro, a bricklayer who lived in a *favela* overlooking Botafogo Bay in Rio de Janeiro. Pedro walked to his work in Copacabana, and afterwards he dug crabs on the beach. The home lacked running water and sewers but did have electricity. Extra money earned by his wife by taking in washing could be put aside for emergencies. Their new home in a distant housing project financed with United States aid funds has a bathroom and kitchen, but the family is still crowded within an overall area of 12 by 18 feet. Mortgage payments take 18 percent of Pedro's wages, and a further 12 percent goes for transportation. The journey takes four to six hours, so that he must leave at 4 A.M. and doesn't get home until 9 P.M. He no longer has time to go crabbing, and his wife has also lost her clients. Saving is impossible, and they often fall behind on their monthly payments. The rich breathe more easily when the poor are rendered less visible by this kind of reform. But it is a problem pushed underground, not solved.[9]

Disillusionment because of the failure of foreign aid to achieve its promised benefits and its misuse to increase the distortions in Latin American society has undoubtedly played a part in the growth of anti-United States sentiment mentioned earlier as one of the big changes in the emotional climate. A much bigger factor, however, is the open take-over by the international conglomerates—most of them owned and controlled by United States interests—of nationally owned industry, banking and distribution services. The Council of the Americas, formerly called Council for Latin America, an organization headed by David Rockefeller and comprising the two hundred companies which between them represent 90 percent of United States private investment in Latin America, takes a positive view of this development. A report[10] issued in January, 1970, claims that United States private investment earned an average of $4.5 billion a year in foreign exchange through exports in recent years, and saved Latin American countries a further $4.8 billion in foreign exchange through import substitution. Sales of almost $13 billion represented about 13.7 percent of the region's aggregate domestic product. Taxes of $1.6 billion constituted 14.7 percent of total fiscal revenues. Employees number more than a million and a quarter and the number is growing constantly. In manufacturing enterprises, only 7.5 percent of the managerial staff and 2.6 percent of the technical and professional staff are from the United States. Profits have averaged $1.3 billion a year between 1960 and 1968, a return of 12.7 percent on accumulated investment. The average in manufacturing investments was 10.4 percent, "lower than the rate of return on many manufacturing investments within the United States." The level of investment had risen from $8.1 billion in 1960 to $12.5 billion in 1968, and the Council looked forward to a continuation of this process. Its formula for "the optimum contribution of private United States investment to Latin American economic and social development" is a minimum of restrictions so as to "maximize the availability of capital, technology and management skills."[11] Substantially the same view is expressed in Governor Nelson Rockefeller's 1969 report to President Nixon. "The United States," it says, "should provide maximum encouragement for private investment throughout the hemisphere."

Osvaldo Gómez, member of a family which pioneered the creation of a series of consumer-goods industries in Colombia, including food processing, paper products, paint, and plastics, takes a different view. I first met Osvaldo in the 1940s. He had just returned home from two years in a business school in the United States. Since then he has been twice married, the first marriage ending in a Las Vegas divorce. An expert skier, he retains his youthful fondness for sports cars, driving them at terrifying speeds on the precipitous Andean roads.

"You remember all those factories we helped to get started down in the Cauca Valley back in those years while I was in the United States and after I got home. Well, they are still going, of course, but we don't control them any more." He gave me his broad, slow smile and shrugged his shoulders. "You sold out?" I asked. I could hardly believe it. When I had first visited Colombia in the 1940s, I was immensely impressed by the industrial development, especially in the Antioquia region and in the Cauca Valley. Begun in the 1930s, it gained a major impetus during World War II when the traditional sources of consumer goods were cut off. The Antioquians have a reputation among Colombians for being very enterprising, and they showed it at that time. I remember visiting one factory that made rayon fiber. It had started with a single extrusion unit imported from Glasgow, Scotland, and it had built scores of additional units in its own machine shop when it found it couldn't import any more. Later, industry expanded also to the Bogotá region, always with local capital, management, and skilled labor. Foreign capital was concentrated in the development of new specialized activities, such as automobile assembly and parts which required a direct relationship with a foreign parent company.

"Yes," Osvaldo said. "We have been selling out for some time. One couldn't afford not to. Now it's the day of the big international conglomerates. They have the capital, the technology and the contacts. They will pay you a good price, if you go along with them. And if you don't, they will simply swamp you. So now we invest our money abroad and enjoy the dividends." Osvaldo laughed again. "I don't understand these things," he said, "but that's the way they work. We send our money to the United States and they send their money here. I know that most people think that money is exported from these countries by people who are afraid of revolutions and want to have an anchor to windward. I suppose that factor exists, but it's not the principal one. The way things are set up we have no choice."

Osvaldo had invited me to meet him at the exclusive Jockey Club in Bogotá. It was the early evening of the Thursday of Holy Week, and the place was nearly empty. Everything closes down in Colombia for the three last days of Holy Week, and those who have country homes leave the city for the long weekend. Osvaldo had been detained for business reasons and planned to leave later that evening to join his family. We came out of the club and started to walk toward my hotel. Suddenly, Osvaldo gripped my arm. "Look," he said, "there you can see for yourself why we can't compete with United States business." The wave of his free hand encompassed the entire scene. The street was filled with people, young and old, all in a holiday mood. "We have passed six churches and four movie houses since we left the club. Did you notice? There was a good stream of people going into the churches. But they were mostly older people. And did you see the lines for the movie houses, stretching for blocks? It's very funny. Holy Week was always the great religious festival of the year for Latin Americans. Everyone prayed and did penance and went to church. On the evening of Holy Thursday, all that people did was to visit the churches. And on Good Friday, from noon to three o'clock, everyone was in the church for the sermons on the Seven Last Words. So now what do we do? We go to the movies. Of course, they are all religious movies. Did you see the titles as we came up the street: *The Ten Commandments, The Way of the Cross, The Greatest Story Ever Told, Quo Vadis, Samson and Delilah?* That makes the people feel it is all right. Tomorrow, it will be the same. The old people will still go to church for their devotions, but the long lines will be at the movie houses. That is something that nobody here knows how to fight. Even our religion now comes from the United States."

We walked along in silence for a few blocks, Osvaldo studying each store window we passed. "That's another thing," he finally said. "Every single store advertises from one to a half dozen credit cards. You have Diners' Club, American Express, Bank Americard, Barclay's, Uni-Card, Master Charge, and I don't know how many others. Ten years ago, these were just for the tourists. Now it's for everyone. I don't know where this deluge of consumer credit is going to lead us, but with unsophisticated people unused to easy credit, it's going to cause a lot of trouble. It's just another sign of the times. The things that now concern people are status, money, and bad breath. If it's good for the United States, it must be good for us, I suppose."

The phenomena which Osvaldo describes have become commonplace in most of Latin America in recent years. Following the classical colonial pattern, the local entrepreneur is squeezed out of his own market by metropolitan firms which monopolize trademarks, technology, and credit, and he sends his accumulated capital to invest in the metropolitan money market where it is used by the very firms which had bought him out. Instead of creating new industries in previously undeveloped areas of the economy, international capital is increasingly taking over existing local industry, often at bargain prices, and simultaneously it is stimulating the mentality of the United States consumer society among the people who are within the money economy. "Much of the economic life in Latin America is dominated by foreign business, mostly American," according to Swedish economist Gunnar Myrdal. "Directly or indirectly, through joint enterprises and other arrangements, United States corporations now control or decisively influence between 70 and 90 percent of the raw material resources of Latin America, and probably more than half of its modern manufacturing industry, banking, commerce, and foreign trade, as well as much of its public utilities. These are rough estimates but are probably not far from the truth."[12] Even when a national of the country heads a firm controlled by a conglomerate, he does not make the decisions, according to Leo Model. The principals in the United States give him his orders. The major research is also conducted in United States laboratories, producing a condition of technological retardation in the host country by denying opportunities to its scientists. "Too often the

United States branches and subsidiaries constitute a sort of technological enclave—foreign-owned, foreign-manned, and foreign-directed—in an economy that remains essentially primitive."[13]

Brazilian economist Celso Furtado, who like so many of his country's best brains is today in exile, has made a profoundly disturbing analysis of this development. He notes that the companies which the international conglomerates have taken over are the most dynamic in Latin America; that is to say, the industries with the greatest potential for development and the highest level of profits. The take-over has involved a minimum of investment of new capital. In addition, it would seem that the limit of penetration is determined exclusively by the conglomerates themselves. Within the existing system, no local company can successfully challenge them. If they decide that it is worth buying, they can exercise leverage to acquire it at a price that ensures profits for them.

I found officials in the embassies and other United States agencies extremely reluctant to say anything worthwhile about any subject, but particularly about this. However, one young man in our embassy in Buenos Aires, after extracting the universally demanded promise that his words would not be attributed to him, did sketch what seemed a significant allegory.

"Let us imagine, just as a hypothetical illustration," he said, "that an Argentine firm has for twenty years been providing a product to a manufacturer in the United States, which he in turn utilizes in his own operation. He becomes dissatisfied with the quality, delivery schedules, or price. He sends down his top men to survey and recommend improvement in management procedures, accounting, operations. In spite of everything, he fails to get what he wants. So in desperation, he finally tells his Argentine supplier that he must take charge or buy elsewhere. The Argentine, in turn, now has no choice. If he loses his principal customer, he might as well go out of business. So he sells control, at the price the buyer determines."

The allegory is illustrative. No doubt, such cases occur. Still, it leaves many elements unresolved. It does not explain why all United States manufacturers, after a long period of satisfactory relationships with their Latin American suppliers, should suddenly discover a deterioration in their ability to fulfill their commitments. Nor does it explain why the Latin American industrialists who are supplying consumer goods to their home markets should equally suddenly decide to sell out. And these are the ones principally affected.

The basic reasons are, in fact, quite different. Even within developed countries like the United States, the small or medium company has, since World War II, found it increasingly difficult to maintain itself against the conglomerate. The latter's greater access to technology and credit and its ability to spread its risk through a multiplicity of products and markets give it overwhelming advantages. The international conglomerate's edge over a local Latin American company is even greater, with technology the key factor. Each year sees an acceleration of technological obsolescence, tipping the scales further in favor of the rich countries which devote huge sums to research. The poor countries must buy, and usually all they can afford is last year's model. The most up-to-date comes only under the control of the company which developed it.

The extent of this process of denationalization of private enterprise varies considerably from country to country. Mexico is the only one that makes any serious effort to prevent it. Starting in 1944, it has enacted a series of laws excluding foreign capital from certain types of enterprises and limiting the proportion in others. But these laws provide for exceptions by administrative decree, and a substantial number of exceptions have been granted. In addition, various devices circumvent the laws, the most obvious being the sleeping partner, known in Mexico as the "name-lender." Shares are registered in the name of a citizen, with a foreigner as real owner and beneficiary.

Elsewhere, the process is determined by the judgment of the conglomerates in the light of the worldwide opportunities. When the United States government promulgated regulations in 1968 calculated to reduce the rate of investment in Europe as part of a program to protect the dollar, and at the same time authorizing an increase in investments in Latin America, it was doing little more than accepting the decisions already made by United States business. Significant excess capacity for manufacturing had developed in the area of the European Common Market. Whereas United States investment there had been $2.4 billion in 1967, the projected average for 1969 and 1970 was down to $2 billion. Latin America, on the contrary, was slated to rise from $1.3 billion in 1967 to over $2 billion in 1969 and the same figure in 1970.

In consequence, as many indignant Latin Americans, including various members of the oligarchy, pointed out to me, when Nelson Rockefeller recommended in his 1969 report to President Nixon the creation of a more favorable climate for private investment, he was pleading less for Latin American impresarios than for international cartels. Figures I was given in Brazil, the biggest and one of the most industrialized countries of the continent, illustrate the relative importance of the two groups. Foreign capital exceeds local private capital 72 to 28 in the production of capital goods; 78 to 22 in that of durable consumer goods; and 52 to 48 in that of nondurables. Only in commerce and services is local private capital still in control.[14]

Where the process is not occurring, the reason is either that there is no significant local industry to take over, or it is so stagnant as not to appeal. Uruguay offers a perfect example of the latter situation. Its meat packing, textiles, beverages, and chemicals industries serve a miniscule market and survive only by reason of high protective tariffs. With the projected development of the regional common market, they will simply disappear.

Osvaldo Gómez and the other Latin American businessmen who are unable to compete are not the only opponents of the growing influence of the international conglomerates on development in Latin America. A more basic criticism is being made by economists and other social scientists. "The large corporation with its advanced technology and high capitalization," says Celso Furtado, "particularly when backed by numerous privileges, produces the same effect in an underdeveloped economy as large exotic trees introduced into an unfamiliar region: they drain all the water, dry up the land, and disturb the balance of flora and fauna."[15] Pointing out that only these large firms have the capacity and the means to operate abroad, he asserts that both the United States Congress and the administration have shown considerable concern to create conditions for the effective operation of political guarantees and economic incentives in favor of such companies. Guarantee agreements have been signed with Latin American governments to give them privileges they do not enjoy in the United States. The Hickenlooper Amendment and other measures operate as political "super-guarantees" and subject local governments to a permanent threat. If in the United States the large corporation is a cause of growing concern because of its un-controlled power, in Latin America, he concludes, "because of a number of privileges, outside the control of the United States antitrust legislation, and with United States political and military protection, the great American corporation must, of necessity, become a superpower."

Governments representing the wealthy still welcome both United States government aid and private investments, even though their concern at being squeezed from both ends is causing them to press for a better deal for the interests they represent. But an increasing number of other Latin Americans want to stop the whole process. "The more help we receive, the more debt we incur," says Joel Gajardo, the theologian mentioned earlier. "Therefore, the best way to help us is to permit us to find our own way, without enslaving aid or loans."[16] The influence of such views has grown enormously in recent years with the rapid change of the official stand of the Roman Catholic Church, traditionally a pillar of conservatism. As will be seen in the next chapter, many of its major spokesmen have declared war on "the international monopolies and the international imperialism of money." It is pertinent to enquire what impact this change will have on Latin American society in the 1970s.

5

THE CHURCH

The Catholic Church finds itself in "a new role" today in Latin America, Governor Nelson Rockefeller of New York told President Nixon after his riot-punctuated hemispheric overview in 1969. After four hundred years of "working hand-in-hand with the landowners to provide 'stability'," it has become one of "today's forces for social and political change," recognizing "a need to be more responsive to the popular will." It reminded him of the situation of the young—"a profound idealism, but . . . vulnerable to subversive penetration, ready to undertake a revolution if necessary to end injustice, but not clear either as to the ultimate nature of the revolution itself or as to the governmental system by which the justice it seeks can be realized."[1]

The above evaluation is from the Rockefeller Report's section cataloging the elements whose dynamic interplay gives life in Latin America its characteristic qualities. The later section on policy and action omits reference to the church, suggesting that the author sees it as part of the problem but not part of the solution. That position would be in line with the tradition of the American academic community. Standard textbooks present four institutions as dominating the power structures: the big landholders, the business and professional community, the army and the church. But when the dialectical interplay of these four forces is discussed, the church disappears from the paradigm. One who identifies progress with the sociopolitical system of the United States will have difficulty in conceiving of a church as exercising a different role from the one it plays here.

Mr. Rockefeller and his advisers seem unaware of a radical departure from this simplistic approach by some contemporary scholars. Instead of dropping the church from the equation, the latter project it—in what may well be a process of overcompensation—to the center of the screen, as the *deus ex machina* to resolve all the problems of the continent. A typical advocate of the new trend is George C. Lodge, a member of the faculty of the Harvard Business School and a former assistant secretary for international affairs of the Department of Labor. His book, published in 1969,[2] criticizes current United States policies as calculated to solidify the status quo and to strengthen anti-democratic oligarchs. Leadership for innovation, enterprise and initiative must, he contends, come from outside the established order. He places his hope principally in Christian Democracy, as offering the best opportunity for the philosophical regeneration of Latin America; in "the radical wing" of the Roman Catholic Church; and in new-style young entrepreneurs highly influenced by the philosophy of the Christian Democrats and of the radical Catholics who are trying to break the stultifying grip of the business establishment.

Mr. Lodge leans heavily on church-related initiatives to support his thesis: cooperatives in Bolivia and Peru which have grown out of a movement started by a Belgian priest-sociologist; peasant unions in Brazil with 150,000 members, organized by two priests; the already mentioned Veraguas program for the integral development of a rural area of Panama, begun by Archbishop Mark McGrath. He is scathingly critical of United States support of the "free" trade unions (which Mr. Rockefeller sees as part of the solution), branding them as historical misfits, creatures of the status quo, corrupt, and frightened of the revolutionary forces. The unions of Christian inspiration, on the contrary, are "representative of a revolutionary force which is bound to be of importance in the hemisphere," have "the fire of conviction and the energy of youth," constitute "the wave of the future."

A more nuanced analysis[3] comes from Ivan Vallier of the Institute of International Studies of the University of California, Berkeley. Catholics occupy "a strategic place in

Latin American social dynamics." There are still many conservatives, whom he labels *politicians* because they are "oriented to the power structure of secular society." In their
world the laity are ignored, "rituals are carried out *pro
forma,* the sacraments are available to those who can pay the
fee, and social evils are defined as implicit in the human
situation. The new pressures that have come from the Second Vatican Council, having to do with changes in the
liturgy, relations with other faiths, and lay involvement, are
strongly resisted, even satirized."

Three other Catholic elites are identified by Vallier as
papists, pastors and *pluralists.* All three reject the traditional
dependence on the state, but in different ways. The papists
would create a strong, autonomous church within the molds
of Catholic Action—lay participation with the hierarchy "in
full obedience to and with full supervision by church authorities." For the pastors, the main task is to build up
strong, worship-centered congregations. Holding that Catholicism is a minority faith in Latin America, the pluralists
turn away from traditional concerns to grass roots ethical
action in the world. "Coalitions with the 'good' are to be
made wherever and whenever possible. Community enterprises, aimed to further economic development and social
integration, are viewed as essential religious tasks. Special
attention is given to the needs and the deprivations of the
poor and the exploited. Ecumenical ties and cooperative
undertakings are established with other faiths."

Vallier sees these three new elites as complementary to
each other rather than in competition. The pluralists represent for him the final stage of evolution, the one offering
most hope for social progress. "Latin American development
increasingly centers around the secular reformers' willingness to tie their forms of production, their political objectives, and their concepts about social revolution to Catholicism's 'new face'. . . . Instead of simply more capital or shiny
tools, support is needed to help the new Catholic elites
transform their system in order that the 'Catholic' factor
and its cultural power can be applied to the whole task of
social development. In short, religious reform is a requisite
of social reform." While Vallier sees the pluralists as offering

the final, socially desirable situation, he insists that the logic of evolution calls for orderly development from the traditional politicians through the stages of papists and pastors. This becomes more difficult in proportion to the strength of the politicians in a national hierarchy, encouraging the temptation to leapfrog and end up simply as *neopoliticians.*

The Vallier thesis is not shared by all sociologists. David E. Mutchler insists that the new Catholic elites are not very different from the old. "If church development is a requisite for social development in Latin America, this is indeed unfortunate, because the Latin American church is not developing. It is fragmenting on a massive scale. The conflicts with which it is now riven do not derive from scholarly quarrels over biblical exegesis nor from the differing psychic needs of the faithful. The conflicts are based, instead, upon opposing and incompatible institutional interests."[4]

A distinctive feature of all the new elites is that they visualize and project the church as a hemispheric reality. Traditionally, the church played a major role in each country, closely related to and usually controlled by the national government which named the bishops and paid the bills. The only external relations were directly with the Holy See, and these also remained within the ambit of the national government because of the parallel contacts of the state through the nuncio and its ambassador to the Vatican. The bishops of Latin America got together only once between colonial times and 1955. That was in Rome, in 1899, at the invitation of Pope Leo XIII, to work out a common ecclesiastical discipline. The 1955 meeting in Rio de Janeiro, summoned by Pope Pius XII, led to the creation of the Latin American Episcopal Council (CELAM), an organization for contact and collaboration between the bishops' conferences of the various countries. From the outset, it was given its tone and direction by such progressives as the late Bishop Manuel Larraín of Chile, Archbishop Helder Camara of Brazil, and Bishop Sergio Méndez Arceo of Mexico. However, its early efforts to fulfill its stated function of "adapting pastoral activity to contemporary needs" were effectively aborted by a parallel body set up in Rome—the Commission for Latin America (CAL)—staffed by reactionary members of the Roman Curia. That situation continued until the Second Vatican Council which brought all the bishops of the world to Rome for each of four sessions between 1962 and 1965. Progressives among the Latin American bishops seized this opportunity to revise the constitution of CELAM and establish its autonomy.

The most dramatic success of the progressives was the promulgation by the Second General Conference of Latin American Bishops in August, 1968, of a program of action known as the Medellín Statements. The victory was preceded by a public clash which began when *O Jornal*, a conservative daily of Rio de Janeiro, published a harsh attack on a professor at the Recife seminary, José Comblin. A Belgian sociologist and theologian, Father Comblin has worked for twelve years in Latin America, first in Chile and more recently in Brazil. A big man, with a disarming smile and an engaging manner, he holds progressive views and has a penchant for inflated language which have made him staunch friends and dedicated enemies throughout the hemisphere. *O Jornal* belongs in the latter category. It happily precipitated a scandal by printing confidential comments on the working paper for the upcoming Medellín conference, which Comblin had prepared with a view to having its language strengthened. The Brazilian press denounced him as a bad priest, as author of a "new Mein Kampf," and as a "Leninist theologian." In Colombia, *La República* compared him to Camilo Torres and described the document as designed "to incite Catholics, on the occasion of the bishops' conference, to armed conflict and an alliance with Marxists." A member of the city council in Recife called on the government to expel the subversive priest "in order to save the religious patrimony of Brazil and its democratic security."[5]

Leader of the opposition to the progressives was the sixty-year-old archbishop of Diamantina, Brazil, Geraldo de Proença Sigaud, a man as fiery and flamboyant as Comblin himself. Sigaud had come into prominence during the Vatican Council by organizing the International Group of Fathers as a caucus for the intransigent minority seeking to block the Council's efforts to update the church. More recently, in Brazil, he had formulated his oppostion to land reform in theological terms by declaring that he would refuse the Eucharist to any peasant who accepted a title to land distributed under the law. He had also collected a thousand signatures—including that of the wife of the country's president—for a letter to Pope Paul deploring "the communist subversion which is at times to be found hidden in the priest's cassock." And he had persuaded twelve Brazilian bishops to join him in signing a letter which warned the president that "the techniques of the left and subversive activities calculated to push Brazil into social chaos are becoming widespread among bishops, priests and the laity." Thanks to the efforts of Sigaud and his friends, the list of theologians invited to the bishops' meeting was revised and several regarded as too progressive were eliminated. Sigaud himself went to Bogotá, where Pope Paul opened the meeting during his visit to that city, and he had the satisfaction of hearing the pope refer sarcastically in public to the "new theologians" who "arrogate to themselves the permission to proclaim their own personal opinions." At Medellín, however, where the bishops moved for their deliberations after the formal opening, his success was limited. The meeting "made an unambiguously clear choice for radical transformation."[6] The documents that emerged constituted a 40,000-word call to revolution. They offered a concept of a liberating God to replace the God of private property. They denounced the oppressing power used by institutions to impose violence, the neocolonialism of the national oligarchies, and the external neocolonialism of "the international monopolies and the international imperialism of money," on which the entire system rests. They listed specifically the growing distortion of international commerce caused by decline of raw material prices while those of manufactured goods rise, the flight of capital, the brain drain, the tax evasions, and the export of profits and dividends by foreign companies "without contributing adequate reinvestments to the progressive development of our countries," the growing burden of debt. "Many parts of Latin America are experiencing a situation of injustice which can be called institutionalized violence. The structures of industry and agriculture, of the national and the international economy, the cultural and political life all violate fundamental rights. Entire peoples lack the bare necessities and live in a condition of such dependency that they can exercise neither initiative or responsibility. Similarly, they lack all possibility of cultural improvement and of participation in social and political life. Such situations call for global, daring, urgent, and basically renewing change. It should surprise nobody that the temptation to violence should manifest itself in Latin America. It is wrong to abuse the patience of people who have endured for years a situation that would be intolerable if they were more aware of their rights as human beings."[7]

Henri Fesquet of *Le Monde* of Paris, who covered Pope Paul's visit to Latin America, entitled the book he wrote on his return *A Church in the State of Mortal Sin*.[8] Comblin's words are still in the final texts of Medellín, harsh as those of Fesquet: a church burdened with wealth, an accomplice of oppressive government, guilty of preaching an alienating formulation of the gospel. But the influence of Sigaud and his allies is also evident. The self-condemnation is now hedged around with reservations. Instead of concrete reforms, we have exhortations to virtue and pious hopes for personal conversion. "We hear complaints that the hierarchy, the clergy, and the religious orders are rich and allies of the rich. In this context we have to make clear that appearances are often taken for reality. Many elements have contributed to this image of a rich church: the great buildings, parish houses, and convents better than those of the people; personal automobiles that at times are in the luxury class; a style of dress inherited from past ages; the exaggerated secrecy surrounding the income of schools, parishes and dioceses. . . . The reality of the very many parishes and dioceses which are extremely poor, and of so many bishops, priests and members of religious orders who lead lives of privation and serve the poor in the midst of hardships, are generally overlooked. . . . It is our desire to have a modest home and life style. . . . We urge priests to give a witness of poverty and detachment from material things. . . . We want our Latin American church to be free from temporal ties, from situations that give tacit approval to wrongdoing, and from ambiguous honors."

Having incorporated fully the analysis of Latin America's problems made by most of today's progressive Catholics, the Medellín Statements departed significantly from their approach to a solution. They reject equally "the liberal capitalist system" and "the temptation of the Marxist system"—the former, "because it starts by assuming the primacy of capital, of its power, and of its right to indiscriminate use in order to make profits"; the latter, "because, even if ideologically it can support humanist values, it is more concerned with collective man, and in practice it ends up as a totalitarian concentration of power in the state." Instead, the Statements call for a restructuring of the economy according to "the directives of the social magisterium of the church." What this somewhat vague expression meant for them was spelled out in a passage which showed that they had in mind the corporate state as projected in a series of encyclicals from Leo XIII's *Rerum novarum* to Pius XI's *Quadragesimo anno*. "We make an urgent appeal to businessmen and their organizations, as well as to the political authorities, to modify radically their system of values, their attitudes and methods as they affect the purpose, organization and operation of their enterprises. Those entrepreneurs who individually or through their organizations try to operate their business in accordance with the directives of the social doctrine of the church deserve every support. Only through such initiatives can social and economic change in Latin America be directed toward a truly human economy."[9] Apart from this statement, I did not in my travels find a single voice in favor of the solutions proposed in these encyclicals to upgrade the workers and renew the social order. Many dismissed them as applicable to the conditions of nineteenth-century Europe. Others went farther, denying that they ever had any validity anywhere. "They were purely theoretical constructs derived from abstract principles in scholastic ivory towers," was a typical comment. "They had no foundation in lived reality."

Catholic publications around the world, most of which are dominated by progressive intellectuals, hailed the

Medellín Statements as the opening of a new era. Priests and lay people in Latin America, who had taken seriously the Second Vatican Council's call for church renewal, welcomed with equal enthusiasm the denunciation of "institutionalized injustice," and placed little stress on the divergence regarding proposed solutions. Within a period of a year, the national conferences of bishops of each country had issued their own parallel statements, reaffirming the broad lines of Medellín and applying its general evaluations to their own situation.

An important practical result was to take some of the heat off priests and lay people who had previously been denounced as communists because of their rejection of the existing economic and social system. They could now appeal to Medellín as their authority. The Quito Reflection Group in Ecuador, for example, early in 1970 sponsored a meeting attended by a hundred priests, a tenth of all priests in the country, and also by three bishops as observers. It endorsed a program demanding support for a poor church dedicated to man's liberation; priests who contribute to the human and Christian advancement of the people; authority to be exercised in terms of service and coresponsibility, ending feudal domination by the powerful; a department for relations with the Vatican in the bishops' conference to replace the nuncio; a united struggle of priests and people against unjust capitalistic and feudalistic structures; optional celibacy; ordination of married men and readmission to the active ministry of those who had withdrawn and remarried; a civil profession for priests so that they could earn their own living.

It soon became clear, however, that the changes were more apparent than real. Even if talk was now freer, the speakers remained as removed as ever from the levers of power which they would need to control before they could implement their ideas. Soon they were recalling ruefully an abiding Latin American reality. In colonial times, the decrees of the Spanish king were always received with elaborate honors—received, recorded and filed. When the colonies became independent, they imported from Europe the most advanced ideas for popular government: demo-

cratic and egalitarian. They wrote them into their constitutions. And then they went on living and governing in
the same autocratic and oligarchic way as before. Today
many are asking if the Medellín Statements have any more
validity than Latin America's civil constitutions.

The archbishop of Lima is one of those who has moved
out of a medieval palace. His new home, nevertheless,
continues to identify its occupant as a member of the
upper class in an upper middle-class neighborhood. It does
little to narrow the gap between him and Lima's half-
million slum dwellers. The new home of the archbishop of
Santiago de Chile, if more modest, puts its owner on a level
with company presidents and corporation lawyers. Another
bishop I met, however, lives in the sacristy of an old church
and sleeps under the high altar. But in general, there was
little evidence of more than token divorce from "capitalistic" ownership and use of property, or from the boarding
schools and other institutions which identify the church
with the wealthy. Church finances continue to be shrouded
in secrecy. Programs to divest the church of its estates and
hand them over to the peasants have been initiated in
various dioceses, but their progress is often as ambiguous
as that of the reforms undertaken by governments under the
Alliance for Progress. Meanwhile, all too often, the pastor
is still the landowner's paid employee, and his Sunday
sermon is a call to the peons to virtuous resignation.

Where the persistence of the system is most evident is
in the continuing partnership of church and state authorities to prevent development of movements not under
their control. Restrictions on the already mentioned Golconda priests in Colombia provide a good example. At the
the first sign that they were making an impact on the
deprived masses, just a year after the Medellín Statements,
their principal leaders were jailed briefly by the government,
then suspended by their bishops.

At almost the same time, in December, 1969, the
bishops of Chile shut down the Latin American Institute
of Economic and Social Studies (ILADES), the most important Catholic training center in Latin America in the
theology of liberation and in the techniques for implement-

ing it. A statement issued by forty priests from thirteen Latin American countries at the last seminar held by ILADES no doubt helped to seal its fate, even though it is in full accord with the spirit of Medellín. "Our church remains for the most part silent in the presence of injustice. Groups and movements which contradict the teachings and attitudes of the Vatican Council and of Medellín are not censured. Instead, they are implicitly or explicitly approved and backed. Even more incomprehensible is the contradiction between the documents that were signed in the exercise of a pastoral mission and the . . . disapproval of expressions and undertakings of priests and lay people who want to live their faith fully and authentically." The closing of ILADES was announced as a suspension; at the time of this writing it was scheduled to reopen under new management—and minus its teeth.

In Brazil, church and state have conspired to silence every progressive voice. Dom Helder Camara's name has disappeared from the communications media since 1968. The media now publish only distorted extracts from statements of "the archbishop of Recife," mixed with rumors and slanders. All that Brazilians are told of his international appearances is that he is defaming his homeland. His only remaining outlets are a hand-delivered weekly newsletter to the priests and a talk to the people of his diocese each Monday on a local low-powered radio station.

The Third World priests in Argentina have similarly failed to achieve any significant victory. Their 1969 manifesto calls for a society which "will be socialist and will totally eliminate private property from the means of production." They strongly oppose Argentina's military dictatorship as insensitive to the needs of people. Most of the bishops support the regime, but a few favor the views of the Third World movement. In 1969, when student and worker demonstrations against the government and against the United States erupted into violence and were put down with considerable loss of life, Archbishop Antonio Plaza of La Plata commented: "When entire populations live in complete dependency, lacking all initiative and responsibility, with no possibility of advancement or better participation in social and political life, there is a great temptation to reject injustices with violence." A short time later, the regime tried to reaffirm its identification with Catholicism by an elaborate ceremony of consecration of the country to the Immaculate Heart of Mary, but it only succeeded in provoking new conflict. "What do we have to consecrate?" asked the Third World Movement. "God rejects all religious acts which are not accompanied by justice and brotherhood. The Argentine people have something very important to consecrate—their hope to be free, and their release from an economic and cultural dependency."

A major effort to promote reform within the church itself has, however, produced nothing better than a stalemate. After a long period of negotiation with Archbishop Guillermo Bolatti of Rosario, twenty-eight of his priests resigned their posts in mid-1969 to protest his refusal to modify his conservative policies. They charged that he was not implementing the reforms ordered by the Second Vatican Council and by Medellín. Soon the conflict escalated with countercharges that the priests were "influenced by Marxist ideologies, promoters of subversion and revolutions, acting against the armed forces, backers of guerrilla movements, and violators of ecclesiastical and civil rights." Three hundred priests from other dioceses came to their aid. They rejected "the tyrannic exercise of authority in the church," denounced the absence of dialogue and contact with the grass roots church, the failure of the national conference of bishops to intervene, and the restraints imposed on priests "who are opening themselves to new pastoral experiences." After efforts to have the Holy See retire the archbishop had failed, the priests announced in mid-1960 that they were withdrawing completely from the diocese.

While the stand taken by the Holy See shocked some, it surprised nobody. In spite of a series of superficial reforms introduced by Pope Paul VI under the prodding of the Vatican Council, the Roman Curia, the Vatican's civil service, continues to exercise a mishmash of executive, judicial and legislative functions in the tradition of a seventeenth-century absolute monarchy. Some of its top cardinals have openly backed the traditionalists around the world in their efforts to impede reforms legislated by the Council. Its attitudes run parallel to those of reactionary Latin American governments, most of whom still exercise the *patronato,* the right to name bishops enjoyed by Spain's kings from medieval times, and who also pay salaries to the clergy or subsidize the church in other ways. The total result of these combinations is that Rome sides with the conservatives and mortgages the future by concentrating power in safe hands. The two latest Brazilian prelates made cardinals leave that group without a single progressive voice. The Brazilian government, for its part, has adopted a policy of ignoring the national conference of bishops, in which Dom Helder Camara and his friends have a voice, doing business instead with the club of cardinals. In El Salvador, in 1969, fifty of the country's 350 priests protested the promotion of their archbishop to the rank of cardinal as a countersign, on the ground that he is "a friend of the rich and of the politicians in power."

I talked to several of the theologians who helped to draft the Medellín Statements. Why, I asked them, would bishops go on record as supporting policies in complete contradiction with what they really believe? "These documents," I was told, "were drafted by five or six priests, several of them of European origin and all of them exposed to the progressive trends in the church in France, Germany and the Low Countries. You must always remember our cultural colonialism. For the people it is the consumption society of the United States, but the church and many intellectuals still slavishly accept European leadership. The 156 bishop delegates at Medellín did debate and revise the documents, introducing the inconsistencies which always result when politicians take over from experts. More than five hundred other Latin American bishops were not present, and few of these have ever read the final statements or would understand them if they did. Taken globally, perhaps 10 percent of the region's bishops have progressive ideas, and most of these have been exposed to currents of thought of other parts of the world. An even smaller number form the reactionaries and conservatives who have the knowledge and skill to offer a reasoned defense of their stand. In between, you have a mass of simple functionaries, men with a limited formal education who would be hard put to get a job as a primary teacher if they needed it. In the conference hall, they follow the leader. Back home, however, they vote with their feet like every silent majority does. They won't change anything, because they know no alternative way to function. They simply await the word from Rome. When Rome tells them to turn the altar around, they turn it around. Tomorrow they would with equal alacrity turn it back."

Some young priests have a more open outlook, but the structures are completely self-protecting. "We had a short period of optimism under the influence of the Vatican Council," I was told. "But the experience of would-be reformers is the same in the church as in the rest of society. Everyone approves of a pilot program, but when it threatens the structure, you've had it. The Catholic secondary schools for the education of the children of the wealthy have not changed. The pastors in the parishes continue to teach the traditional fatalism and resignation. In many places, the only substantive function performed by the parish priest is to baptize infants. Baptism is a social ceremony essential for the children of every class. It integrates the child into the society, giving him the support of godparents without whom it is impossible to make one's way in the world. A priest will have 25,000 people in his parish, and with the high birth rates, he will have 2,000 or more baptisms each year. For each he receives an established fee, and that provides his basic living. He derives some additional income from marriage fees, though most don't bother to go through a marriage ceremony. As a rule, there is not much income from masses, because the social function of the mass is limited. However, people will have a mass said at the time of a death, often for the superstitious purpose of placating the spirit of the dead person and fending off harm from the survivors. Mass is also important as an element in the celebration of local festivals, and it may then signify for the people an act of propitiation or sacrifice to their own traditional gods."

What emerges is a picture of the priest who serves his parish as an outside functionary engaged in formal activities, but without vital relationship with the people. Even if a native of the country where he works, he comes from that other society and is as much its representative as the mayor or the policeman: part of any army of occupation. His purpose is not to teach religion or anything else but to perform a series of ritual actions which express on both sides an aspect of the incorporation of the conquered into the system of the conqueror.

This underlying reality had been clearly described for the bishops by Father Comblin in his analysis of the draft working document, already mentioned. "The concepts of North American or European sociology regarding the social classes, social mobility, and allied issues are not applicable in Latin America," he wrote. "The inequality here is far greater than the simple inequalities of social classes. What we have are two races, two civilizations which have not yet interpenetrated each other. The aristocrats find the extraordinary social or socioracial inequality normal. Latin America consists of colonies in which the conquerors established themselves. They were not driven out by the wars or revolutions of independence. On the contrary, their power was increased. . . . The clergy identifies itself with the dominating group. It consists exclusively of persons who have been assimilated into this group. Its education is along the same lines as that of the upper classes, and its social relations are with them."

What this means, according to Comblin, is that the church is "one of the most underdeveloped of all Latin American institutions," and "linked far more closely to underdevelopment than the church in Asia or Africa." It neglects the peasants and slum dwellers. "The people of the slaves and of their descendants are not cared for. Their situation has grown worse since independence. The institution of 'absolution' (a declaration that the peasants were not obligated to attend mass on Sundays) constitutes one of the most serious errors in the history of the church. Not even the peasants of medieval Europe were treated in this way. The absolution recognizes implicitly that the peasants are second-class citizens. Their conscience is legally unbound, but the assumption remains that they do not have spiritual needs. The church leaders found a way to salve their own consciences by suppressing the obligation of Sunday mass, thinking that in this way they were taking care of the religious formation of souls. Had the church been seriously concerned about the peasants, it would have come up with another solution. But it is clear that it did not regard the peasants as of any value. The result is a rural population which, in practice, receives no spiritual aid from the church, depending exclusively on family tradition to transmit its religious beliefs and practices from one generation to the next."

A concrete example of the coexistence of the two civilizations is provided by the fiesta mass in Brazil. On December 8, the Feast of the Immaculate Conception brings everyone to church, and the devotion is overwhelming. But for millions, the rite is not in honor of Mary, mother of the Christian God, but of Yemanja or Janaina, an African goddess of the sea and of fertility. Later in the day, the worship is continued under the presidency of a *candomblé* priest or priestess in shrines or temples designated exclusively for these rites. Other Christian feasts similarly serve to worship traditional gods, St. Lazarus being identified with Omolu, St. Barbara decked out in her arrows with Shango, the sword-carrying St. George with Oshosse, god of the hunt. Also important are such other sword wielders as Joan of Arc and Cosmas and Damian, similarly identified with African war gods. Many Brazilian priests spend all their working years ministering to this cult, yet so unrelated to the people of their parishes that they do not have the slightest idea of the real role they play in the community. The original reason for the cloaking of the traditional religion in Christian costume was that its practice had been outlawed from the earliest times, a prohibition lifted only during the presidency of João Goulart in the early 1960s. During all that period, the people kept this and many other secrets from the strangers among them. Even today, although the facts have been fully established by social scientists, the church in Brazil has no experts on the subject of indigenous religions, preferring to ignore it.

A similar pattern of hybrid practices is found in many places. The voodoo rites of Haiti and other parts of the West Indies incorporate elements of the Catholic mass. The Pacha Mama, the earth goddess to whom the Quechua and Aymara Indians of the highlands of Bolivia and Peru offer animals in burnt sacrifice, is identified in their minds with the image of the Virgin Mary. The *brujo* (wizard) of the Guatemala Indians takes his followers to worship their traditional deities in the Catholic church of the village as well as in other holy places. In Panama, according to a missionary, the people see the church "as something apart from themselves, principally as the hierarchy. The priest is from another class, another culture, usually from another continent. His presence in popular Catholicism, while important, is marginal. Take the burial rite as a good example. This rite in its fullness embraces everything that happens from the moment of death (which almost always occurs without a visit by the priest) to the completion of a nine-day mourning period, or even longer. You have the arrangement of the room, the candles, the statues, the prayers, the ceremonial weeping, the procession to the church, the ceremonies in the church, the attempts to throw oneself into the open grave in the cemetery. In all this, the priest has his ten or twenty minutes. It is a perfect model of the entire situation of the official church in the framework of popular Catholic religious life. The church has its ten or twenty minutes. The rite of baptism follows exactly the same pattern."

In the view of this same missionary, many of the elements of this popular Catholicism are expressions of the situation of oppression in which the people live. "If the world of their experience is a hierarchy, is it not natural to assume that the supernatural world is similarly structured? If in this world the relationships of cause and effect are not under man's control, does it not make sense to seek the aid of prayer by turning to a saint who is closely related to the one who decides? And if this is the way God has made the world, the best thing is to learn to live with it. Here we are obviously touching on what Marx called 'alienation' and Freud discovered as a 'projection.' The church has tried to answer these criticisms by saying such is not the effect of true Christianity. However, that is an idealist defense, because it does not take into account the concrete situation of most of the people. The only valid answer would be a new praxis, a radical change of approach."

The institutional church has not made such a change for a variety of reasons. One is its lack of resources. What can one man do who is charged with the spiritual care of ten, twenty or thirty thousand illiterates? How can he even face up emotionally to the fact that his predecessors and he have done no more than establish a meaningless conformity? Then there is his vested interest. The present arrangement provides a livelihood and a status which any change could jeopardize. And finally, as Comblin has pointed out, he has been assimilated into and identifies with the dominant group, not with the people. The dominant group wants to keep the people the way they are.

That there exists within the institutional church a dynamic minority trying to change the praxis, and that it has succeeded at Medellín in getting formal approval for its approach, is due in large measure to the new wave of foreign missionaries from Europe and North America who swept into the region after World War II. The movement was strongly promoted by the Holy See, alarmed by the inroads of Protestantism (especially in its Pentecostal forms) in Latin America, as well as the growing imbalance between population and indigenous priests. These foreign priests arrived with an optimism engendered by the success of the Marshall Plan in Europe. They shared the belief of the international agencies who were simultaneously promoting the economic development of Latin America that they possessed the know-how to remake the church in Latin America in the image and likeness of the churches of their respective home countries. Many Latin American seminarians and young priests were caught up in this movement, and it seemed for a short time to be accomplishing a basic transformation of the system. Before long, nevertheless, it became apparent that the successful, but highly subsidized pilot programs were no more than tokenism. Like foreign aid in the civil sphere, what was being done was admirable, but each year the problem grew bigger and the possibility of solution dimmer. To provide more ample and efficient techniques for bringing the rites of religion to the people while leaving them in their present conditions would merely advance the cause of superstition. To make men religious, they first had to be made men.

The updated self-image achieved by the church at the Second Vatican Council strengthened this revised view. The stress on service to mankind, and especially to the poor, encouraged the trend to give preference to social action over traditional religious activities. The emphasis on the primacy of the local church taught the foreign missionaries to recognize that it was a form of spiritual colonialism on their part to attempt to impose the structures and attitudes of their home churches elsewhere. This self-questioning was greatly encouraged and given new perspectives by an article entitled "the Vanishing Clergyman"[10] published by Ivan Illich who, as head of the Cuernavaca Institute, had introduced many U.S. missionaries to the Spanish language and the culture of Latin America. The Roman Church, said Illich, is "the world's largest nongovernmental bureaucracy," employing 1,800,000 full-time workers. For all its efficiency, "men suspect that it has lost its relevance." The traditional clergyman is "a folkloric phantom," "a member of the aristocracy of the only feudal power remaining in the world," "a man sentenced to disappear, whether the church wishes it or not, by the changes in modern society." Instead, Illich sees the leisure society as opening a part-time ministry to laymen "mature in Christian wisdom" through prayer, study of scripture and a life of service, without removal from their careers or incorporation into a clerical caste.

The self-questioning of the missionaries is by no means unique. Many members of the Peace Corps and of other foreign aid programs have gone through a similar process of enlightenment, often quite traumatic. Here is the story told me by one, not atypical, United States priest. "I was in Brazil about four years, doing all the things I had been taught, baptizing, saying mass, preaching, signing forms, all that jazz. I was doing a good job. You couldn't knock it. I was working in a slum and it was a period of rapid inflation. The people who came to my office seemed to have only one problem: how to make ends meet. Someone suggested a protest march to dramatize the hunger of the people. It was perfectly legal, and I agreed to join. But the cops came after us and they beat up the students unmercifully. Several were hospitalized. I had never seen anything like it in my life. We fled into a school and we stayed there all night, fearing further punishment if we broke into small groups to go home. The entire night was spent in discussion of our problems and proposals for remedying them. It was then I realized that the poor have no rights, and that if my priesthood was to have any meaning, it should be devoted to changing that unjust situation."

Another who has described the process of his radicalization is Thomas Melville, a former Maryknoll priest, who was expelled from Guatemala along with three other United States missionaries—one of them his brother—after working for fifteen years among the highland Indians. They were charged with having helped a guerrilla group. "Having come to the conclusion that the actual state of violence, composed of the malnutrition, ignorance, sickness and hunger of the vast majority of the Guatemalan population, is the direct result of a capitalist system that makes the defenseless Indian compete against the powerful and well-armed landowner, my brother and I decided not to be silent accomplices of the mass murder that this system generates. We began teaching the Indians that no one will defend their rights, if they do not defend themselves. If the government and the oligarchy are using arms to maintain them in their position of misery, then they have the obligation to take up arms and defend their God-given rights to be men. . . . This is a situation which is not an accident of history but an international perversion of the natural order effected by a wealthy minority, supported by the national army, which is in turn backed by the government of the United States and blessed by the hierarchy of the Catholic Church. . . . The fact that the United States is training the armies of the countries of Latin America to help maintain the state of exploitation is a further reason why we, as citizens of the United States, should struggle to correct this shocking situation."[11]

This type of radicalization, involving a deep questioning—if not total rejection—of both civil and ecclesiastical structures, is widespread and growing among missionaries from the United States, Canada and Europe, especially those under forty years of age. Even priests from Spain and Italy, traditionally pietistic and conservative, are well represented. The expulsion of missionary priests for their advanced views, sometimes by the church authorities, sometimes by the state, often by the two powers in collusion, has become commonplace.

For the United States missionary, the deepest trauma occurs not with the rejection of local civil and church structures, of which he never thought much in the first instance, but with a subsequent step, the repudiation of the American Way of Life. This occurs when his reflection on the misery of the poor forces him to recognize that the Medellín Statements were correct in placing the ultimate blame for the situation on the built-in imperialism of international capitalism. Some of the older missionaries still see the American presence as the rich man's burden, bravely and selflessly borne, but most of the young ones have reached the point of doubt or gone beyond it. One young United States priest in Bolivia told me that hell for him would be to have to readjust to the Cadillac and $30,000-home routine into which his seminary colleagues had already settled within a few years of ordination. "All my colleagues think the same way," another told me in Chile. "It's common knowledge that United States business methods and even our foreign aid are harming the Chilean economy." Typical of the conclusions reached are those expressed by a group of Anglican and Catholic missionaries from the United States at the end of a week of prayer, reflection and discussion together. "We have discovered that as American missionaries we are failing the Brazilian people. . . . Even our number has increased markedly with the number of foreign businessmen, until the foreigner encompasses 50 percent of the economic and religious potential of the country. . . . We protest against the American business corporations who are reaping the cream of financial dividends, . . . against a United States foreign policy indifferent to Brazil's right to determine her own

destiny, against United States assistance given to development programs which unjustly disregard the needs of the
majority of the people. . . . For the majority of the people
progress is a spectacle. Their participation in economic
growth is to look on as 'progress' parades by, to clear their
throats and spit on the newly paved parade routes. . . .
The United States has injured, is injuring, and will continue to injure the lives and liberties of many Brazilians,
if it continues to render aid because of the fear of communism and the fear of inevitable social change. . . . We
could say nothing, but if we did, we would betray the very
people we have come to serve. The misery, the slavery, the
underdevelopment will not be cured by silence, just as it
will not be solved during the present economic occupation
by foreign capitalistic empires, among which the United
States stands most culpable for her overpowering and self-
preserving presence. It is difficult as well as embarrassing
for us to say these things, . . . but we must express the truth
as we have experienced it with our Brazilian brothers."

Some of the younger Latin American priests share the
views of these missionaries, but they are a small proportion
of the total, and it is doubtful that their number is rising.
The modernization of many seminaries after the Second
Vatican Council brought a substantial rise in the number
of candidates to the priesthood. But the exposure of the
students to progressive ideas quickly caused them to change
their minds, as they saw the enormous gap between what
they were expected to do as priests and the structures within
which they would have to function. About a thousand of
Brazil's 12,000 priests abandoned the ministry over a period
of five years. The seminary of Recife was down to thirty
students in 1970 from a former level of 120. Fortaleza,
which used to have a hundred, had closed down. The same
trend exists in the entire region. A seminary in Chile that
used to have 120 students was also down to thirty. Those
who leave the priesthood or the seminary because of their
progressive attitudes tend to drop out of the church structures altogether. The same process is visible among progressive lay people. A study of a representative Catholic Action
group revealed that half of those who were activists six
years earlier had subsequently left the church in disgust.

The radicalized priests who stay within the church structures, like the radical intellectuals and students, are placing all their bets on the peasants and the urban slum dwellers. Most of those who have committed themselves to this new approach continue to offer the traditional church services to any who seek them, but without stressing that aspect of their ministry. The boast is no longer that "I had 2,000 baptisms last year," but that "I baptized only ten children, and in every case the parents had first taken a complete course of instruction in Christian doctrine." These priests do not see themselves as conduits of grace to tens of thousands of people. They are satisfied if they can create a few small islands of Christian life, leaving the future radiation to the Holy Spirit.

As a concrete example of the application of these concepts may be cited two United States priests who concentrate their energies on ten families in their slum parish of 20,000 people. They hope that in a few years, five or six of the heads of these families will be ordained deacons and that after a further interval of experimentation and preparation these deacons can be ordained to the priesthood. The current discipline in the Roman Catholic Church permits the ordination to the diaconate of married men, and there are strong pressures for extension of this provision so that mature married men can become priests. Those who are working to create a revolutionary mentality among the peasants and slum dwellers regard this as absolutely necessary. The present system of preparation of celibate priests in seminaries effects a total emotional estrangement from the people, even in the rare cases in which the candidate is one of them.

Another priest, a Brazilian, in a rural parish with 15,000 people, works with five groups of fifty persons each, seeking to develop them into true Christian communities. "It will then be up to each to determine the structures it finds necessary to lead its Christian life," he says. "Some may want a member to be ordained to serve as community president. Others may be content with the occasional visit of an outside priest. Others may find other solutions. Who knows?"

The parish of a third priest is a shanty town without

light, water, or roads, two hours from a major city. When it rains, there is a sea of red mud both inside and out. The pastor lives on the spot, and at no better material level than many of his parishioners. Convinced that the sacramental system as traditionally practiced lacked all Christian significance for these people and served to alienate them in the Marxist sense, he has no church and performs no liturgical or sacramental activities. He is proud of his calloused hands. On a typical day, he helps one of his parishioners to build his home. It is a job that calls for more patience than skill. Some light saplings are tied together to make a frame. The walls are mud, the roof either tile or a thatch woven from palm leaves. The pastor's main continuing work is an informal conscientization program with a few teenagers.

All engaged in these experiments agree on one point. They deny the long held claim that Latin America is a Catholic continent, stressing instead the failure over five centuries of the church—as of society—to incorporate the common people in any meaningful way. They see themselves as not even starting from scratch, but rather forced to tear away a mass of superstitions and distortions in order to begin. The new church they envision would be strikingly different; as one slum dwelling priest expressed it, "a truly popular Catholicism in Latin America would likely assume a pentecostal or sect appearance. Hopefully, it would also be political, that is, related to the problems of man living in society. It would therefore be involved in the concrete and controversial. In order to avoid alienation of the people, it would have to foment rather than diminish class consciousness." In consequence, this new "Catholicism of the masses" would not be structurally subordinated to the present upper-class church, or even associated with it in conventional ways. "It would not easily 'integrate' with other Christians organized in parishes and dioceses. On the contrary, it would assert its dissimilarity in dialectic militancy; not in violation of Christian unity, but with the honesty which is essential to unity. It would be in the hands of its own popular leaders."

To the extent that these forces and directions grow within the church, it will certainly be a force for "social, economic and political change," as Governor Rockefeller has described it. But it is far too soon to prophesy with any assurance that they will prevail. The church in Latin America is as fully incarnated in the colonial-dependent system as are the other social organs. What is clear at present is that the efforts to update in the spirit of Pope John XXIII and the Vatican Council have produced signs of the "inner rebellion," the "self-demolition" which worry John's successor, Pope Paul VI. It is also clear that the church is the only social and moral institution in Latin America powerful enough to survive the destruction of "intermediate structures," which is a primary objective of contemporary military dictatorships. In that sense, the best hope for the people would seem to be a victory of the progressive elements within the church itself.

6

THE
ARMED FORCES

Major Mauro Itacarambi lives in a modern apartment building with his wife and three children at Ipanema Bay, less well known but more fashionable than neighboring Copacabana, on Rio de Janeiro's fabulous waterfront. Life has treated Major Itacarambi rather well. His father, a bookkeeper in Petropolis, had business connections who obtained a place for him in the War College. He graduated as a second lieutenant just in time to share the upgrading of the armed forces that followed the coup d'état of April, 1964. When he had joined the army, he had figured out that if he lived right and cultivated the proper people, he should in twelve or fifteen years make colonel and live at the level of a lawyer or a professor. Now he found a much more attractive progression. Almost immediately, still a lieutenant, he was making as much as a medical doctor employed by the state, and his social standing was higher than the doctor's.

He further improved his situation by marrying the niece of a retired general. The main use for Brazil's estimated 2,400 retired generals had long been to provide material for cartoonists who portrayed them lounging around their country estates in gold-braided pajamas. But just then, Brazil incorporated a technological advance that had already proved itself in the United States. Business firms found that the easiest way to deal with a government of colonels was through the intermediary of a general. Whether one wanted a loan from a state bank, a building permit, or a licence to import or export, the winning approach was to put a couple of retired officers on the board of directors.

Itacarambi was only vaguely conscious of the change of national atmosphere that accompanied his good fortune. It was not till much later that he realized he had helped, in his small way, to turn the country into a huge military barracks. All Brazilians were subjected to the disciplinary regulations of the armed forces, and the armed forces themselves were transformed into political police charged with the duty of maintaining a status quo in favor of a small group of privileged Brazilians and foreign monopoly businesses. What Itacarambi saw was the introduction of his superior officers into every important post in federal and state government and in the state-owned sector of industry. In due course, his turn would come. Meanwhile, he improved his prospects by having the ex-general pull strings for him. In this way, he went to the Dominican Republic in 1965 with the "police force" from Brazil which turned the United States invasion into a "Pan-American" operation. Subsequently, he took the "intensive training in jungle survival and combat" at Fort Sherman in the Panama Canal Zone, as well as the courses at neighboring Fort Gulick in counterinsurgency and pacification of civilian populations.

He was back home in time to attend, in a subordinate role, the Eighth Conference of the American Armies held in Rio de Janeiro in September, 1968. His courses at the School of the Americas in Panama had been ideological as well as technical. In consequence, he had no problem in agreeing with the formulation of the role of Latin American armed forces offered the Conference by General William Westmoreland, recently named chief of staff of the United States Army after four years as commander in chief in Vietnam. "One only needs to read his newspaper," he told his fellow generals, including his Brazilian hosts whose expertise in torturing political prisoners can hardly have been unknown to him, "to know that the communists have used insurgent warfare throughout the world with varying degrees of success. . . . I feel that the prospects of repeated 'Vietnams' around the world present a very real danger to the security of every freedom-loving people. For this

reason I believe that the techniques of insurgent warfare
are high on the list of threats which each of us must consider. As I said, we must not expect to find the patterns
identical or the techniques always similar. Lenin built his
revolution around the proletarian worker. Mao used the
peasant as the backbone of his movement. In South Vietnam, Ho Chi Minh is relying on an insurgent trained
outside the target country and on an army infiltrated from
the same direction. Two things, however, are likely to
remain the same: the propaganda describing each insurgency will picture what they term as an 'oppressed' people
rising to overthrow the alleged oppressor. The objective—
a communist dictatorship—will persist. . . . The insurgency
environment is dynamic. The world has many dissatisfied
people whom the communists can exploit in their quest for
destruction of free society. This poses a threat that will be
present for a long time."[1]

Itacarambi was so impressed that he shortly afterward
obtained a copy of the prospectus of the College of Inter-
American Defense, Fort McNair, Washington, D.C. This
super-academy was established in 1962 as an element in the
response of the United States to the Cuban revolution. As
the prospectus explained, it "provided courses on the inter-
American system, dealing with the political, social, economic and military factors which form essential components
of inter-American defense, with the object of furthering the
preparation of selected personnel of the armed forces and
high officials of civil governments." Itacarambi knew that
he would have to make colonel before they would accept
him at Fort McNair, but he was confident that he could
accelerate that process. And after Fort McNair, the sky
would be the limit. He could count on getting immediate
charge of a detachment of the special troops trained in
counterinsurgency in the Panama Canal Zone.

At this point, however, Itacarambi discovered the
fickleness of fortune's smile. His wife's uncle became the
center of a business scandal that exploded on the front
pages of the newspapers. The official enquiry established
that he had built up an enormous empire, a dozen director-
ships of leading firms, consultant fees, stock options and fat

expense accounts for bribing government officials. He was
packed off to jail and his protégé lost all leverage.

As a species of compensation, however, Itacarambi
found a new comradeship with his fellow officers of equal
and lower ranks. Formerly, their relations with him had
been correct but distant. Now many of them joked at his
discomfiture but within a friendly atmosphere that gradually
revealed a very different evaluation of the military life
they shared. They scoffed at the hypocrisy of their superior
officers who jailed the one whose crimes had been exposed,
while they made fortunes by graft through their control of
the machinery of government. And behind the scoffing was
a deeper self-questioning. What was their real role? Were
they really soldiers defending the fatherland from hidden
communists committed to destroy free societies, as their
Panama-trained instructors and General Westmoreland
kept telling them? Or were they mercenaries subsidized by
foreign interests to block their own people's legitimate self-
expression?

These are questions being asked more often in all parts
of Latin America, both by soldiers and by civilians, as the
military progressively take over the role of policemen, and
as the police acquire automatic arms and dress in uniforms
that make them harder to distinguish from soldiers. Those
who ask the question have no need to identify the foreign
interests involved. Although not stamped "Gift of the
people of the United States," as is by law the rest of our
foreign aid, arms and uniforms are easily recognized by
anyone who watches television coverage of the war in Vietnam or the Berkeley riots. They constitute one of the most
visible elements in the United States presence. Only the
details differ from country to country. The armed cops who
crowd Bogotá airport and lounge in hotel lobbies carry
armbands which identify them as "tourist police." Others
in the hotels and at office entrances are stamped "Burns of
Colombia." As the traveler reaches Brazil from Paraguay,
eight officers of immigration, police and other security
forces are needed, with an impressive show of firearms, to
check his travel documents. Each of the armed services—
army, navy, airforce and police—has its own security

organization at every Brazilian airport; all of them over-shadowed by DOPS (the Department of Political and Social Order) whose secret police are authorized to arrest on suspicion and hold indefinitely without trial. In Monte-video, Uruguay, the guard stands in battledress, his finger on the trigger of his submachine gun, at the door of every public office.

The display of armed might reflects in part the labor surplus. Political motives encourage the expansion of all branches of the public service far beyond needs. But the specific expressions of the new militarism are not accidental. They flow from a deliberate policy developed by Washington since World War II. That policy began from the correct assumption by the United States defense planners that Latin American armies had not played and would not play a role in the world balance of power, and that their military value would become progressively less with the growing sophistication of weaponry. But they could be effectively used to counter the more insidious threat to the world power balance which those same defense planners believed they had discovered—the process of internal subversion by the forces of international communism.

Washington, being willing to pay the cost, had no difficulty in selling the program. The ruling classes in Latin America saw the communist conspiracy theory as a gift from heaven. They realized that the winds of change were blow-ing on this side of the Atlantic as well as in Africa. The volcanic tremblings and rumblings of the suppressed masses had become so insistent as to require strong counter-measures. So enthusiastic, in fact, was the support of the oligarchs for measures to curb internal subversion that in several countries they revived the old tradition of private armies to support the common cause. Of these the most notorious are *La Mano Blanca* (the white hand) in Guate-mala, and the CCC (Comando Caça-Comunistas: communist hunting commandos) in Brazil. Nobody knows how many thousands have been killed in terror and counterterror operations in Guatemala in recent years. Carlos Guzmán Böchler, professor of sociology and political sciences in the national university of Guatemala, gives an estimate of 6,000 for one twelve-month period between April, 1967 and

April, 1968.[2] What is generally agreed is that *La Mano* is responsible for 90 percent of the slayings. In Brazil, the "death squads" of the CCC operate with impunity in the countryside, terrorizing, burning, torturing and killing.

Those who seek basic reform welcome the evidence that the former sham is no longer viable, even if the immediate response is a hardening of repression. They interpret the agreement between conservatives and liberals in Colombia to suspend the constitutional process for sixteen years from 1958, sharing rule on a basis of equality, as the first open admission that the era of pseudodemocracy is ending. It demonstrated that elected governments in Latin America were creatures of the ruling classes just as much as the open dictatorships which have heavily punctuated their existence.

When the Treaty of Rio de Janeiro for mutual defense was signed in 1947, Washington was already well on its way to its new concept of the role of the Latin American armed forces. The Cold War had just started, and the freeze promised to be a long one. The world for the foreseeable future would divide along ideological lines, the atheistic communism of the Soviet Union challenging the democratic Christianity of the United States. The tasks of the Latin Americans, as subordinate allies, would be to protect their own coasts against invasion, and to deal with internal subversion.

The rapid development of long-range missiles changed the strategy of major war. In practice, it eliminated the role of Latin American navies as defenders of their coasts. The parallel success of Castro in Cuba and the expansion of Castro-inspired guerrillas in other countries increased the emphasis on internal defense. The program for training and equipping anti-insurgency forces was initiated in 1963. It was a responsibility of the United States Southern Command (USSOUTHCOM) located in the Panama Canal Zone. It proceeded with dispatch and enthusiasm to persuade the Latin American armed forces to exchange their jet planes, tanks and warships for jeeps, helicopters, hand grenades and automatic pistols. They took readily to the new toys, though without ever completely outgrowing their love for the old.

The headquarters of USSOUTHCOM are located on

and inside a steep hill overlooking Panama City and the Pacific Ocean. While its primary mission is stated to be the defense of the Canal, its secondary task of combating "the forces of communism that threaten the peace and prosperity of the western hemisphere today as never before" (to quote from its current official release) has occupied a substantial part of its efforts in recent years. Land, sea and air elements are all located here. United States military training programs in South and Central America, including the counterinsurgency training provided by Special Forces units, are all responsible to this command, and it supervises United States support of the "civic action programs" of Latin American armies. It also commands United States troops engaged in combat or "stability operations" in Latin America, such as the 1965 intervention in the Dominican Republic. A team of sixteen Green Berets was sent to Bolivia in 1967 to direct the Bolivian army action against the guerrillas headed by Ernesto Che Guevara, and this team's role in organizing the operation in which Guevara was killed has been officially admitted.

USSOUTHCOM thinks of itself as having ultimate responsibility for Latin America's defense both against external aggression and internal subversion. It takes the lead in encouraging "interservice and regional cooperation," in establishing "integrated command and control centers with common operating procedures," in developing "joint military plans," and it participates "in combined exercises with regional organizations and individual Latin American countries."

An important element in encouragement, development and integration is the military mission responsible to USSOUTHCOM but stationed in a Latin American republic. At the headquarters in Panama, in March, 1970, I was told that there are missions in seventeen Latin American countries, varying from a low of three individuals in Costa Rica to "about eighty" in Brazil. Other informants insist that the number in Brazil is substantially higher. Figures developed for a committee of the United States Senate in 1967 by Edwin Lieuwen, an outstanding authority on military affairs in the Americas, showed that there were then forty-three missions in seventeen countries, ranging in size from five in Panama to "well over a hundred" in Brazil, with a total of 737 officers and enlisted men assigned to these missions in the region.

The military missions are separate from the military attachés on the staff of the American Embassy. They are directly responsible, not to the attaché or even to the ambassador, but to USSOUTHCOM in the Canal Zone. They are linked to headquarters by "a complex military communications system which has its nerve center in the Canal Zone." This nerve center, built underground in the hillside and heavily reinforced, also serves the United States diplomatic missions, and the armed services of the host countries. The head of the military mission, not the military attaché at the embassy, is the principal military advisor to the United States ambassador in each country. He directs the military assistance and advisory activities of his army, navy and air force section chiefs as they work with their counterparts in the armed forces of the host country. In this way, the Pentagon infiltrates and short-circuits the State Department.

The defense planners, I was told, do not discount the possibility of general war, but they consider internal security the primary concern. "The armed forces of each Latin American country must be able to cope with communist-supported insurgency and guerrilla infiltration. In recent years, most of the military efforts have been toward this end. Success in meeting the threat of guerrilla bands in such countries as Bolivia, Colombia, Guatemala, Peru, and Venezuela illustrate that these efforts are bearing fruit."

It is USSOUTHCOM training of Latin Americans that has caused the widest controversy and apprehension. The enormous increase in the military role in repression in Brazil and Argentina, and the development of military regimes in Peru and Bolivia committed to populist aims and consequently in a state of tension with the United States, have thrown the spotlight on the situation from different angles. Helio Jaguaribe told the Latin American Council of Social Sciences at its 1968 meeting in Peru[3] that military denationalization raised two principal issues: the seizure of power by the armed forces, and the assimilation of these armed forces into the defense system developed by the United States for its own protection. These two aspects, he said, were interrelated, the former depending on the latter. The dependence of the armed forces of Latin America on an outside source increased their ability to control power within their own countries. And the fact that they are the repositories of internal power increases the United States' motivation to assimilate them. Here we have an additional reason, though perhaps not the ultimate one, for anticipating that the phase of Latin American political life we are entering will be characterized by direct military rule.

Denationalization may not be the intention of the USSOUTHCOM training programs, but in the opinion of most Latin Americans it is certainly the result. Training under the Military Assistance Program is provided in Washington and elsewhere, the principal center for Latin America being the United States Army School of the Americas, located at Fort Gulick in the Panama Canal Zone. It offers its courses in Spanish and Portuguese, the only service school to teach in a foreign language. It has trained some 25,000 Latin Americans in various military skills, most of its courses dealing with military civic action and counterinsurgency. Its Irregular Warfare Committee "teaches various measures required to defeat an insurgent (movement) on the battlefield, as well as military civic action functions in an insurgent environment."[4] The civic action instruction, designed to fit into such politico-military activities as the pacification program developed in Vietnam for areas infested by hostile guerrillas, includes courses in water purification, well drilling, and operation of heavy equipment. In addition to those trained at Fort Gulick, an approximately equal number of Latin American military have been trained elsewhere. Department of Defense figures released in March, 1970, listed a total of 50,581 Latin Americans trained under the Military Assistance Program funded by AID. According to Richard S. Winslow, Jr., a former AID employee, "during fiscal 1970, the State Department's Agency for International Development is spending $451,000 on its 'public safety' program in Brazil; $292,-000 is now paying for thirteen United States police specialists residing in Brazil and helping to train thousands of Brazilian police in 'criminal investigations,' 'counterinsurgency,' and the use of the most modern police equipment. AID boasts that in fiscal year 1968, 16,000 Brazilian police were trained under this program, with the number increasing in each successive year. Another $129,000 is being spent this year to bring fifty-eight Brazilian police officials to the United States for an average of four months training in the latest police techniques."[5]

Other training facilities in Panama include the Albrook Air Force base and the Army Jungle Warfare School. Albrook caters exclusively to Latin American personnel and teaches all courses in Spanish. The Jungle School offers intensive training on jungle survival and combat to Latin Americans and those preparing for service in Southeast Asia.

The Latin American charges of denationalization are not based simply on the fact of this training but on its nature. Here it becomes significant that Fort Gulick is the headquarters of the Special Action Force (official title of the Green Berets) for Latin America. The unit has eight hundred members who travel in mobile training teams to supplement the work of the resident military missions with special instruction in counterinsurgency. Since its formation in 1962, its mobile training teams have operated in every Latin American country except Mexico, Haiti and Cuba.

The major role played by the Green Berets in the training programs means that Latin America's armed forces are taking on the characteristics of this special force rather than those of the peacetime armed forces of the United States. The distinction is vital. The Green Berets do not see themselves as part of the regular army but as a group with its own purposes and methods, constantly fighting the army to retain its identity and freedom of action.

Established in 1952 as a revival of the wartime OSS, it developed in the Europe of the Cold War, specifically to train and direct partisans behind the enemy lines in East Europe in case of war with Russia. The brink was reached twice in 1956 alone, during the Hungarian revolt and the parallel turmoil in Poland. In its original composition, the force was heavily European. Veterans of World War II underground formations and special forces, they had seen their world destroyed by the advance of the Soviet Union into Europe's heartland. The ultimate threat for them was the further advance of communism to the Atlantic. William Pfaff, a Green Beret for three years in the 1950's, has described his colleagues as insecure, lacking inner discipline, eccentrics and enthusiasts, but above all, free from normal human bonds and commitments. "Both regular and reserve elements of Special Forces must be described as being composed of self-consciously uprooted men, emotionally and intellectually detached from the mainstream of civilian society."[6]

It is in this context that Pfaff places the Green Beret murder case which ruffled the American conscience briefly when it surfaced in 1969. Its significance, he wrote, "lies in the fact that the alleged murder was so doggedly without passion or the justifications of panic or crisis. It is its *administrative* quality which so dazzles us: its reflection of an apparent assumption by those involved that murder is the appropriate way to dispose of a prisoner who presents an obstacle to the orderly conduct of an intelligence operation. . . . Such a clerkly impersonality about killing a prisoner has found a comparison in the administrative routine of the Nazi death camps, whose SS commanders would complain to one another about the bureaucratic difficulties of their task and compare notes on the technical and organizational solutions they had found most satisfactory."

A spokesman at Canal Zone headquarters assured me that the major emphasis of the training given by the Green Beret teams is on civic action, digging wells and driving tractors. Latin Americans who have been through the training in Panama or at local centers tell a different story, one that agrees better with the spirit described by Pfaff. For example, a Chilean pastor who interviewed many trainees in his professional work stated: "Their personality is deformed by an intensive brainwashing which equates all protest with communist conspiracies. There is also the brutalization which results from a regime that turns a civilized Chilean into an animal. Ours is a gentle country, without wild beasts, poisonous snakes or mosquitoes. Our men are unprepared for a training which includes extreme brain stresses, physical stresses, emotional stresses, electric shocks and so on. An average man becomes totally unbalanced. It is very hard to get him back to a normal outlook."

Of course, the two accounts of the training may not be as far apart as they appear at first. In the mentality of the Green Beret, Pfaff insists, well digging and brutalization can coexist comfortably. "I vividly remember a CIA man, a bespectacled doctor of philosophy, I once met in one of Vietnam's northern provinces. An automatic pistol under his arm, an AR 15 rifle in his jeep, he ran a 'revolutionary development' team which 'rooted out' the Vietcong infrastructure in a village at the same time that it built schools and dug wells for the peasants. He was entirely pleased with himself; he made much of his ability—he mentioned it to me several times—to nominate men to die. He said that he had chosen a Nung rather than a Vietnamese as his bodyguard because when he pointed out a man to be killed he wanted no hesitation. He said that he was very happy in Vietnam, and no doubt he was an idealist, doing the Lord's work."

The ideological motivation, the "doing the Lord's work," is an integral part, perhaps the most important part, of the training given by USSOUTHCOM to the Latin American armed forces. The entire rationale and justification for the satellitization of these forces was the hypothesis of a threat by outside agents to an assumed democratic way of life. Such was the basis for the first formulation of postwar United States foreign policy. Not without some continuing ambivalences, the United States has gradually withdrawn from this oversimplification in its domestic life. It has solid working arrangements in its direct relations with the Soviet Union which are incompatible with belief in its Cold War philosophy. Nevertheless, the rest of its foreign policy remains based on the old assumptions, as the history of the past ten years in Southeast Asia demonstrates so tragically.

In Latin America, the survival is equally total. In his memoirs published in 1965, President Eisenhower was still defending his Latin American policies on the ground that all threats to existing order were inspired by international communism, and that international communism in turn was, in the western hemisphere, a kind of foreign intervention, something that automatically entitled the United States to act under the Monroe Doctrine. For General Westmoreland in 1968, the creation of a communist dictatorship was still the goal of the same international conspiracy. USSOUTHCOM in 1970 remains convinced that its task is to combat "the forces of communism that threaten the peace and prosperity of the western hemisphere today as never before."

That no change is in prospect is evident from the formulation by President Nixon in October, 1969, of a policy which he himself stated was "substantially shaped by the report of Governor Rockefeller." It is worth spending a moment with the Rockefeller Report to appreciate what this means. Communist subversion, it says, "is a reality today with alarming potential," and "the subversive capabilities of these communist forces are increasing throughout the hemisphere." Political forces which seek to end stagnation, poverty and oppression are "enemies," the "covert forces of communism," who "exploit" such factors. "Clearly, the opinion in the United States that communism is no longer a serious factor in the western hemisphere is thoroughly wrong. . . . Forces of anarchy, terror and subversion are loose in the Americas."

The underlying problem is that anti-communism has become the cement which holds the entire system together. The ruling classes in Latin America seized on it avidly when it was first enunciated, rightly seeing it as a powerful weapon to defend the outmoded socioeconomic structures which ensured their hegemony. The leadership of the armed forces at that time reflected in large part the views of the ruling classes and consequently found no difficulty in agreeing. Besides, they welcomed the offer of a bigger role in the life of their countries, the more professional training and the prospect of a guaranteed continuing supply of modern arms. Ironically, one significant effect has been to draw a larger proportion of officers—like Major Itaca-rambi—from the middle classes. Modern weapons and war games call for engineers and other specialists. Promotion increasingly depends on talent and drive rather than on family background. But the new officer class has come through the brainwashing of Fort Gulick and the war colleges set up with United States guidance in each country. Recent developments in Peru and Bolivia suggest that they may be questioning the anti-communist doctrine, but elsewhere they continue to maintain a united front.

The fundamental dilemma for the Latin American armed forces, as also for the United States while it adheres to its present policy, is that change has been forcibly prevented for such a long time that any effort to effect a substantial improvement in the living condition of the masses quickly gets out of hand. The generals are forced to lump under the global heading of communism every activity and movement that threatens the status quo. Like Eisenhower in his memoirs, when Guatemalan or Colombian peasants assert their human dignity, the generals can only give credit to the agents of international communism, backed with arms and money by a foreign power. Otherwise, they would be unable to justify their suppression of democratic forms in the name of democracy, and their growing dependency on a foreign power to save them from the threat of a foreign power.

To maintain the status quo is, however, a misnomer. It assumes that the situation is static, when the social tension in Latin America is dynamic. Two factors, as mentioned earlier, continuously intervene to force change, and as they intensify, the counterforce to prevent change must increase correspondingly. One is the growth of population; the other the demonstration effect, the growing consciousness of injustice produced by the communications media. To counter these factors, the armed forces must be constantly enlarged, modernized and kept happy. Brazil upped the proportion of the federal budget spent on the armed forces from 15 percent in 1963 to 25 percent in 1967. The United States projected for 1970 military sales of $61.4 million to Latin America, more than twice the 1969 level. Not only must the strength of the armed forces increase, but it must express itself more visibly, leading to a direct take-over when the tensions have passed the point of control within the conventions of civilian rule.

The resulting repression is, according to Helio Jaguaribe, a kind of fascism. It differs from the fascism known in Europe before World War II in that its dynamic center is not within the country but outside it. Like the European form, it represents a ruling elite which, while self-perpetuating, bases its power neither on a traditional status nor on popular representation. Instead, it uses technical control processes to reconcile policies of economic modernization and the preservation of political and social immobility. The characteristics of the Brazilian regime, Jaguaribe says, are "a substantial reinforcement of the state," the "tightest possible economic and political integration of the country into the Western system, under United States leadership," and "a free market, assuring private enterprise full control and management of the economy." This, he says, is colonial fascism: fascism, because it is "a model for promoting economic development without changing the existing social order"; colonial, because it depends "on the West in general and the United States in particular, due to its need for foreign assistance and foreign markets."[7]

The two most developed examples of colonial fascism in Latin America are Brazil and Argentina. In both cases, the armed forces have effectively replaced the people as the seat of sovereignty and the source of power. In both cases, the body of laws they have developed conceive of the country as a military barracks and of the people as a vast army whose task it is to execute national policy made and centrally directed by the military elite. Jaguaribe insists that these regimes could not survive without the active support of the United States. An analysis of the role attributed to the Latin American military by the Rockefeller Report, the

only significant policy document on Latin America produced by the Nixon administration, confirms his view. Mr.
Rockefeller sheds no tears over the failure of the democratic
revolution which President Kennedy's Alliance for Progress
had proposed. It does not worry him that the large landowners still dominate agriculture, or that dictators rule over
most of the region. In the political area, his formula for
order is more law enforcement muscle. The failure of the
United States to realize that the forces of anarchy, terror
and subversion are on the march in Latin America, he says,
has caused many Latin Americans to doubt the determination of the United States to face up to this serious threat
to freedom, democracy and the vital interests of the entire
hemisphere. They are growing cynical. "Many of our
neighbors," states the report, "find it incomprehensible that
the United States will not sell them military equipment
which they feel is required to deal with internal subversion.
They have been puzzled by the reduction in U.S. military
assistance grants in view of the growing intensity of the
subversive activities they face."

Circumstances surrounding the Rockefeller Report
have encouraged many commentators to dismiss it as of no
more than passing significance. The way it was publicly
framed left much to be desired. Rockefeller, an enormously
busy man as governor of New York, was to spend a few
hours in each Latin American capital, listen to a narrow
spectrum of officialdom, then tell President Nixon what the
region wanted and what it should have. Popular reaction
in Latin America further limited the opportunities for fact-
finding. Riots accompanied Rockefeller's presence in Colombia. Protesters in Quito forced a change of route from
the airport to the president's palace. Six students were
killed in street clashes with the army. The stop in Bolivia
was cut to three hours at the airport. Peru refused an invitation. Chile and Venezuela felt obliged by the public
outcry to withdraw the invitations they had issued. What,
it was asked, could a report produced in such circumstances
contribute to hemisphere understanding?

Even if nothing new was collected by the visitors, other
than the fresh evidence of widespread discontent, the report

is important because of the interests represented by the man who signed it. The Rockefeller family retains substantial holdings in four oil companies derived from the original Standard Oil trust created by John D. Rockefeller, Sr., all of which have major production, refining, transport and sales activities in Latin America. They are Standard Oil of New Jersey, Mobil Oil Corporation, Standard Oil of California, and Standard Oil of Indiana. Standard Oil of New Jersey, for example, owns 95 percent of Creole Petroleum Corporation, the Venezuelan giant. The Rockefellers also are deeply involved in industry, distribution, banking, and investment services in Latin America. They set up the IBEC corporation in 1947 to diversify family holding in areas other than petroleum, and they retain 70 percent of the shares of this $160 million company. While IBEC operates worldwide, it derives more of its income from Latin America than from any other region. Its 1969 report showed assets of $54.4 million in Latin America, revenue from the region for that year of $114.5 million, and 4,600 employees.

An important aspect of the Rockefeller interests is that they straddle the two types of United States investment in Latin America. The older type was concentrated in the production and export of primary materials, petroleum, mining, and agricultural. Having no interest in a local market, it identified with the traditional oligarchy in its concern to have a massive labor force living at the lowest possible level consistent with the ability to work. The newer industrialists, retail distributors and bankers also seek to take advantage of the low wages which result from a surplus of labor. However, they need higher labor skills, as well as the level of incomes required to provide internal markets for their manufactures and services. The relative importance of the two groups fluctuates. A recession in the manufacturing sect:on in the late 1960's, for example, brought a revival of interest on the part of international capital in the primary sector. Mining companies raised their investments in the poor countries by 31 percent in 1968 in relation to the previous year, to an annual level of $1.2 billion, and they hoped to double it to $1.8 billion by 1970. Petroleum interests similarly increased their external investments in 1968 by 14 percent to $3.5 billion, and they also anticipated further expansion by 1970. Taking Latin America as a whole, 85 percent of the sources of raw materials are controlled by United States operators.[8]

Just as there are differences of interest between the traditional elements in the local oligarchies whose power is based on landholding and the more modern elements involved in industry and commerce, so are there parallel differences in the two groups of United States investors. The former would, for example, channel foreign aid to such infrastructure works as roads and ports which directly benefit the export of primary products. The latter prefer aid for industry and the expansion of the communications media through which they develop the consumer mentality required to sell their products. The range of the Rockefeller interests made the New York governor acceptable to both groups. What he says is not merely what he gleaned on his lightning tour but the distilled wisdom of United States business and finance as filtered through the thirty-five specialists who accompanied him on his journeys and joined in formulating the conclusions.

It is this background that makes the Rockefeller Report so important, especially as it explicitly confirms the interpretation of those Latin Americans who claim that the United States is steadily, and at an accelerating rhythm, expanding its imperialistic control. Like these critics, Rockefeller affirms that the Latin America countries have reached or are rapidly approaching a state of such instability that only military governments can keep order. The difference, of course, is in the interpretation of the fact. They want a reversal of the procedures which produced the situation of instability. He denies that there is any internal instability, blaming the condition on "outside subversives." His logic compels him to call for more force, in quantities that can only be determined by the level of the aggression from without.

The report makes an evaluation of all the factors encouraging change in Latin America. They are, first of all, the impersonal factors of science, technology and communications, factors which are in themselves neutral and capable of being directed towards whatever ends men decide. Then there are the less easily controllable human factors: the workers, the businessmen, the youth, the church, the armed forces, the communists. Each of these is evaluated in turn, and all but two get short shrift.

The workers are dismissed in a single paragraph, of which perhaps the most significant observation is that a large part of the work force is under communist leadership. Businessmen are dismissed with a couple of paragraphs of conventional rhetoric. Youth comes off better with four paragraphs, but the message remains constant. "The very fact of their idealism makes some of the young vulnerable to subversive penetration and to exploitation as a revolutionary means for the destruction of the existing order." Four paragraphs also suffice for the church (as mentioned earlier), and they are perhaps the most devastating of all. It, too, is no longer dependable.

That leaves us with our friends, the armed forces, whose importance in the equation is measured by ten long paragraphs; and our enemies, the communists, whose importance is only slightly less. It guarantees them eight.

Having warned United States readers that they are not sufficiently conscious of the threat to the "free nations" of the western hemisphere which results from the machinations of "hidden communist forces," the report recalls the important work already done by the armed forces, including police forces, of Latin America. "Two decades and more ago, in the presence of an open and worldwide Soviet threat, the United States response was realistic and flexible. It included, in the western hemisphere, the training and equipping of security forces for hemisphere defense.

"Fortuitously, the military capability thus achieved subsequently enabled the individual nations of the hemisphere to deal with the initial impact of a growing, covert communist threat to their internal security. However, the threat was shifted from one based in the rural areas to one centered around urban terrorism. Realistic efforts to deal with this increasingly dangerous development are necessary, on an effective, hemisphere-wide basis. . . .

"In addition, there is not in the United States a full

appreciation of the important role played by the police. There is, in the United States, a tendency to equate the police in other American republics with political action and repression, rather than with security. There have, unfortunately, been many such instances of the use of police. Yet well-motivated, well-trained police, when present in local communities, enforce the laws, protect the citizens from terror, and discourage criminal elements. At the present time, however, police forces of many countries have not been strengthened as population and great urban growth have taken place. Consequently, they have become increasingly less capable of providing either the essential psychological support or the internal security that is their major function."

The armed forces are for Rockefeller the last line of defense for the order which he continues to call, following a long established tradition, the free world and the democratic way of life. Having no choice, he is prepared to back them. But even he sees dangers, and he analyses them at some length. The armed forces are constantly tempted to hark back to the role conventionally played by the armed forces of sovereign nations, the role in which they had seen themselves before the United States had assumed responsibility for the protection of their borders from outside aggressors.

"The United States must face more forthrightly," he wrote, "the fact that, while the military in the other American nations are alert to the problems of internal security, they do not feel that this is their only role and responsibility.

"They are conscious of the more traditional role of a military establishment to defend the nation's territory, and they possess understandable professional pride which creates equally understandable desires for modern arms; in addition, they are subjected to the sales pressures and blandishments of suppliers from other nations—East and West— eager to sell. The result of all this is a natural resentment on the part of the military of other American nations, when the United States refuses to sell modern items of equipment.

"Thus many military leaders in the other American

republics see the United States acting to hold them back as second-class citizens, and they are becoming increasingly estranged from us at a time when their political role is on the rise. Our dilemma is how to be responsive to their legitimate desires for modern equipment without encouraging the diversion of scarce resources from development to armaments, which in some cases may be unrelated to any real security requirement."

Rockefeller offers no solution to this very real dilemma. What at first sight seems such is merely a suggestion for influencing the political role of the armed forces to which he had referred just before he presented the dilemma. As Rockefeller analyses that role, he sees that it has grown important as an element for "constructive social change," because the armed forces have developed "increasing impatience with corruption, inefficiency, and a stagnant political order." Yet it is not free of dangers, the worst of which is that "authoritarian governments, bent on rapid change, have an intrinsic ideological unreliability and a vulnerability to extreme nationalism. They can go in almost any doctrinal direction." They are even capable of becoming "radicalized, statist and anti-United States." In a word, they are open to being infiltrated. "Special mention should be made of the appeal to the new military, on a theoretical level, of Marxism: (1) it justifies, through its elitist-vanguard theories, government by a relatively small group or single institution (such as the army); and, at the same time, (2) produces a rationale for state-enforced sacrifices to further economic development."

While he names no names, nothing could be clearer than the contrast Rockefeller here makes between such military governments as those of Brazil and Argentina on the one hand, and those of Bolivia and Peru on the other. He knows that he cannot distinguish between them on the ground that one group is oppressive and the other respectful of the rights of the people. If freedom is a criterion, his Brazilian and Argentine friends would score worse than the others. Instead, he offers a pragmatic approach, justifying it for those who might still remember the guarantees given by the United States in the Alliance for Progress to favor democratic regimes above dictatorships. "Military leaders throughout the hemisphere are frequently criticized here in the United States. However we will have to give increasing recognition to the fact that many new military leaders are deeply motivated by the need for social and economic progress. . . . In many cases, it will be more useful for the United States to try to work with them in these efforts, rather than to abandon or insult them because we are conditioned by arbitrary ideological stereotypes."

As if the insult to all opponents of dictatorship were not enough, Rockefeller now makes yet another somersault. The new equipment should go only to friendly armed forces, namely, those who dedicate themselves to the unending effort to control the communist menace. Since every popular movement which would impose social controls on capital and increase the participation of the masses in the life of the community is an expression of the communist menace, it has now become possible to award the good military of Brazil, Argentina, Guatemala, Nicaragua and even Haiti, while withholding the new toys from the deviationists in Peru and Bolivia until they catch on.

That Rockefeller had reason for his fear that Latin American armies might not be forever content with the role the United States allots them as controllers of internal subversion was illustrated by an interview, published in Uruguay in December, 1969, with the military president of Bolivia, General Alfredo Ovando Candia. Two years earlier, Ovando had led the Bolivian forces who killed Che Guevara and stamped out his guerrilla movement.

His first frank admission was that he had realized in 1965 or earlier that his government had sold out to United States interests. He had to wait, however, until 1969 for his chance to overthrow it. Next came an equally frank evaluation of the changed role and function of the armed forces.

"*Gutiérrez.* The role of the armed forces in this process of liberation is a parody, General, and I'd like to hear your explanation. The sectors of these countries most deeply compromised in the imperialist scheme of things are the national ruling classes and the armed forces. This is even truer of the armed forces than of the others, because they have been fitted into structures which are managed by the Inter-American Defence Council and the Pentagon. Can you explain how the armed forces can become a factor of development or liberation until they move out of these strategic arrangements which now place them at the service of objectives not those of the nation? Don't you think that the first thing they have to do is to get out of those structures?

"*Ovando.* Yes, I believe that is so. If there is not the education, if there is not the personal formation, you see that this would not be possible. And that was precisely the task we gave ourselves. What we set out to do was to develop this spirit, to educate the future officer step-by-step in the essentially nationalist spirit. Bolivia's armed forces lend themselves to this purpose. They have never been a caste institution. The officers come from middle-class families of modest resources. Some even come from peasant stock. And I believe they have a great revolutionary spirit, even if they perhaps do not yet have a total understanding of the Latin American process. But, beyond doubt, they do already have a revolutionary spirit. Perhaps it is still somewhat romantic, but before too long it will be right on the beam.

"*Gutiérrez.* I was referring not to the human elements but to concrete facts which place the armed forces of Bolivia within a certain framework. These run all the way from the professional preparation with training outside the country to the drawing up of plans of hemisphere defence which are geared to the national interest of the United States. I am also thinking of other factors which, as General Torres has recognized in the Inter-American Defence Council, are the expression of a purpose of external control. Does your government think that, if it is to carry out its revolutionary objectives, it must take the armed forces out of these structures? For example, should Bolivia resign from the council? Should it stop training its people abroad? Should it cancel the arms agreements with the United States?

"*Ovando.* The answer is definitely yes. In that sense, the armed forces must get a high level of independence. They must move to some extent out of that framework which undoubtedly tends to direct the institution and its members to predetermined ends. Bolivia's armed forces are not going to need technical supervision. To a large extent they already have their own professional schools. Thanks be to God, they also have their own distinctive military doctrine. One reason is that both the officer school and the school for higher officers have always been under exclusively national control. No military missions of any kind ever got inside them. Besides, the United States military mission has never exercised a broad range of activities here. We are on our way to the total independence already mentioned.

"*Gutiérrez.* Are there no United States training missions at this time?

"*Ovando.* There is a mission, but it is a very small one. And just between ourselves, it isn't active.

"*Gutiérrez.* On that point I'd like to put a question to you in your capacity as a general, not as president. The strategy of the high commands of Latin American armies before World War II, and in some cases even more recently, was always based on the danger of attack from without. United States policy forced us to adopt a different line, namely, to prepare for counterinsurgency. This meant a change in the training methods, in the kind of arms, and in the tactical plans. In the Third World as a general rule, the plans of the high command prepare the armies for warfare as guerrillas, not as counterguerrillas. This they regard as the best means of national defense available to them. In other words, they have simply returned to a strategy based on the danger of attack from without. Bolivia, however, has up to now been armed and trained for counterinsurgency. Will the new orientation of your regime also change this aspect of Bolivia's insertion into the apparatus of imperialism?

"*Ovando.* Yes, we will return to a guerrilla strategy as our method of national defence. However, I think that, more than anything else, the basic organization of the armed forces here should not be either in terms of an attack from without or of preparation for counterinsurgency, but rather one that seems outside the military sphere yet is highly appropriate for the purposes of the military institution in an underdeveloped country. The army should be geared to help the national revolutionary process as an instrument of development. At the same time, however, as I see it, Bolivia has to adopt the guerrilla approach to its problems of national defence."[9]

Ovando's frank comments raise the question whether the withdrawal by a Latin American army from its satellite status in order to lead the country on an independent populist course provides a viable way to liberation of the people. Many progressives tend to hail as indications of progress the military regimes which came to power in Peru and Panama in 1968, and in Bolivia in 1969. All three justified their seizure of power as necessary to protect the people from the exploitation of the local oligarchs and their international business allies, and all three did, in fact, introduce changes which were calculated to reduce privilege and share well-being more widely. Peru, for example, has made significant progress with land reform. More effort is being devoted to increase the supply of food for local consumption than to expand exports. And the government has had some success in getting investment capital under conditions that are less offensive to national sovereignty. On the negative side, all three military governments have proved unable to maintain order without curtailment of civil rights. The control of the press by the oligarchy has been broken in Peru, but in its stead has come state control. And in all three countries police repression of legitimate citizen complaints is rampant.

The historic problem of the military dictatorship is that uncontrolled power corrupts. No matter how good the original intentions, the erosion of politics soon follows, especially in a small country which depends for survival on outside markets and suppliers. The political pressures surfaced in Bolivia during the summer of 1970, less than a year after the coup which brought Ovando to power. Amid rumors of a secret deal with Washington, the Ovando regime ousted and exiled several of its more extreme left-wing supporters and retired General Juan José Torres, the armed forces chief who had gradually moved from a conservative position to one of extreme radicalism. Encouraged by these evidences of dissension, a conservative group in the armed forces staged a coup in October which overthrew Ovando, only to be ousted within twenty-four hours by a countercoup led by Torres. But the area of maneuver of any regime in Bolivia, as in Peru or Panama, is always narrow. The best it could hope for, even in theory, would be to transfer—like Cuba—from one orbit to another. And even that possibility is today no more than theoretical. Nobody imagines that the United States would permit a second Cuba. What some observers stress is that the existence of nationalist regimes in Peru and Bolivia is an encouragement to elements in the armed forces of Brazil and Argentina favoring a Nasser-type evolution. That such elements exist at the middle and lower officer levels—men like Major Itacarambi who have been disappointed by the system, and idealists who have been humiliated by their repressive role—is undeniable. The trend is particularly strong in Argentina. Because of Washington's choice of Brazil as its major satellite, the opportunities for advancement and enrichment for officers are lower in Argentina and the level of frustration correspondingly higher. The size, geographic location and level of economic development of Brazil and Argentina would make Nasser-type regimes potentially viable in either of them. But, for reasons that will be developed in a later chapter, the likelihood of the installation of such a regime is remote.

7

La Cía

La Cía (lah-SEE-ah) is how Latin Americans refer to the CIA, and the expression is the universally used shorthand to describe the more-or-less hidden United States presence and influence. The words are spoken with the conspiratorial reverence with which more devout ages honored the devil's name. According to Latin American folklore, every North American is a card-carrying member of the CIA, and it also employs a vast mercenary army of Latin Americans. There is an agent under every bed, a bug in every vase of flowers.

In all parts of Latin America there is an amazing amount of literature purporting to document the activities of *La Cía*. In some countries it is quite open, in books and magazines. In others, it takes the form of clandestine booklets and leaflets, turned out mostly by students with duplicating machines in university basements. Much is invention or highly elaborated rumor. But an impressive amount is either concretely documented or so circumstantial as to add up to rather persuasive evidence.

The Central Intelligence Agency (CIA) was created as an independent executive bureau of the United States government by the National Security Act of 1947. The wartime Office of Strategic Services had expired in 1945 but was so missed that President Truman, by executive action, set up an agency the following year to gather strategic facts from abroad and report them to him. The Central Intelligence Act of 1949 made possible the monster which Latin Americans and many others consider the CIA to have become. Its director does not have to account for the way he spends a budget in excess of $3 billion. The size of the staff is classified, but is reportedly more than 20,000.[1] Employees are exempt from civil service procedures. The agency makes and enforces its own rules for hiring, investigation, and firing. And, as transpired in 1969 when it refused to allow its members to testify at a court-martial of Green Berets charged with murder, it is not even answerable to the nation's judicial system.

Latin Americans, however, use the name generically. *La Cía* in common parlance covers the totality of the United States presence; the embassy staffs, the AID officials, the Peace Corps, visiting university professors and roving newsmen, social workers, and missionaries. Everyone is automatically suspect, and solid proof must be furnished in order to break through the barrier of fear and persuade the Latin American to express his thoughts. The obstacle to communication is not just a general opposition on ideological or ethical grounds to the idea of being surrounded by secret agents. It is a personal fear, in extreme cases for one's life, but always for one's job and liberty of action. To be listed on *La Cía*'s card index as undesirable or even suspicious is one of the worst things that can happen. For the student, the professor, or the labor leader, it is presumed automatically to close off opportunities for scholarships, research, and study abroad.

Officials of the United States embassies and of AID in Latin America seemed to me to be leading much more isolated lives in 1970 than ever before. Of course, there was an obvious reason for caution. They moved about in constant fear of kidnapping, both of themselves and of their families. That, however, did not seem to me to explain an evident lack of contact with United States missionaries and others engaged in teaching and social work. My inquiries among such nonofficial personnel produced the astonishing information that they had deliberately cut themselves off from fraternization with officials. Time and again, I got the same answer. "If you are friendly with them, the people tag you as an agent. To do our work, we have to keep clear." And more than one added: "Besides, I have nothing in common with them. They are all CIA agents. Everyone knows that."

Latin Americans are, paradoxically, more familiar with current happenings in the United States than with those of their neighbors or even of their own country. Newspapers depend overwhelmingly on the United States agencies for their coverage. Few have correspondents even in neighboring capitals. Their home coverage is usually superficial, often deliberately vague or misleading because of official or unofficial press controls. Radio and television similarly depend preponderatingly on United States sources for both entertainment and news. Many stations are owned or managed by the United States networks. Most of the widely read news and opinion magazines are either published in the United States or controlled by United States interests.

One result of this news focus on United States concerns is that the Vietnam war has long occupied the center of attention, and with traumatic impact. For the first time, Latin Americans have followed a war blow-by-blow, not only in the newspaper but on the television screen. The students are particularly fascinated. Everywhere I went, they discussed it. Their identification with the Vietcong tended to be total. They saw themselves at the receiving end of all the United States firepower and napalm. They admired the enormous ability of the Vietcong to survive. They took courage from the fact that the greatest power in the world was unable to impose its will on people like themselves.

They were equally aware of what the Vietnam war had done to the United States. "Between 1945 and 1968, you spent a thousand billion dollars on armaments," commented Miguel Cardozo, a young trade union official. "Your present spending is in the neighborhood of $80 billion, which is equal to the entire gross national product of Latin America. In Vietnam alone, you continue to pump $32 billion a year into an imperialist war you have already lost. Ten percent of the United States population is engaged in production for the war, and a quarter of the work force is devoted to underpinning the military machine. Ending the war production would lift unemployment to 25 percent."

In the view of people like Cardozo, the military structure which they describe generically as *La Cía* has become the biggest business in the country. It raises capital, determining the nature and quality of production, the price, the delivery dates, all this for nearly $50 billion worth of industrial work a year, more than the combined activity of the four or five biggest private companies. "*La Cia,*" says Arlindo Salazar, "is transforming the United States into a military dictatorship not very different from those we have in such Latin American countries as Brazil and Argentina. It is rapidly taking over the decision-making power from the president and congress. In response to the violent protests of students, blacks and other suppressed groups, the level of internal repression is being progressively increased. It is quite clear that you have a military super-government which manipulates all official agencies, including the State Department, the AID program, and the Peace Corps."

Substance was given to that analysis when the head of AID, John A. Hannah, disclosed on a radio program in Washington, in June, 1970, that his agency had been used as a cover for operations of the CIA in Laos.[2] The decision was made during the Kennedy administration in 1962 and persisted under the two following presidents. Nobody should expect Latin Americans to believe Dr. Hannah's further assertion that this constituted a unique exception.

What seemed more logical was a news report from Washington shortly after the Hannah disclosure. The administration, it said, was drawing up plans to shift numerous economic and social programs in South Vietnam and Laos from civilian to military control. The defense department would assume responsibility for balancing the defense budget of South Vietnam and pacifying the rural areas, for public health, for the training of the police and the care of refugees. All such activities in Latin America are technically part of the AID program, and their effect is already seen as a paramilitarization of foreign aid so that it no longer promotes development but serves rather to repress legitimate political movements of a popular nature.

The process of distortion is particularly visible in Brazil. Washington, in 1962, suspended disbursement of aid funds approved in 1961 in an effort to influence government policy. The restrictive policy continued until the army ousted the constitutional president in April, 1964. Within three months, loans totaling $65 million were granted, and a short time later a commitment was signed for $150 million as part of a $1 billion "international program of aid for Brazil's economic recovery." The Brazil program was still at a level of $187 million in 1970, at a time when AID programs were being slashed across the board. A significant slice of the money went to subsidizing a federal budget of which 25 percent was spent on the armed forces in 1967, up from 15 percent in 1963. Deliveries of United States military equipment to Brazil, just over $1 million a year on average between 1950 and 1964, jumped to $13.3 million in 1964 and $17.7 million in 1969. Peru, by way of contrast, which had gotten $3.5 million more than Brazil in the 1950–64 period and which was up to $4.7 million in 1968, fell from grace in that year. A military junta overthrew the constitutional government, which would not have bothered Washington except that, in Rockefeller Report terms, it was "radicalized, statist and anti-United States"; qualities which it put on the record by nationalizing the International Petroleum Company. Its deliveries of United States military equipment were cut to $700,000 in 1969.

While the United States military mission to Brazil, the biggest in Latin America, was training 2,255 Brazilians in interrogation of prisoners and other techniques of guerrilla warfare between 1964 and 1968, the AID people gave counterinsurgency courses to more than 55,000 police officers in the Northeast alone, the most depressed area of Brazil and the one in which peasant organization for self-protection and self-advancement was most highly developed.

The United States reaction to any disturbance anywhere in Latin America has now become apparently automatic. In 1970, when conflict threatened in Colombia and in the Dominican Republic at election time, police cars, trucks and riot-control equipment were rushed from the United States under the so-called Public Security Program. Similarly, when riots exploded in Trinidad, arms and equipment were immediately airlifted to the authorities. The end result is to create an image of the United States as a world policeman, not a popular metaphor, but a bloody reality.

For the Latin Americans, all of this falls into a perfectly logical historical pattern. "You have always asserted and exercised a right of unilateral intervention in our countries for your own interests," one group of students told me, "and all that has changed is the method, in deference to the political realities of today. You play it as cool as you can, but when you must be openly brutal, you do not hesitate."

The bulletin board of a university student center in Montevideo, Uruguay, provided a specialized review of history, listing dates and incidents that seem to enter every discussion by students or intellectuals of inter-American relations.

1845	One third of Mexico's territory annexed.
1854	Nicaragua invaded.
1860	Honduras invaded.
1871	Dominican Republic invaded.
1881	Peru supported in war against Chile, in return for port of Chimbote.
1885	Creation of the Central American Federation opposed and boycotted.
1895	Intervenes in Venezuela.
1898	Further attempts to create Central American Federation blocked. Annexes Hawaii. Annexes Puerto Rico, Philippine Islands and Guam. Sets up the Republic of Cuba, which it controls until 1934 by means of the Platt Amendment.
1905	Dominican Republic invaded. Occupation troops remain in charge of customs until 1941.
1913	Panama invaded and Canal Zone occupied, starting a "protectorate" which continued until 1941.
1915	Haiti invaded. Occupation continued until 1934 and control of customs until 1941.
1917	Costa Rica invaded.

1919   Honduras invaded.
1926   Nicaragua, which had been a "protec-
         torate" since 1911, invaded. Occupation
         continued until 1934.
1961   Cuba invaded (Bay of Pigs).
1962   Cuba blockaded—the missile crisis.
1964   United States marines rushed to Brazil to
         back military seizure of power. They did
         not have to go ashore.

The foregoing are public facts of history. What went on
behind the scenes is often obscure, but significant elements
are on the record. In his account of his first term in office,[3]
President Eisenhower spoke quite frankly of a network of
intrigue in the Caribbean and Central America. What most
riles Latin Americans about this and similar confessions is
the tone, the insistent assumption that the United States is
legally and morally justified in unilaterally determining the
fate of sovereign nations, the absence of any regret or purpose of amendment. We airlifted arms to Honduras and
Nicaragua in May, 1954, Eisenhower reported, in order to
bring pressure on the Arbenz government in Guatemala,
which was "openly playing the communist game." Eisenhower also made clear our connection with the following
month's invasion of Guatemala from Honduras by a force
headed by an exiled Guatemalan colonel, Castillo Armas.
At first, things went smoothly for the well-equipped international force. But then they lost two of three bomber
planes used to buzz Guatemala City and bomb the ordi-
nance depot.

That same afternoon, President Eisenhower, John
Foster Dulles, Secretary of State, Allen Dulles, head of the
CIA, and Henry F. Holland, Assistant Secretary of State for
Latin America, met in a crisis session in Washington. "The
sense of our meeting was far from unanimous," Eisenhower
wrote. "Henry, a sincere and dedicated public servant and
a real expert in Latin American affairs, made no secret of
his conviction that the United States should keep hands off,
insisting that other Latin American republics would, if our
action became known, interpret our shipment of planes as

intervention in Guatemala's internal affairs. Others, however, felt that our agreeing to replace the bombers was the only hope for Castillo Armas, who was obviously the only hope of restoring freedom to Guatemala."[4]

The one who insisted that military considerations were more important than the political scruples of Henry Holland, the "real expert in Latin American affairs," was the head of the CIA. After an evaluation with Allen Dulles of the impact on the invasion of a failure to replace the planes, Eisenhower made his decision. "Our proper course of action—indeed my duty—was clear to me. We would replace the airplanes."

The story of Eisenhower's second administration[5] also has some revealing details about United States manipulations in Guatemala and elsewhere in Central America as part of the plans the CIA developed and financed to overthrow the Castro regime in Cuba, with whom the United States, at the time, maintained diplomatic relations. "Covert training of exiles for any possible future operations against Castro were going forward. Units were growing steadily in strength and efficiency against the time when actual tactical planning could be undertaken. In December [1960], I suggested to the State Department that the time might now be propitious for organizing a 'front' against Castro among the refugees, with the United States recognizing the leader and his associates as the legal government of Cuba, with the proviso, however, that the exiles themselves would voluntarily select from their own number an acceptable 'head of government.' I added that if they could do so at once, 'I'd like to see recognition accorded promptly—if possible, before January 20.' [January 20 was the inauguration of the new president.]

"On the morning of January 10, the *New York Times* carried an article, with a map, describing the training of anti-Castro forces in Guatemala. Although some details in the article were inaccurate, it told most of the story. I decided that we should say nothing at all about this article. Believing that my successor might want some day to assist the refugee forces to move into Cuba, I considered that we were limited in what we could say about them.

"So, to the incoming administration, we left units of Cuban refugees busily training and preparing hopefully for a return to their native land. Because they had as yet been unable to find the leader they wanted—a national leader known to be both anti-Castro and anti-Batista— it was impossible to make specific plans for a military invasion. . . ."[6]

Castro originally came to power with the approval of the United States, and Washington did not turn against him until it became clear that he intended to remove Cuba from United States political and economic tutelage, even if that meant substituting the hegemony of Soviet Russia. The Kennedy-Khrushchev agreement resolving the 1962 missile crisis recognized the fact of Cuba's defection. To ensure that it was not imitated by other Latin America nations, many of whose people had shown sympathy and admiration for Cuba during the crisis, Washington decided it would, in the future, concentrate on nipping in the bud any movement that threatened to degenerate into socialism.

Such a situation seemed, in fact, to be developing in Brazil. Fifth in the world in land area and eighth in population, this country had begun a meteoric expansion in 1955 under President Juscelino Kubitschek. Enthusiasm surged through the country, arousing the expectations of the masses and spurring migration to the cities. Kubitschek and his successors tried to speed up social improvements while avoiding tax reforms which they feared would alienate the wealthy. The resulting inflation increased labor unrest and popular pressures for more reforms. Janio Quadros, Kubitschek's successor, resigned in 1961 after six months in office, in favor of his vice-president, João Goulart. But Goulart seemed equally unable to stabilize the situation. The United States showed its displeasure in 1962 by suspending the disbursement of AID funds. Toward the end of 1963, conservative politicians in Brazil began to plot with the army leaders. By early 1964, the plotters were boasting that the United States Embassy was on their side. After one abortive attempt, the coup began on March 31, 1964. The following day, President Goulart fled to Uruguay and an interim president was sworn in. Within twelve hours, President Johnson sent "his warmest good wishes," an action which disillusioned the many Latin Americans who had taken seriously the United States commitment signed at Punta del Este in August, 1961, to deny recognition to military regimes which over-threw constitutional governments. Secretary of State Rusk also voiced his approval. His concurrent denial of the widely published charges that the United States had "or-dered and financed" the revolt was greeted with some skepticism, as was the subsequent official evaluation by Thomas Mann, Assistant Secretary of State for Inter-Amer-ican Affairs, who stated in his annual report for 1964 to the president that "the people of Brazil achieved a new national consensus and have begun an important program of economic and social reform."

In 1968, it was the turn of the Chileans to learn that the CIA was active in their midst. An unusually big and impressive group of social scientists from the United States had been working in the country for some time. They had excellent academic qualifications and were connected with top universities in the United States. They identified them-selves as engaged in high-level academic research on human motivation. But, as it turned out, Operation Camelot was an elaborate spy project to evaluate the defense capabili-ties of Chile. Rather significantly, the Pentagon and CIA had embarked on it without bothering to notify the United States ambassador to Chile. Chileans found the insult all the more gratuitous because theirs is one of the most stable countries in the hemisphere and because the Chris-tian Democratic regime of President Frei was scrupulously democratic at home and pro-United States in foreign pol-icy. The United States ambassador did what he could to make amends but the bad taste remained.

The taste turned sourer in December, 1969, when Chile's Senate met in closed session to discuss a complaint formulated by a Christian Democratic member concerning "the activities of the CIA in the country and the pressures it exerts." This time, the offending party was the Penta-gon rather than the CIA, a detail Chileans understandably consider secondary. The Pentagon had started a study in the Chilean army to find out if the officers were "satisfied with their living conditions," and to determine the kind of circumstances under which "they could envisage the possibility of their intervening in public life;" in other words, what would it take to get them to seize power. The last coup d'état in Chile occurred in 1932, and the possibility of a repetition seemed utterly remote to Chileans.

Possibly the Pentagon understands better than the Chileans how the mentality of Latin American armies has changed since it took over their technical training and political orientation. It had information that a top officer, General Roberto Viaux, had for several months been indicating a more than academic interest in the program of the military government of neighboring Peru. Following a military coup which brought General Juan Velasco Alvarado to power in October, 1968, Peru had succumbed to the temptation of radical military dictatorship so luridly painted by Rockefeller in his report to President Nixon. Although all the facts are not on the record, the theory is plausible that the Pentagon's inside information and evaluation had something to do with the sudden retirement of General Viaux early in October.

It seems, in any case, to have been interpreted as such by the Young Turks in the Chilean army who sympathized with Viaux and who a few weeks later precipitated a mini-revolt of the Tacna garrison. The stated cause was to protest the salary levels of the officers, but some of those participating did not exclude political projections. Prominent among these was a Captain Mora, a close associate of General Viaux. Mora is a Black Beret, the Chilean version of the Green Berets—a tough soldier, but one who sees no reason why the power the army enjoys should not be used to get things done. From the United States viewpoint, the formation of a military regime in Chile with an outlook similar to that of Peru would have been disastrous, and appropriate moves were made to strengthen the right-wing elements in the armed forces, specifically the top ranks of the navy and air force and the colonel in command of the Black Berets.

Peru also has had CIA attention. The United States had been aware for some time before the coup of October, 1968, that the military were plotting. Specifically, the Pentagon had been informed by the Rand Corporation, which it had commissioned to study the situation, that "the Peruvian military, if they decided to intervene, would do so for reasons of social order and not for personal reasons."[7] In terms of the stated interest of the United States that it welcomes clean government dedicated to social betterment, this should have been reassuring. For the Pentagon, nevertheless, and for certain other United States interests, it indicated an intention to stray from the task allotted to Latin American armed forces.

United States interests in Peru had organized a Protection Plan, an organization whose stated purpose was to protect the installations of United States companies in the country. The installations most immediately threatened were those of a Canadian company, International Petroleum Company (IPC), a wholly-owned subsidiary of Standard Oil of New Jersey. Peruvians had asserted for years that IPC owed back taxes, and the company had used its influence to delay a definitive ruling by the courts. General Juan Velasco, named president by the leaders of the coup, now took a course which he knew would be highly popular. He expropriated IPC in February, 1969, proclaiming his willingness to pay full compensation just as soon as it paid Peru the $690.5 million debt assessed by the tax authorities. He indicated that his government would accept a court ruling, if IPC challenged the assessment.

About this same time, the Peruvian government began to protest the activities of the Protection Plan on the ground that it was not a genuine trade protection association—but a vast spy ring. Peruvian investigation services announced the seizure of a list containing hundreds of names. United States Embassy personnel were declared *personae non gratae*.

All this, Peruvians claim, proves that the United States will stop at nothing to keep them from modernizing their economy and society. A social scientist specializing in Peruvian politics and economics offered the following evaluation. "I do not favor a military government," he told me, "but I see no viable alternative while we are subjected to such intolerable external pressures. I do not support this government because it conflicts with my committment to the democratic system, but I do approve both of what it has done up to now, and of its proclaimed policies. You must, however, realize that its area of maneuverability is extremely limited. The 'club' still exists, and its economic power can always be translated into political wallop. What has changed is the composition of this club. Formerly the decision makers, what one might call the executive committee, were our leading oligarchs—the big landowners and heads of commerce. Today, these are still club members, but they no longer make the big decisions. That role has passed to the *apoderados* of the United States companies, the Peruvian lawyers and accountants who head their operation here, men who have lost faith in their own country and thrown their fortune in with the *gringos*. If we have a countercoup, and we could have one any day because all it takes is one false step by Velasco, it is they who will bribe the army officers, who will secure the cooperation of the CIA, who will arrange for Washington recognition."

But even short of a countercoup, Washington can create problems for Velasco. In Lima, for example, they talk about Ernest V. Siracusa, a fifty-year-old diplomat, a hardliner formerly in Mexico, Guatemala and Argentina, who arrived in Peru as head of the mission in 1969. He wanted to get tough right away and urged Washington to suspend arms sales and apply the Hickenlooper Amendment, a provision of United States law which makes mandatory the cessation of all foreign aid if prompt and adequate compensation is not paid for expropriated United States property. Delivery of arms was cut back immediately, from $4.7 million in 1968 to $700,000 in 1969. After long hesitation, however, Washington decided not to apply the Hickenlooper Amendment. It was judged prudent not to risk the negative impact on Latin American opinion which resents the claim to judge unilaterally that another sovereign state has violated international law. In this instance, there were the further factors that the expropriated company was Canadian, and that a substantial legal doubt existed as to whether any payment was due to it.

Disclosures about CIA activity also quickly followed the military coup in Bolivia in September, 1969, which brought to power a regime committed to a nationalistic and anti-United States line similar to that of Peru. The coup coincided with the appointment as United States ambassador of the same Mr. Siracusa who had just made headlines in Lima. The Bolivian authorities charged a little later that Mr. Siracusa's arrival had marked an upsurge in the activities of the United States secret services in the country. Before the end of the year, they officially announced that a CIA spy network had been discovered. According to Interior Minister Ayoroa, Bolivia's security services had been infiltrated during the CIA-directed counterguerrilla operation against Che Guevara in 1967, and the network continued to function after the Green Berets withdrew.

The revelations caused little surprise to Bolivians. They were long accustomed to multi-level pressures from the United States. The Bolivian writer, Sergio Almaraz Paz, has recorded a typical example.[8] In its anti-Castro campaign in the early 1960's, Washington became extremely annoyed at Bolivia's unwillingness to agree to break diplomatic relations. Victor Paz Estenssoro, head of the Nationalist Revolutionary Movement (MNR), which had nationalized the tin mines and broken up the big estates during the previous decade, refused to go along. A vicious anti-government campaign was unleashed in the controlled Bolivian press. When Paz Estenssoro protested, United States Ambassador Henderson explained that he was the man in the middle, being himself under pressure from the Pentagon's political officer, a Colonel Edward Fox. At one point, Paz Estenssoro lost his patience and said to Henderson, "If that's how things are, let Fox come and replace me as president." When the chancellors of the American republics met in Washington under the aegis of the Organization of American States to vote the diplomatic isolation of Cuba, a Bolivian delegation, headed by the economics minister, was also in Washington seeking to negotiate commercial credits. A few hours before the decisive vote, President Johnson sent a cable to President Estenssoro demanding that his delegation vote against Cuba. It was for the record only, because Washington already had a substantial majority in its pocket. Paz Estenssoro refused. And the economics minister came home without a dollar.

Ironically, the pressures on Paz Estenssoro finally caused him to yield on far more important issues, and even to return to United States control a large segment of the nationalized mining industry. Ousted in 1964, he settled down in Lima, and remained there until December, 1969, when he moved to Washington while President Ovando publicly warned that "a conspiracy against us is being hatched outside the country."

Also denounced by the Ovando regime as part of the CIA operation and placed under government control was the American Institute for Free Labor Development (AIFLD), an organization sponsored by the AFL-CIO and other United States interests for promoting trade unionism in Latin America. Since World War II, the labor movement has been fragmented by three currents, each represented by an international federation, identified respectively as Free, Socialist and Christian. Organized labor has always been weak in Latin America. Apart from Cuba with over 20 percent and Argentina with 11 percent, the proportion of unionized workers is everywhere very low, varying between Colombia's 7 percent and Haiti's 0.1 percent. The basic conditions, political, social and economic, for successful unionization have generally been absent. Legal protection and guarantees do not exist or are ineffectively applied. Public opinion, determined by media of communications controlled by business interests, is apathetic or hostile. The worker-employer gap is so wide as to make the worker's efforts to assert his rights seem an outrageous violation of the established order. The vast and growing imbalance between the labor force and the labor requirements of agriculture, industry and services facilitates strike-breaking and union-bustings. Replacements are always available from the bottomless pit of the destitute unemployed, to whom the prospect of work inevitably outweighs any theoretic consideration of fraternal solidarity.

The Socialist and the Christian Internationals and their affiliates are agreed on the basic postulate that in such circumstances the function of the trade union is largely, if not primarily political. Social structures have to be changed before unions can acquire bargaining power. The Free Trade Unions, on the other hand, are dominated by the philosophy of the AFL-CIO that what's good for us has to be good for them. Labor in the United States had prospered by staying out of politics and concentrating on the strictly economic issues of wages, working conditions, health and pension benefits, and so on.

United States companies in Latin America welcomed this approach. They fought unionization of their plants, but when it was unavoidable, they preferred union leaders who spoke the language to which they were accustomed back home. Sheltering under the umbrella of the Cold War and the slogan of democratic institutions, the United States government and business joined the AFL-CIO in a vast program to sell their brand of trade unionism. Thousands of leaders at all organizational levels were trained in labor schools in the United States.

An evaluation made by Enno Hobbing explains how United States business benefited. Mr. Hobbing is staff director of the Council of the Americas, an organization, headed by David Rockefeller, grouping two hundred corporations responsible for more than 80 percent of United States investment in Latin America. It is, in its own words, "the principal spokesman for all North American businesses operating in Latin America."

"Both Latin American and United States businessmen," wrote Mr. Hobbing, "looked at the deteriorating situation and realized they would have to do more than tend to business. If their enterprises—and Latin America—were to have a future, they would have to support the constructive, democratic elements in labor movements and on university campuses; they would have to devote more effort to helping the private sector solve pressing social problems.

"A primary concern was the Latin American labor movement. The communists were making headway toward gaining control of it, but in the early 1960s supporters of democratic principles found in the American Institute for Free Labor Development (AIFLD) an imaginative way to help turn the tide. Essentially an organization for training labor leaders in enlightened labor practices, AIFLD has been given financial support by corporations, and business-men have sat on boards of directors beside George Meany and other leaders of the AFL-CIO. Latin American entre-preneurs have likewise assisted and welcomed the work of AIFLD. It has trained tens of thousands of democratic labor leaders in its schools and seminars in practically every Latin American country and at its advanced study center in Washington. It has taught them the workers' stake in pro-ductivity, techniques of union organization, collective bar-gaining, and the generally vigorous defense of the legitimate rights of labor."[9]

"That is a complete distortion of the facts," according to Luis Escobar, a labor organizer in Medellín, Colombia. "We saw what happened here during the industrial reces-sion we experienced in 1969 and 1970. Did these so-called Free unions use their influence to get the United States to eliminate its quotas and tariffs—as it had promised—so that we could keep our factories going? Not at all. They were too busy making deals with management at the expense of their members. The problem is that the training they re-ceived in the United States distorted their values. Just like the army people who go to Panama, the union leaders who attend the institute in Washington undergo an intensive brainwashing. Life becomes for them a constant conflict with the evil forces of communism. The bosses are the good guys making the world safe for democracy. Those of us who protest a lock-out or the introduction of scab workers are trouble makers and subversives."

Miguel Cardozo, also a labor organizer, agrees. "The AFL-CIO functions as an instrument of the State Depart-ment and the CIA to divide and control our trade union movement," he says. "This imperialist organization uses the AIFLD to corrupt and control popular movements in all parts of the world, as we in Latin America know all too well. The AIFLD financed an eleven-week strike to the tune of $700,000 to bring down the Jagan government in

Guyana. It backed the invasion of Cuba and United States intervention in the Dominican Republic, just as it supported the war in Vietnam."

Financial support of AIFLD by the United States government and business has helped the Free Trade Union movement to survive. The outlook for it is, nevertheless, far from bright. Many members in such countries as Colombia and Brazil, have become disillusioned by the defection of leaders to the side of the employers in moments of crisis. The rise to power of the Christian Democrats, closely associated with the Christian trade unions, in Venezuela and Chile, has also hurt the Free unions, and they will not benefit by Chile's further movement to the left in the 1970 presidential elections. In addition, the philosophy underlying the Free Trade Union movement is being vigorously challenged by Latin American social scientists. Economic development, they insist, will not automatically bring social progress as long as the monopoly of political control, combined with the enormous labor surplus, restricts the benefits to a small segment of the population. Rather, as was suggested in an earlier chapter, it actually increases the distortion between the developed and undeveloped sectors.

The presence of transistor radios, bicycles, toothpaste, and Coca-Cola, according to Mexican anthropologist Rodolfo Stavenhagen, "does not automatically imply the development of these areas, if by development we mean an increase in per capita output of goods and services, and in the general social welfare. Often this diffusion of products is nothing but the diffusion of the culture of poverty into the backward, rural areas, for it involves no basic institutional changes." Instead, "the spread of manufactured industrial goods into the backward zones often displaces flourishing local industries or manufactures, and therefore destroys the productive base for a significant part of the population, provoking . . . economic stagnation."[10] Helio Jaguaribe agrees. We are in a vicious circle, he says. Economic development within our satellite economy "is of its nature not viable, because it tends to perpetuate and aggravate the disproportion between a modern sector and an archaic sector, a ruling sector and a ruled sector, with a progressive shrinking in size of the modern sector in relation to the whole."[11]

The substantial United States contribution to modernizing the Latin American university is being reevaluated in equally negative terms. Medellín again provides an example with an eye-catching slogan on the road leading to the university: "Get the Yankee assassins out of the University of Antioquia." The "assassin" epithet simply reflects the almost universal condemnation of the United States involvement in Vietnam, a sentiment which many personalize because they are familiar with and share Martin Luther King, Jr.'s presentiment that Latin America is next in line for napalming and saturation bombing. The reason for wanting the "Yankee assassins" out of the University of Antioquia is a little more complicated. Like almost all Latin American universities, that of Medellín experienced an enormous expansion during the 1960s, a growth some would call cancerous—from 1,600 students to 8,000. The inrush of students imposed great stresses on the institution, requiring more classrooms, books, professors, laboratories and other training facilities. The United States aid program stepped generously into the breach, as in scores of similar cases. Substantial grants and loans helped to build a new campus, with an academic and administrative organization modeled closely on those of United States universities. Libraries were enriched with versions in Spanish of United States school and college texts. Professors came on loan to organize departments and establish directions.

At first, the academic community was understandably pleased to find itself in the spotlight, and it did not object to modernized facilities and new salary scales. But the honeymoon was brief. It soon became obvious that the help being provided was not completely altruistic. The United States methods and texts were producing a more thorough integration into the economy of the United States and also reinforcing the already enormous cultural invasion. Revelations in the mid-1960s that CIA funds were underwriting studies that had been presented as strictly academic, and that CIA agents sometimes masqueraded as university professors, brought student riots. Many institutions have cut down on exchange professors, but AID money is still being offered and accepted, in spite of continuing protests by students and other progressive groups.

The impact of the United States programs is most immediately obvious in medicine. Medical schools receive up-to-date installations from the United States, and textbooks instruct the students in the latest techniques. By the time the young doctors graduate, they are ready to step into practice—in any thriving suburban community in the United States. They know when to use a fluoroscope, when to call for X-rays, when to demand a cardiogram, urine analysis, or blood tests. The trouble is that in the Colombian countryside, no such facilities are available. Even in the cities, the cost is such that they are accessible only to a tiny minority of the wealthy. Unequipped by their studies to diagnose or treat even common ailments under these conditions, many frustrated doctors get on a plane to the United States, where an AMA-controlled shortage of medical doctors exists. Those who stay cluster around the technical facilities in the major cities. The people in the country continue to be born and die by their own devices.

Similar distortions occur in engineering, chemistry, architecture, and in general, wherever operating techniques are dependent on the type of plant and research facilities available for the practice of the specialization. But even in the more abstract and intellectual branches of knowledge, the introduction of the United States model produces a graduate whose evaluations and judgments of reality are based on conditions in the United States rather than those in his own country. The economics school of the Catholic University of Santiago de Chile, for example, has been completely revamped over a period of years by a team from the University of Chicago. The program covered administration, academic structures, and course content. Visiting professors established the tone, and the faculty was upgraded by graduate training in Chicago. The technical results are admirable. But the Chileans are profoundly disillusioned because the graduates are so oriented toward the economic reality and needs of the United States as often to be incapable of relating to the problems of their own country.

The integration of higher education into the United

States market for professionals is not new. But the foreign aid programs have intensified it and given it new characteristics, especially in the areas of the physical sciences, mathematics, medicine and the social sciences. The trend is encouraged and accelerated by expanding opportunities for continuing studies in the United States, another relatively new phenomenon. Until World War II, the Latin Americans looked to Europe for higher studies. Since that time, however, the United States government and industry have cooperated in developing a worldwide system of incentives to attract foreign students. The total enrollment in colleges and universities in the 1969–70 academic year was 134,950, of whom 24,540 were from Latin America. Meanwhile, most Latin American students who study abroad study in the United States.

The Institute of International Education is the principal instrument in the United States for promoting this process. Established in 1917 by business groups who saw the potential value of foreign students for their international operations, it acquired its dominant position in 1939 when it began to serve as the operational agency for government exchange grants. Its directors and members at any given moment are a cross-section of the top echelons of industry, commerce and banking. It is closely related to the most prestigious foundations: Rockefeller, Ford, Carnegie. In the 1960s it also came to light that the Dodge Foundation, the Hobby Foundation, the McGregor Fund, the Aaron E. Norman Fund, the Rubicon Foundation, and other contributors to the Institute of International Education were in fact conduits for the flow of funds and personnel from the CIA to organizations which represented themselves to the world as nonpolitical and nonideological.

The style of the Institute of International Education, to which the foreign student arriving in the United States is introduced, has been described as one "of sophistication and internationalism, a style which denies the existence of fundamental conflicts of interest, which says the world can be run just like the college campus—a controlled environment where people can be channeled in subtle ways, where everyone can be made to believe that he is a participant in a community of free men and where questions of control need never arise and raw uses of power need only be occasional."[12]

The function of the Institute is, however, more concrete. As it explains in a promotional pamphlet, United States corporations "recognize—abroad as well as at home—that education offers the best means for stimulating purchasing power, encouraging political stability, and most important of all, developing a reservoir of the trained manpower so necessary to their overseas operations. However, the United States corporation faces difficult decisions and alternatives in undertaking sound and profitable ventures in international education. Unfamiliar cultures, complex situations, unskilled manpower, and frequently a thin layer of educational and technical resources present serious problems in foreign settings. In approaching such problems, many corporations have benefited from the Institute's wide experience and counsel."

One such function is to provide information on available personnel to United States firms operating abroad. These firms, as the Institute points out in its literature, usually "find it necessary or desirable to employ nationals with United States academic training." Accordingly, the Institute each year publishes a census of foreign students and scholars studying, teaching, or doing research at colleges in the United States, as well as a similar survey of United States students and scholars abroad. It includes fields of study, country of origin, and sources of support. Additional data, including home addresses, are available as a further service. The Institute's services also include the "recruitment of professional staff members, contractual salary negotiations, purchase of equipment and material, fiscal management, and other services hand-tailored to each particular undertaking."

How American international companies view these activities is clear from an article in *Think*, a magazine published by IBM for its shareholders and other opinion makers among its worldwide contacts. "Foreign students will ultimately be helpful to United States business. The man who wants to start a cotton gin in the Congo will find it easier if he has a Congolese buddy from college, especially as the Congolese will probably be a high official. And then, American corporations, gradually turning their operations in foreign countries over to the people who live there, will need trained personnel."

The obvious importance of a buddy as a high official is stressed similarly in an article in *The Lamp*, the Standard Oil of New Jersey magazine. "In Brazil, business is playing a big part in supporting the Inter-American University Foundation, which selects those students who look like the country's leaders of tomorrow and gives them a sophisticated orientation course, in Brazil and in the United States, on the world in which they live."

From its point of view, official Washington also sees the benefits that result from the integration of Latin America's higher education into that of the United States. One aspect is developed in the *U.S. Army Area Handbook for Ecuador*. "With the financial support of AID, missions from the University of Pittsburgh, the University of Houston, and St. Louis University have been assisting the Central University, the University of Guayaquil and the Catholic University of Quito, respectively, in improvement programs. The principal areas of activity include the reform of central administration, the institution of basic studies programs for all students before further university work and the strengthening of the *facultades* (faculties) dealing in disciplines related to social and economic development. Plans also call for the promotion of greater stability and a calmer, more exclusively academic atmosphere."

One of the more bizarre aspects of the university reform promoted with United States help in almost all the Latin American countries during the 1950s and 1960s, is its failure to deal with the system's most glaring defect, while creating conditions which magnify it. This is an open admissions policy which enrolls vast numbers with minimum aptitude and low motivation. Those who fail courses may repeat indefinitely. Many students stay for ten, fifteen or twenty years before they finally fade away. Mexico's University City has 70,000 students, of whom only 10 percent graduate. Guatemla City has an enrollment of 12,000, but an annual graduation level of three hundred. The students who will never graduate are doing enormous harm. They occupy classrooms, libraries, and laboratories which are in such short supply that universities are running two and three shifts a day. They consume the time of administrators and professors. And their marginal interest in the education process acts to dissipate the enthusiasm of the serious and committed students. Yet United States aid is being spent on perpetuating this system by providing new classrooms and facilities.

Latin Americans are increasingly concerned by the total impact of all these influences. While the governments keep silent because they want to maintain the flow of aid, intellectuals and serious students grow frustrated. Many see the entire process as a huge conspiracy to provide benefits for the United States at the expense of their countries. The United States gains by the big and growing brain drain. The most dynamic and talented graduates can easily find work in the United States. The local branches of United States industry and business can also offer inducements which local government or business cannot match. Finally, the others who have been trained in United States universities, or locally under professors trained in the United States and in academic programs oriented in its direction, serve gradually to transmit to the entire community the norms, standards and objectives of the American Way of Life.

The brain drain is the most obvious and measurable part of this complex process. Until recently, it was mainly a question of the attraction provided by better jobs, higher salaries, more stability of employment, greater opportunity, facilities for research in the academic and scientific world, and the availability in industry of the equipment to enable one to exercise knowledge and skills. Such are the elements that have always attracted large numbers of young people. More recently, a new and even more sinister factor has been added. The spread of dictatorial regimes committed to the suppression of all opinion judged by them subversive is forcing substantial numbers of university professors and other top thinkers to emigrate. Brazil, since 1964, has lost hundreds of these people, many of such a level that they had no difficulty in relocating in the most prestigious institutions of higher learning in the United States. The negative impact on the cultural life of Brazil has been enormous. The leaders have gone, and their followers are terrified to express their ideas. The same process is occurring elsewhere. "Argentina, when the military took over, had an outstanding group of scientists," Norman Dervas told me. Dr. Dervas is a United States social scientist who has lived several years in Argentina. "As part of its program to neutralize the university, the regime got rid of some eight hundred key professors. The faculties that suffered most were the exact sciences, the ones related to the process of national development. Since these men were among the most scientifically advanced in Latin America, their departure caused a watering down of the entire educational system. In addition, as is normal in Latin America, these professors also worked in research institutions and in industry outside the university. When they left the country, they took with them a whole sector of its technological capability. Such is the extent of the tragedy." I talked to many of these teachers, and they are convinced that they are victims of *La Cia*. Ironically, there is no pressure to prevent their moving to the United States to hold important jobs in the universities or in industry. The system there is too well-entrenched to be threatened by some refugee scientists.

Estimates of the brain drain vary widely. A study published in 1970 by the International Monetary Fund showed that the Latin American countries with the highest outflow are Argentina, Colombia and Mexico. Between 1962 and 1966, Argentina lost 3,834 professionals; Colombia, 3,572; and Mexico, 3,005. What is generally agreed is that the vast expansion of the universities combined with the far smaller rise in the demand for graduates will intensify the hemorrhage in the 1970s.

It is obviously not reasonable to blame the CIA for all of Latin America's ills. But as long as half a dozen poorly coordinated and bumbling Washington agencies continue ill-concealed efforts to manipulate the political and cultural life of the hemisphere, the suspicions and hatreds they arouse will stultify the most disinterested efforts of other North Americans.

8

THE
FUTURE PRESENT

Although Brazil has already figured substantially in earlier chapters, it is probably the best country in Latin America to study in more detail as an illustration of current developments. Its population (90,000,000: twice that of Mexico) and size (3,286,000 square miles: three times that of Argentina) of themselves justify such treatment, but the more important reason to stress the Brazilian experience is that many Latin Americans fear that it represents the direction in which the continent is moving. To understand what that means requires a more organized analysis of its recent history.

With extensive natural resources and enough people to create a market for a modern industrial economy, Brazil set out aggressively after World War II to transform its colonial economy which had been based on the export of coffee. Industrialization had already progressed significantly in the 1930's, beginning with textiles and other light and medium industries. Wartime restrictions on international trade speeded the process of Brazilian industrialization and allowed the accumulation of reserves of foreign currency obtained from exports. This double process set the stage for a major advance between 1945 and 1960. Heavy industry producing capital goods was started. President Juscelino Kubitschek, whose campaign slogan had been to achieve fifty years of progress in five years, initiated his term in 1955 with an ambitious "Target Plan" for self-sustained growth in energy, transport, food, basic industries, and education, plus a new capital, Brasilia.

During the previous five years, the gross national product had increased impressively by 29.5 percent, and the Target Plan brought a further increase of 41.1 percent between 1955 and 1960. But the advance was won at a price that proved excessive. It involved a truce with the country's reactionary forces, leaving intact the foundation of their power, their ownership and exploitation of the rural-agricultural complex. Landownership is more highly concentrated than in almost any other Latin American country, and the landowners are concerned with power even more than with profits in their use of the land. Kubitschek's planners hoped that development of the urban-industrial sectors would unleash market economic forces to modernize the rural-agricultural system and unify the domestic market. The landowners blocked the process. They were able to hold the 50 percent of the population represented by peasants at their traditional subsistence levels of living, thereby denying to industry this potential market for its products. Even the food supply increased at less than half the 12 percent rate of increase of the urban demand for food. Prices naturally rose, and half the urban population, earning the minimum wage, spent its entire income on food. That left only a quarter of the population as the potential market for industrial goods.

Kubitschek's successors, Jánio Quadros and João Goulart, tried to break the stranglehold of the landowners. Alarmed by the growing gap between the impoverished rural Northeast and the industrialized South, they favored projects to correct that situation. They proposed to modernize agriculture by means of farm cooperatives and large state farms. Many of the new industrialists became frightened; alarmed at the growing role of the state, the increased taxes and the inflation, they moved closer to the landowners in opposition. This in turn drove the government further toward revolutionary change, seeking the support of the popular forces aroused by the prospect of active participation in public affairs. It proclaimed goals of land and income redistribution, economic nationalism, nationalization of large sectors of production, political mobilization of the urban and rural masses, and international neutralism and nonalignment. This in turn frightened the policy makers of the United States and with official encourgement, a coalition of politicians, businessmen, and the military overthrew President Goulart in 1964.

The military regime promised a quick return to constitutional government, and presumably intended to do so. First, however, it undertook to undo the policies and programs of the ousted government. Laws providing for the distribution of certain noncultivated lands to peasants were annulled. In return for the United States' support and its promise of major loans, the regulations limiting the export of business profits were withdrawn, and the nationalization of oil refineries was rescinded. Controls on wages effected a sharp reduction in the inflation rate without a serious reduction in business profits. The first of a series of so-called "institutional acts" was a decree suspending some constitutional guarantees and increasing the power of the executive. Mass arrests followed. Many political leaders, including the last three elected presidents, were stripped of their political rights for ten years. Congress was purged of 112 members, and several state governors were deposed. Two thousand military men were retired.

Organized labor and university students received special attention. Leaders of key unions were ousted and federal nominees substituted. Peasant leagues were disbanded. National and state unions of students were outlawed. Thousands of military commissions of inquiry were created, endowed with wide and judicially uncontrolled powers, to investigate local bodies and institutions throughout the country and eliminte every potential enemy of the regime.

The first of several attempts to relax controls and return at least in part to the forms of democracy was made in 1965. Elections for governors were held in several states in October, the major political opponents having been eliminated by decree. But any opposition was more to the people's liking than the candidates of the regime. It was the easy winner in the more important contests. The military junta replied with Institutional Act No. 2 which ended popular voting for state governors, dissolved all political parties, and gave to the purged Congress the task of electing the president of the republic and state governors. Two new political parties were created under rigid government controls, one to be the government party, the other "a loyal opposition." But even the loyal opposition could not accept its role for long. When the purged Congress elected General Costa e Silva to the presidency in October, 1966, only the government deputies participated. The others abstained in protest against what they called "an electoral farce."

Meanwhile, the regime pressed forward with its constantly proclaimed major goal of a total realignment of Brazil, both economic and political, with the United States. Decrees favoring foreign investment and capital movement were promulgated. Priority was given to private capital and free enterprise in future development, although the resistance of nationalistic elements within the military prevented the sale of existing state-owned concerns or the proposed abandonment of the state oil monopoly. In return for these policies, Washington kept absolute silence about the destruction of democratic institutions and the curbs on freedom. Senator Wayne Morse was a lone voice when he protested Institutional Act No. 2 and urged an end to economic and military aid. Lincoln Gordon, U.S. Ambassador to Brazil from 1961 to 1966, vigorously defended the political, as well as the economic policies of the Brazilian regime when questioned by a U.S. Senate commission. And in April, 1966, an AID report to Congress praised the conduct of the Brazilian government since the coup.

Early in 1967, another attempt to legitimate the regime was made by the promulgation of a new constitution. It incorporated the institutional acts issued since 1964 and authorized the president to promulgate laws and declare a state of emergency without consulting Congress. A press law followed, with harsh penalties for criticism of the government, and a national security law gave the military courts power to treat all opposition to the regime as treason. In spite of these laws, a belief that pressures were being eased gained wide currency. In March, accordingly, thousands of students gathered secretly in Rio de Janeiro to reorganize the student movement and condemn the dictatorship as a servant of Yankee imperialism. In August, 350 student representatives traveled clandestinely from all over Brazil to reconstruct the National Student Union and hold its 29th annual congress. The first task they gave themselves was to mobilize popular opposition to the dictatorship. In the same month, the *Frente Ampla* was formed, a broad coalition of the major pre-coup politicians. It brought together the militantly anti-communist Carlos Lacerda, a principal plotter of the 1964 coup, with ex-President Kubitschek and most of the Center-Left. The attempts to recreate popular organizations, however, quickly revealed a level of opposition to the regime which the regime found unacceptable. When police killed a student during a peaceful demonstration in Rio in 1968, the funeral became a mass protest, and army tanks occupied the city. Students clashed with police the following month in Rio, São Paulo, Brasilia, Salvador and other cities. Workers soon joined the students in massive condemnation of the dictatorship and of the United States support for it, leading to mass arrests. June became known as "the month of blood." It saw the dissolution by decree of the *Frente Ampla,* the killing of six people during demonstrations in Rio, and massive police interference as demonstrations grew in size and frequency. Toward the end of the year, radical resistance movements staged a number of bank holdups and bombings of government buildings and of offices of the United States companies and government. Extreme right-wing organizations responded with assassinations and tortures. In October, the leadership of the student movement was wiped out when the police arrested a thousand delegates meeting secretly in Sãn Paulo for the 30th congress of the National Student Union.

By this time, the dilemma of the military government had become clear. It was on a treadmill. Reconciliation of its policies of economic modernization with the preservation of political and social immobility, while concentrating the economic benefits in the business community and the armed forces, required a progressive increase in the level of repression of popular movements. The inbuilt stagnancy of the economy, because of its inability to bring most of the people into the market for industrial products, prevented expansion of the labor force to keep step with population growth. Ever harsher methods had to be used to prevent starving peasants from migrating to the cities to swell the explosive marginal masses.

Institutional Act No. 5 (December 1968) brought a significant stepping-up of repression. Described as a coup within a coup, it ended all pretence at representative government, giving the president unlimited dictatorial power. He can recess the National Congress and all subordinate legislatures indefinitely, meanwhile exercising their legislative functions. He can oust state governors and city mayors, and substitute his replacements. He can suspend the rights of any citizen for ten years and cancel all elected terms of office—federal, state or municipal. Suspension of citizen rights, in addition to prohibition of trade union or political activity, may involve subjection to police surveillance, exclusion from specified places, or confinement to one's home. He can dismiss any public employee, regardless of office or security of tenure, without having to state his reasons, and without appeal to the courts. Finally, the decree suspended habeas corpus, enabling the political police to hold suspects indefinitely on charges of crimes "against the national security, economic and social order, and the popular economy."

On signing the decree, Marshal Costa e Silva recessed Congress and ruled under its terms until his death from a stroke in October, 1969. The election of his successor was one of the most extraordinary performances in the history of any country. The 239 senior officers in the armed forces (118 army generals, 61 air force generals, and 60 admirals), constituted themselves an electoral college and proceeded to select a president from among their membership. At first, there was considerable backing for the candidate of the troops of the Northeast, but he was finally ruled out because he was only a three-star general. Instead, the electors settled on General Garrastazú Médici, commander of the Third Army. Congress, which had been purged several times, was then called back into session to "elect" the new president. To preserve the pretence of choice, two other names were submitted along with that of General Médici; the Army

Chief of Staff, and the chief of staff of the Armed Forces. Congress approved the top name, that of General Médici.

The situation inherited by this tall and graying sixty-four-year-old cavalry officer, was a somber one. The inflation rate, though cut impressively from the 1964 level of 85 percent, was still at a disturbing 23 percent. The most obvious effect of the investment which had poured into the country under the new guarantees was an increase in the foreign domination of the private sector of the economy. It controlled 72 percent of the capital goods sector, 78 percent of the durable consumer goods sector, and 52 percent of the nondurable consumer goods sectors. Wage controls had cut by 25 percent the real income of most Brazilians, lowering the demand for manufactures. Factories built by SUDENE, the development agency for the depressed Northeast created by President Kubitschek in 1959, were particularly affected by the fall in the purchasing power of that region. The cost of shipment to the more developed South made their products uncompetitive there, and many had to close or operate on limited schedules. Health, education, sanitation, and other vital services remained grossly inadequate in most parts of the country. While the industrialists and financiers of São Paulo, Rio, and the other big southern cities continued to back the regime, it was in a state of smouldering war with professionals, intellectuals, students, progressive segments of the church, and the voiceless masses trapped in growing deprivation.

The new president started with a conciliatory gesture. Acknowledging that his regime "could not be called fully democratic," he promised that "at the end of my term [1973], I hope to leave democracy definitely installed in our country, as well as fixed bases for our economic and social development." His predecessor had taken office in October, 1966 with a similar pledge to "humanize" the revolution. The rhythm of events, however, had proved stronger than Costa e Silva's intentions, and continued to dominate his successor. At his first news conference, in March, 1970, General Médici publicly confessed that his promise of liberalization had been premature. "The military will continue in office as long as it takes," he said. The Institutional Act

No. 5 will not be annulled "soon." Rather, "it was instituted too late, and it is still too early to revoke it." There was no letup in the tough tactics of DOPS (Department of Political and Social Order) and of the security organizations operated by each of the armed services to exercise surveillance over all citizens. They went ahead with mass roundups for questioning, detentions, and torture in search of terrorists who robbed banks and stole arms from military installations. They continued to muzzle the press, to deprive citizens of their political rights, to oust professors and students. An estimated 12,000 of the 30,000 persons arrested on charges of subversion since 1964 remained in jail, most of them untried.

By 1970, the issue of torture had become critical. The government had long admitted incidents, but blamed the excessive zeal of individuals. Friends of the victims, who ranged all the way from members of the outlawed Communist Party to priests and nuns, clandestinely compiled and smuggled out of the country massive dossiers which established the existence of a pattern impossible without official involvement. A committee of scholars, writers, religious leaders and spokesmen for civil liberties was formed in the United States to evaluate the evidence. It included Ralph David Abernathy of the Southern Christian Leadership Conference, John Bennett of Union Theological Seminary, Louis M. Colonnese of Catholic Bishops' Conference, Stanley J. Stein of Princeton University and Charles Wagley of Columbia University. In a report[1] issued in April, 1970, this committee said that "torture, terror, and repression are the order of the day; the privation of fundamental human rights continues unabated; the Brazilian—student, worker, intellectual—joins the ranks of the world's political refugees. In all, a critical situation now exists." Specific cases of torture documented in this report include a statement signed by thirty-eight priests from Belo Horizonte. They testified that they had firsthand accounts from political prisoners of "violent blows and tortures practiced by the police as a means of obtaining confessions . . . or simply for reasons of vengeance; the imprisonment of citizens without time limit; . . . an incalculable number of arbitrary detentions of innocent persons; . . . absolute contempt for the rights of parents to know the whereabouts of their children; . . . the imprisonment and torture of relatives as a means of pressuring prisoners to reveal information; . . . violence done to women, who are stripped naked and beaten and have electric shocks applied to their breasts."

The report further stated that the use of torture "now appears to surpass all other techniques of police investigation and inquiry. Torture has become so commonplace that the three armed services have organized courses." For example, it said, a class in torture was conducted in October, 1969, at the headquarters of the state police of Minas Gerais, in Belo Horizonte; and twelve male political prisoners used as guinea pigs subsequently described the proceedings in a collective document. "On October 8, a class in interrogation was held . . . for a group of about a hundred military men, the majority of them sergeants from the three branches of the armed forces. Just before the class, Maurício [de Paiva] was given electric shocks 'to see if the equipment was in good working order,' in the words of a private named Mendoça. At about 4 P.M., just before the class was to begin, the [following ten] prisoners were led up to the classroom where the session was already in progress: Maurício de Paiva, Angelo Pezzuti, Murilo Pinto, Pedro Paulo Bretas, Afonso Celso Lara, Nilo Sérgio, Júlio A. Antonio, Irany Campos, and a former MP from Guanabara and another prisoner known as Zezinho. Immediately after, they were ordered to enter the room and strip. While Lieutenant Haylton was showing slides and explaining each type of torture, its characteristics and effects, Sergeants Andrade, Oliveira, Rossoni, and Rangel, together with Corporals Mendoça and [an illegible name] and the soldier Marcelino were torturing the prisoners in the presence of the hundred military men in a 'live' demonstration of the various torture methods in use. Maurício suffered electric shocks, Bretas had a finger put in irons, Murilo was forced to stand on top of cutting edges of tin cans, Zezinho was hung from the '*pau de arara*,' and the ex-MP was clubbed, while Nilo Sérgio had to hold his balance on one foot while heavy weights were hung from his outstretched arms."

About the same time, the International Federation of the Rights of Man and the French branch of Amnesty International sent two lawyers, Jean Louis Weil and L. E. Pettiti, to Brazil for an on-the-spot survey. Having interviewed public and private citizens, including members of the clergy, they reported that "the situation in Brazil today is considerably more serious than that observed in Greece last year. Torture in Brazil has a systematic and generalized character. These are not any longer isolated incidents, but a true political instrument used for the purpose of terrorizing." They said that nearly 12,000 political prisoners were held in jails all over the country, the average age of these prisoners being twenty-two years.[2]

A little later, in July, 1970, the International Commission of Jurists charged at its Geneva headquarters that the government of Brazil was continuing the "systematic and scientifically developed" practice of torture. "It is no longer a mere aid of judicial interrogation but has become a political weapon." The commission, supported by 50,000 lawyers and judges from almost all noncommunist countries of the world, has consultative status with the Economic and Social Council of the United Nations and with the eighteen-nation Council of Europe. Sean McBride, a former Minister of Justice of Ireland, is its secretary general. The commission said its report was based on documents secretly removed from Brazilian prisons and concentration camps, documents and statements from former political prisoners who had escaped or been sent into exile, and other materials gathered by visitors to Brazil. Noting that the spreading use of torture was "corrupting Brazilian society," it commented that "there is little hope of ameliorating the repression in view of the ever increasing number of civil servants and military officers who have incriminated themselves by torturing their fellow citizens."[3]

All these reports match perfectly with my own observations when I visited Brazil in April and May, 1970. Everywhere I went, torture was the constant subject of discussion. Everyone had stories about the experiences of friends and acquaintances. What had caught imaginations most vividly was the *pau de arara*, the "parrot's perch" already referred to as one of the techniques used in the course of instruction in torture methods in Belo Horizonte. The perch, a fixture in the traditional Brazilian country home, was a branch or pole on which the family parrot swung as he squawked noisily and flashed his gaudy plumage in the sun. Later it was applied to the rail to which the landless laborers clung when they fled by truckloads in the rainless 1930s from the drought-parched Northeast to the slums of Rio and São Paulo. Now it means the form of torture in which the victim is trussed, with a pole under his knees, and swung back and forth, head down. For added impact, clothing may be removed and electric shocks applied to the genitals, breasts and tongue. Brazilian mothers no longer threaten naughty children with the local equivalent of Brer Fox or the bogey man, but with the *pau de arara*.

One of the things which understandably frightens Brazilians is that innocence of crime is no guarantee of safety. In Belo Horizonte, Dona Vanda Souza, a physician, recounted a visit she had paid that same day to her brother who was being treated for attempted suicide. A chemist by profession, he had once been a left-wing politician, but had abandoned politics to work as a chemist long before the 1964 military putsch. In 1968, some former political associates came to him with a proposal to join them in clandestine activities. He turned them down and forgot the matter. His wife never learned of the single meeting in their home. But one of the conspirators was seized nearly two years later and under torture gave the Souza home as the meeting place. When the police came for Souza, they also arrested his wife. In such situations, the wife is invariably seized as a pawn, often tortured in the husband's presence to encourage him to talk. It was with the hope of saving his wife that Souza had cut his throat.

An education specialist told me two of his friends had similarly attempted suicide. In Rio I talked to a professor who was getting a legal separation (the law does not provide for divorce) for his sister. Her husband was an active member of the underground, and the professor hoped the legal separation would save his sister if the husband was taken alive. Several others told me of legal separations for similar reasons.

In Recife, I put together the facts about some students who, after having been forced out of the university, had gone to live with the peasants, with the intention of organizing them in defense of their rights. According to the *Diario da Justiça* (October, 1969), the legal office of the Seventh Military Region charged that "Elenaldo Celso Texeira, Luis Medeiros de Oliveira, João Batista Franco Drumond and Zacharias Joaquim Gomez had disguised themselves as workers at the Noruega sugar mill in Escada, Recife, for the purpose of stirring dissension and promoting class war, their intention being to overturn the government, establish a people's dictatorship, and destroy Brazil." After several weeks in custody, two of these accused, Luis and Elenaldo, were moved to a Recife hospital, still under guard. There they were visited by the archbishop of Recife, Dom Helder Camara, who immediately asked the state governor, a military officer, to hold an inquiry. It was obvious, he wrote, that Luis's condition was far more serious than two broken arms (the effect of a fall while trying to escape from the hospital). "Luis insists that, having been tortured already beyond endurance, he decided to try to escape in any way available, when he saw they were going to renew the tortures." The inquiry, the archbishop urged, should call the doctors to explain whether the marks on the bodies of Luis and Elenaldo, including those on their genital organs, could be explained as other than the result of torture. Eight months later, Luis was still in the hospital, paralyzed—apparently permanently—from the neck down. The governor's reply was still awaited.

People everywhere also stressed that right-wing terrorist organizations operated with impunity and with evident connivance of the authorities. One of their many dastardly crimes was the assassination of a young priest, Antonio Henrique Pereira, active as a youth leader in Recife. He was waylaid one night, barbarously tortured, mutilated around the head and neck, then shot three times through the brain. According to an official report of the Recife diocese, the press and radio were forbidden to report the assassination or notify the public of the mass and funeral, and there was an "excessive and provocative" presence of the military at these ceremonies. The report called for an investigation of the part played in the crime by the CCC, "our national Ku-Klux-Klan, the political counterpart of the death squad." A preliminary investigation produced several important leads, and a prime suspect was jailed. The matter was then allowed to peter out, leaving the suspect in jail without trial. A similar crime by guerrillas brings into immediate play the entire, highly efficient, investigative apparatus of the state.

Brazilians universally believe that the United States is responsible for the torture, not simply in the sense that the regime is its puppet and incapable of independent survival, but more directly as the one who trains the Brazilian police and prescribes this technique of pacification. "It is not our style at all," they comment wryly. "This government has a non-Brazilian efficiency at every level, from tax gathering to torture, which is for us conclusive evidence of the omnipresent American know-how." According to the report of the United States committee already cited, since September, 1969, "United States security agents flood Brazil. Mass arrests, terror and tortures of political prisoners are conducted in a volume and brutality far exceeding the wanton brutality of Cuba under Batista." In August, 1970, an Italian Catholic magazine, *Il Regno* of Bologna, published a report from its correspondent who testified that he was one of a group of political prisoners who had been tortured "by Brazilian police and an unknown group of people who spoke only English." It is possibly significant that two of the instructors at the Belo Horizonte class in torture described above have non-Brazilian names, Lieutenant Haylton and Sergeant Rangel. Not less pertinent is the information published after the assassination by Uruguayan guerrillas of the United States police adviser, Dan Mitrione, also in August, 1970. A former chief of the Uruguayan secret police was reported in the press as saying that he had resigned rather than accept Mitrione's use of "violent methods of repression and the use of torture." That the police with whom Mitrione worked as an adviser in Uruguay were in fact using torture as "a normal, frequent and habitual occurrence" was confirmed by a committee of seven of its members named by the Uruguayan Senate. Before being assigned to Uruguay, Mitrione had worked as an internal security expert in Belo Horizonte and Rio de Janeiro.

Brazil has now acquired the characteristics of a colonial fascist state as described in an earlier chapter by Helio Jagaruibe. It is using "technical control processes" to reconcile the conflicting policies of economic modernization and the preservation of political and social immobility; and it has achieved "the tightest possible economic and political integration of the country into the Western system, under United States leadership." The "technical control policies" include, in addition to the systematic use of torture and other forms of oppression, the abolition of the rule of law, the destruction of intermediate organizations between the individual and the state, including trade unions, political parties and student associations, and an elaborate program of brainwashing through the media of communications and the education system. This program was formalized in 1970 by a decree-law imposing two hours of instruction per week in "moral and civic education" in public and private schools, from first grade through university. The program is controlled, not by the education department, but by a newly created entity, the National Commission of Morality and Civism, headed by General Moacir de Araujo Lopes. This commission started its operations by giving public notice that all guides, charts, manuals, anthologies, and other printed materials intended for use in the courses of moral and civic instruction must first be censored by the commission "to ensure that they do not conflict with the doctrines contained in the decree-law." It is preparing special training programs for teachers of morality and civism, plus crash courses for teachers already graduated. As a temporary measure, the school principal can designate a suitable teacher, being personally responsible for the ideological orthodoxy of the one he chooses. Details of the fulfillment of the program, including reports on the performance of each student, must be reported to the commission. This will permit the creation of a national register establishing the political and social attitudes of every school and college graduate. Significantly, the first text approved by the commission, and the only one generally available in schools in mid-1970, was authored by Plínio Salgado, an active Nazi sympathizer during World War II, and now proponent of a system based on Nazi-Fascist principles which he calls "Integralism."

Only the church survives in Brazil as a social institution not dominated by the dictatorship. For reasons explained in an earlier chapter, however, it offers no immediate threat. On the contrary, the major sentiment within the church is strongly in favor of the policies calculated to preserve the traditional structures. Orders of nuns engaged in operating schools for the children of the rich are completely convinced that everything in Brazil is perfect "ever since we got rid of Goulart," as one mother superior expressed it to me. "Castelo Branco [the general who masterminded the 1964 coup and succeeded Goulart as president] was such a good man. He frequented the sacraments and did everything to facilitate the work of the sisters. His successors have been equally fine people and cooperative. Several of our sisters are closely related to ministers and army officers. They are our friends. The government is doing the most marvelous job for the country. The ministers are absolutely honest and poor. It isn't fair to criticize them for the bad conditions in the Northeast. They had droughts there for months, and last night on the television it was floods. How can you blame the president for that? He is building dams as fast as he can."

Asked about conditions in a slum visible across the valley from the spacious balcony of her hilltop convent, the reverend mother showed little compassion. "You can't do anything for those people in the *favelas*. They are poor because they don't want to work. They will take a job for two days, then stay away the third day to rest and drink their pay. We offer the girls good jobs as domestics but they prefer to be prostitutes. They say that is the only way they can make enough to educate their children. But they neither want to leave the *favela* or to improve their living conditions in it."

Such nuns and the upper-class society whose attitudes

they reflect are strongly anti-communist. They identify all opposed to the regime as communist subversives. At the same time, antipathy to the United States is traditional, "The Americans are interested only in getting a profit from everything they do," was how one nun formulated what she felt to be the common attitude. "President Kennedy saw this, and that is why they killed him." In the long run, that antipathy may prove significant, but two other elements in the reverend mother's evaluation account more for today's dominant attitude of the church to the regime. She is institution-oriented. What counts is attendance at church and "facilitating the work of the sisters." She has a class identity. "They [the army officers] are our relatives and friends." These same two factors weigh heavily with most churchmen. Of the country's 250 Catholic bishops, probably not more than thirty share the social concerns expressed in Pope Paul VI's encyclical on development and in the Medellín Statements. Most of the others are bureaucrats, of limited education and ability. They have generally restricted their protests to situations in which the interests of the institutional church were directly involved. Or they have formulated their criticism in terms which leave a question as to the direct involvement of the government, as when Cardinal Eugenio Sales of Salvador in January, 1970, denounced "the terrorism, the torture of prisoners, and the assassinations carried out by the so-called death squads." The regime has also moved carefully. The Brazilian Society for the Defence of Tradition, the Family, and Property, a rightist group with strong financial backing, is used to spread rumors and libels in the controlled press against progressive leaders. Head-on collisions with troublesome bishops are avoided. Instead, priests and laymen close to them are harassed and imprisoned until they take the hint and lower their voices.

Dom Helder Camara, archbishop of Recife, is spokesman for the small surviving opposition. A diminutive 130-pounder, with an impish smile and a broken front tooth that helps to identify him with the typical member of his flock who never sat in a dentist's chair, he lives and works in the sacristy of an old, rundown church, has neither servants nor automobile. His bed is in a crypt under the main altar. At sixty, he still writes poetry, brief expressions of his fragility, his defenselessness and his staying power.

> When I was young
> I loved to wander
> among mountain peaks.
>
> Why, I asked myself,
> when I saw a gap between two peaks,
> why not jump right over?
>
> And all my life,
> clutching an angel's hand,
> I have done just that,
> precisely that.

For a time, he exerted considerable leverage within Brazil. His personal dynamism and charm, combined with the international reputation he gained as a spokesman for the Third World at the Second Vatican Council, enabled him to influence the tone of national episcopal statements. He inspired the criticism of the Institutional Act No. 5 formulated by the bishops' central committee in February, 1969. The act, they said, "permits arbitrary actions, including violation of such basic human rights as self-defense, legitimate expression of opinion, and the right to be informed; it threatens the dignity of the person, both physical and moral." But his impact on Brazilian opinion, as noted earlier, has been greatly reduced by the simple expedient of denying him access to the communications media.

The very existence of such a man, nevertheless, has a certain potential dynamic. By word of mouth the news travels that he continues unsilenced in his own diocese, at the meetings of the National Conference of Bishops, and around the world. He himself is convinced that the good news he announces in other countries cannot, in this age of all-pervading communications, be kept forever from the Brazilian people. And his boundless energy carries the prophetic voice of the world's poor in ever widening circles.

In 1970 alone, he ranged through Canada, the United States, France, Belgium, Sweden, Switzerland, Japan, Australia, and New Zealand, honored everywhere as a man of truth and vision. "A few years back," wrote a Paris magazine[4] in June, 1970, "a maximum of 2,000 Parisians came to hear Dom Helder Camara when he spoke in the French capital. But last month, no fewer than 10,000 jammed the Sports Palace for his Appeal to the West; and many more thousands who couldn't get in listened in nearby streets. The story was the same in Marseilles, Orleans, Louvain—in every European city visited by the archbishop of Recife. And in addition, most of his listeners on every single occasion were people under the age of thirty."

What Dom Helder is preaching is a coherent and rounded program of revolution. As he formulated it for me when I visited him in May, 1970, it starts with a critical analysis of the United States. Twice in our lifetime, he said, the world asked the United States to save it; and twice the United States fought a war to save the world. "It is very easy to understand that, after having twice expended such effort to save the world, one might think of oneself as the savior of the world." And, in fact, he says, the United States did assume this role of world savior when it issued the Cold War challenge to Russia. All the power structures of the country were mobilized: the Pentagon, big business, the politicians, and the scientific community as represented by the university research institutes. Latin American armies were given a new role. National war colleges, organized by the Pentagon, taught the higher officers to believe that they had broken through to a level of knowledge not shared by any other group in the nation. "The war college has all the answers; better economics than the economists, more understanding of music than the musicians. It is geared to give quick answers. You press a button, and a card jumps out. What is worse, it has fed an oversimplified poetic philosophy: a world divided into two camps—a capitalist camp with a monopoly of all values, of honor, justice, love, patriotism, religion, everything with a positive content; on the socialist side, all the countervalues. A tragic consequence of this narrow, partial, simplistic anti-communism is that it forbids modification of structures, no matter how distorted. Even marginal changes might let communists and other subversives infiltrate. There has been lots of talk. Basic reforms were demanded as a precondition for the late, lamented Alliance for Progress. But the result was help and maneuvering space for powerful employers to became richer and stronger, so that in their generosity they might share a little of the extra wealth with their collaborators."

Even if the poor countries "have nothing to expect from capitalism or even from neocapitalism," in Dom Helder's view, it does not automatically follow that they should turn to the socialist camp. Soviet Russia has shown itself at the United Nations Conference on Trade and Development (UNCTAD) "as cold and egoistic" as the United States. In addition, he dislikes its rejection of pluralism, the imposition of its own specific model on its junior partners. It flattened Hungary and Czechoslovakia in turn, and Yugoslavia's ability to survive the death of Tito is problematic. And still more serious is its "non-rational dogmatism," its elevation to the level of a scientific finding—like the law of gravity—of its doctrine of dialectic materialism.

For this reason, Dom Helder does not see the Cuban solution as the one to follow even if other Latin American countries could imitate it (which he doesn't think possible). "I respect Cuba's effort. I always protest against the discrimination which forces us in the rest of Latin America to act against our sister, Cuba, a discrimination which has forced us against our will to excommunicate her. But Cuba is not for me a solution. Its only way out of capitalist oppression was to pass from the United States orbit to that of Soviet Russia. It is still a slavery; a mere change of masters."

While he approves of neither side, Dom Helder agrees with the many other Latin Americans who think one is worse than the other. Capitalism offers nothing, but socialism's potential is far from exhausted. "I believe we can have a socialism truly respectful of the human person. What will be its shape? That is our problem. We have to use the experience of others, but must find our own way, one suited to our psychology, to our soul as a people."

Dom Helder, however, has no illusion that any country will be allowed to practice this socialism in freedom until men agree to deal with the issues on a world scale. "The structural changes we need require a change in the structures of the rich countries. They are at the root of the problem of the poor and responsible for it." As to the likelihood of such change, he is more optimistic than most Latin Americans. For all his criticism of its present role, he admires the United States. "Your history is one of the world's finest," he says. "Your forefathers gave up everything for freedom—freedom to believe, freedom for their children." He is hopeful that Americans will come to recognize that current policies threaten that freedom. "Your press freedom is extremely relative. The freedom of the president is relative. What happens when he tries to close bases, to cut the size of the armed forces, to reduce the military budget? At Georgetown University fifteen years ago, I asked how long the Pentagon would take orders from the White House or from Congress, and all I got was a smile which said that the United States is not a banana republic. Who's smiling now? When I read *Seven Days in May,* which was a best selling novel and a hit play and movie, I realized that the hypothesis of a military dictatorship in the United States is not all that absurd. See what happened in the universities. Faced by the challenge of students seizing buildings, the university authorities call for martial law. That really frightened me. If the psychologists, sociologists, and educators cannot read the signs and anticipate the problems of the students, if in an emergency they have no better solution than force, what kind of example are they giving the government of the country? If one day the general situation in the country creates a similar challenge, there is the example of the universities to encourage it to reply with all the force at its disposal."

The analysis of Brazil's military dictatorship is equally precise. It is for Dom Helder strictly counterrevolutionary, a creature of the predatory international capitalism which holds Latin America in colonial underdevelopment. "We do not have a true revolution here. What we had in April, 1964, was a coup d'état, and in December, 1968, there was a second coup within the first. Revolution calls for a rapid and profound change, and that is precisely what is absent. Their anti-communist obsession makes them fear to touch the structures. They believe that the eyes of the masses can be opened faster than they know how to introduce reforms, and the dilemma terrifies them. So all they do is suppress every influence that might open people's eyes. Those of us who have the courage to talk about conscientization and the development of men into rounded human beings are denounced as subversives and communists."

Should one try to work with them? I asked. "I do not think it possible," he continued, "for the church—and that is what I am talking about—to collaborate with the present Brazilian government. I think it would be a serious mistake, because the government is in an impasse. Really valid change cannot be made without the participation of the people, and this it rejects because of its anti-communist obsession. For the same reason, it will never admit the need for basic change in the conditions of our international trade, particularly our trade with the United States. To challenge this relationship is, for it, to favor the communists."

At the same time, the archbishop is not ready to take to the hills. "To opt for underground activities and armed violence shows a lack of political realism. I am not even talking about my personal theoretic pacifist position, simply of the hopeless imbalance. Our situation is not like that of France under the Nazi occupation, at least not yet. There you had a unity against the oppressor which we have not achieved. In addition, there was a level of outside support not available here. I know that people talk about Cuba, but I am sure that the United States will not let itself be taken by surprise a second time in this hemisphere. The Pentagon has taught our satellite governments how to train a sophisticated network of anti-guerrilla troops. They are ready to swoop in any kind of emergency."

A pacifist, Dom Helder is also an activist, but what he can do in Brazil is limited. "It is forbidden, at least in practice, to meet as groups in public. Besides, if I were to challenge the government frontally, it is most unlikely that as a bishop *I* would be jailed. But *my people,* priests and laity, particularly the poorest of the laity, would suffer, would be imprisoned, would be tortured." And even that suffering would be of doubtful value. "When a man is imprisoned here on political charges, you can't believe what the press says about him, or even what he says himself. Even prison becomes an anti-sign when forced confessions and distorted reports give rise to scandal and divisions."

Brazil, nevertheless, does not exist in a vacuum. Censorship slows the flow of knowledge but cannot stop it completely. The process of developing the self-awareness of the poor countries flows across its borders, a process to which Dom Helder himself contributes in his constant voyaging. Like Nelson Rockefeller, he does not exclude the possibility that the armed forces will some day grow discontent with the limited role assigned them by the Pentagon and switch from their pretorian function to a nationalistic one. Like Martin Luther King, who is one of his heroes, he has a dream. "It is within the bounds of imagination that the military of Brazil will reach the point of realizing that what is good for the United States is not necessarily good for Brazil or for Latin America; that they can come to see the stupidity of selling for progressively lower prices and buying for progressively higher prices. And if all our Latin American peoples, including the military, learn to identify the oppressor system which determines those prices, then I believe we will be able to agree on a continental integration in order to end both internal and external imperialisms. We will do this, not to establish a new imperialism of our big countries over the smaller ones, or not to escape from the world community, still less to fall into a new orbit. We simply must make ourselves strong so that we can participate as equals in mankind's task of creating a just world."

The process of creating worldwide awareness of the need for social reform is being dialectically promoted by the Brazilian regime's policy of expulsion of its own intellectuals, as well as of foreigners who express criticism or engage in educational or organization activities regarded as subversive. The latter include Peace Corpsmen from the

United States and the similar organizations from Canada and Europe, as well as missionaries. Brazil in the second half of the 1960s saw the same radicalization of young missionaries from Europe and from North America as did the rest of Latin America. As already noted, the change particularly affected the North Americans. Formerly pragmatic and convinced that hard work and planning could bring progress within the existing order, they began to ask more radical questions. Usually a year or two in a slum setting effected a total identification with the cause of the poor conceived in terms of class struggle.

Following promulgation of Institutional Act No. 5 in December, 1968, scores of the most outspoken of the foreign missionaries were expelled. Those who remain, reduced to silence, have dug in for a long siege. Like most Brazilians, they do not think that either of the developments projected by Dom Helder will easily or quickly come to pass. And they know that the evolution about which the regime itself speaks from time to time is even less realistic. It can move only toward more repression, as is demanded by repression's own intrinsic logic. "We are entering today on twenty years of neo-Fascism," F. C. Santiago Dantas, a former foreign minister of Goulart, told Alceu Amoroso Lima in 1964.[5] No reason to revise that judgment has since appeared. The repression can continue to escalate for as long as the United States is willing to feed it.

9

AFTERTHOUGHTS

Far from its stereotype of siestas and fiestas, Latin America is caught up in a grim struggle for survival as part of the civilized world. The prospects are terrifyingly negative. The gap between it and the developed nations to the north, against which it must measure its material well-being, grows wider each year. One figure quoted earlier dramatizes that process. A typical person in a developed country increases his real income $110 every year; $2.20 in an underdeveloped country. The gap widens by $107.80.

But $2.20, if not much, is something. Doesn't it mean that the average Latin American is a little better, that he has something to hope for, something to encourage him to try harder? Actually, no. The same gap-widening process which occurs between developed and underdeveloped countries is repeated internally in the poor countries. In international commerce, the rich and powerful progressively bend the terms of trade in their favor. They determine the prices at which they sell their manufactures and buy raw materials. In control of their production processes, they adjust rapidly to the fluctuations of demand in a way not available to the producer of raw materials. The rich nations thus monopolize the benefits of technology. Similarly, within the poor nations, the modern sector monopolizes the benefits of technology. The small annual improvement in the gross national product is concentrated in this sector, 20 percent or less of the entire population. The average man in Latin America is not a little better off each year. He is a little worse off.

Progress has brought roads, bicycles, sewing machines, aluminum cooking utensils, toothpaste, transistor radios, and Coca Cola to the Latin American countryside. Industrial consumer products help to make life better for those who have the money to buy them, but their social impact is negative. They achieve no increase in the per capita output of goods and services in the area they reach. The time they save for their users cannot be employed productively where there is already an excess of labor. On the contrary, they increase unemployment by displacing local artifacts. In addition, the money that pays for them is transferred from the rural to the urban sector, thus increasing rural pauperization by a progressive outflow of wealth with no wealth-producing return.

Official statistics speak of unemployment of 20 percent or higher. When one adjusts for such obvious forms of concealed unemployment as lottery vendors, bootblacks and itinerant vendors of vegetables, the figure goes above thirty. And we are not yet at the reality, because all business activities involve a deeper level of concealed unemployment. Scores of clerks make up accounts and bills which one machine could handle more efficiently and accurately. Stores employ three or four times the economically optimum number of assistants. Half the number of workers could easily maintain the present level of economic activity, and the excess of labor over real needs increases year by year. This surplus labor, increasingly concentrated in the para-city slums, represents an albatross around the neck of the productive sector, an albatross whose insatiable appetite adds constantly to its weight. It becomes more demanding as it grows, more threatening, more frightening.

People living in economically developed countries with an approximate balance between labor supply and demand have difficulty in understanding that all this unemployed labor is not surplus to the economic system of Latin America. That system has survived for four hundred years precisely because of the peon labor which costs nothing to produce or maintain, providing for itself at a subsistence level, very much like wild cattle or horses, always available according to need. Of course, the principle is not essentially different from that governing the employment of Chicanos in the southwest of the United States, or of blacks both in the rural South and industrial North. They are cushion sectors, to be utilized when the economy needs extra labor, and to take the shock when the economy contracts. In the United States, however, a dynamic economy has left only a small and declining proportion of the work force in the marginal situation; in Latin America, the surplus has gotten out of control and threatens to smother the system.

One of the first Latin American leaders to be concerned by the threat to political stability of the urban slum dwellers was Juan Peron, dictator of Argentina from 1945 to 1955. But his policies only accentuated the problem by favoring the urban industrial proletariat at the expense of the agrarian proletariat, thereby increasing the rate of population movement from the interior to the cities. Argentina is the most highly urbanized country in Latin America, with more than a third of its people in Greater Buenos Aires and only 30 percent in rural areas. Peron, however, failed to maintain a rate of growth of urban industry to match the influx of labor. At first, he built much low-cost housing. Later, he settled for high walls along the highways to hide the squatters. The rate of influx to Argentina's cities is today lower than that to cities in other countries of Latin America, because of the lower percentage of rural population. But the total number of slum dwellers is a substantial proportion of the country's twenty-four million inhabitants. Squatters alone are estimated to number two million, and many others, who are technically not squatters because they have some title to their dwelling, live no differently.

The outbreaks of violence in the black urban communities in the United States, starting with Harlem in 1964, and peaking in Newark and Detroit in 1967, were followed by the publication of plans in Argentina, Brazil, Venezuela, Colombia, and elsewhere, for the elimination of substantial concentrations of squatters in and close to their big cities. The proposals were all worded in practically the same language, and they were closely tied in with the foreign aid programs, strongly suggesting a common policy developed by Washington in the interest of law and order.

The Argentine government announced its intention of moving a quarter of a million squatters over a seven-year period, building 8,000 houses each year to accommodate them, with the rent of the new houses adjusted to the income of the occupants. Before being given their new homes, however, the squatters were to spend six months in transitory housing, where they would be taught how to live humanly, thus guarding against the danger that the new locations would deteriorate rapidly to the slum level of the old. By early 1970, fifteen transitory areas had been constructed, each holding 150 to 200 families. The houses are of a barracks type, put together with flimsy materials appropriate for temporary accommodations. The military move into a squatter camp and mark the houses to be eliminated the following week. On the appointed day, the armed soldiers return, load the people and their belongings on trucks, then flatten the shacks with bulldozers. Before admission to the transitory housing, people and belongings are sprayed with DDT. The new locations have been planned so as to facilitate police control of the inhabitants. Many are fenced like internment camps, and all have controlled entrances and exits, with federal police or military personnel in charge. Several lie within military areas. Five to 7 percent of the inhabitants are paid by the police as watchmen and supervisors, but no provision has been made for jobs for the others. In addition, nothing has been done about the permanent homes to which the people in these intermediate areas are supposed to move after six months. What seems to be developing is a technique for breaking up potentially dangerous concentrations of people into units easily controlled by the armed forces.

The concern of the public authorities at the increasing militancy of the slum dwellers is understandable. There is widespread discussion of the need to restrict the migration from the countryside to the cities, a kind of internal passport system similar to that in Russia both before and since the Bolshevik Revolution. But more and more, the supporters and beneficiaries of the status quo look to population control to restore a balance between the labor needs of the society and the supply of labor, a policy which has

Washington's enthusiastic endorsement. As a general proposition, it is obvious that an increase in population without a corresponding increase in economic productivity means an all-round lowering of living levels. It is equally obvious that such has been the situation in Latin America, and that the deterioration continues. The data given in the first chapter of this book, however, should also make it obvious that the present concentration on population control, while ignoring all the other factors, is doomed to failure. It is doomed, first of all, because Latin American politicians, like politicians everywhere, won't pursue energetically a policy that would cost them votes. And, as Ivan Illich has said, "only a strong man could afford simultaneously to dare traditional Catholics who speak about sin, communists who want to outbreed the United States imperialists, and nationalists who speak about colonizing vast unsettled expanses."[1]

More basically, however, as Illich and others have also pointed out, the policy will continue to fail because in the present political and social context the message cannot reach the peasants and slum dwellers. They do not believe the propaganda that says that they would have a higher living standard if they had fewer children, because they see that childless neighbors are no better off materially than they are, and less protected against illness and old age. Parents will not plan their families until they see this step as part of a program of community development, a program which they themselves control. That means social change of the kind that the United States, as well as the local oligarchs, will not permit. "Populations are mindless," says Illich. "They can be managed but not motivated. Only persons can make up their minds; and the more they make up their minds, the less they can be controlled. People who freely decide to control their own fertility have new motivations or aspirations to political control. It is clear that responsible parenthood cannot be separated from the quest for power in politics. Programs that aim at such goals are unwelcome under the military governments prevailing in South America, and such programs are not the kind usually financed by the United States."[2]

The reasons why the United States will not finance such programs must be faced sooner or later. Just as there is a mathematical limit to increase of population, so there is an economic limit to increase of repression. To control 5 million Guatemalans or 4 million Santo Domingans is a trivial burden on the United States economy, just as the control of 14 million Czechs is well within the capabilities of the Soviet Union. But our repression of 90 million Brazilians is already becoming costly, and it is illusory to imagine that 250 million North Americans could maintain any semblance of law and order thirty years from now in a Latin America whose 600 million inhabitants live in the economy that present policies are preparing for them. Even the big international companies which are today the major beneficiaries, both of their own efforts and of the contribution of the United States taxpayer, can hardly hope to operate in such circumstances.

But, it is appropriate to ask, Do we even have thirty years? How long can the deterioration continue without an explosion? In 1961, when I was writing *Latin America: the Eleventh Hour,* I thought, as did many, that the practical limit of poverty had been reached. The exposure effect of the transistor radio and other communications media had made the poor conscious of the growing wealth around them. They would insist on a steadily greater share. The reality has, however, proved more complicated. Ten years later, far more people are living in greater deprivation, and in the presence of far more outrageous wealth. Meanwhile, thanks to the training provided by United States experts in counterinsurgency, public armies and private terror squads have been successful in forcing the poor to make do with less. A Brazilian peasant woman told me in 1970 that the landowner formerly let her grow vegetables while her husband cut cane, but now "the sugar cane comes right up to the door" of their shack. Meanwhile, the purchasing power of the man's daily wage is down to 75 percent of what it was six years earlier. There seems no limit to what the poor can support. They simply develop a little less, physically and intellectually, die of hunger a little sooner.[3]

The fact that hunger affects the intellect as well as the body must be fed into the projection. Betty Cabezas of DESAL (Center for Economic and Social Development of Latin America, Santiago, Chile) reported to the Seventh Inter-American Planning Conference, in Lima, Peru, in October, 1969, that between 270 million and 300 million Latin Americans will, in thirty years, be marginal to the economy, that is to say, without opportunity for productive activity; and that between 80 million and 120 million of this group will be urbanized. With the vast majority of the inhabitants of a region living generation after generation at a subhuman level, a deterioration in the quality of the stock is inevitable. In this perspective, the science fiction projection of a Chilean sociologist mentioned earlier acquires more plausibility. One cannot exclude the possibility that the world is heading for an evolutionary mutation, with some branches of the human race reaching upwards technologically and cybernetically to a new plateau, while others are destined to become "by the end of the century, the primitives of the civilized; and in the next century, the apes of a new humanity."

As the gap between rich and poor widens, increased social tension seems to be rapidly bringing to an unmourned end the pseudo-democracy which characterized Latin America's 150 years of political independence. That pseudo-democracy was always punctuated by coups d'état and military dictatorships. Today's trend to army rule, however, appears basically different. In 1970, nearly 60 percent of the people of Latin America (which means some 155 million persons), lived under military governments, military-backed dictatorships, or governments set up by the military after the overthrow of a previous government by force of arms. Since the mid-1960s, the armed forces had seized power in Brazil, Argentina, Bolivia, Peru, and Panama; they had maintained dictators in Paraguay, Haiti, and Nicaragua; they had imposed their will in presidential elections in Santo Domingo, Guatemala, and Honduras. In Santo Domingo, the opposition was such that they had found it necessary to call in foreign troops.

Today's military dictatorships differ from those of the

past in that they no longer represent one of two contenders for power within a country that is politically undeveloped and socially stable. They reflect instead the deep social crisis that results when a politically aroused segment of the population becomes dissatisfied with its share of the national wealth. The workers of Latin America, both urban and rural, lack intermediate structures through which to channel their complaints and negotiate political compromises. In consequence, popular dissatisfaction can express itself only in disordered, negative, often antisocial activities. That is one of many reasons for endemic guerrilla activities in nearly all countries, some of them hardly distinguishable from the banditry which is the traditional outlet for the frustrations of the rural dispossessed. Even where the armed forces are sympathetic to the aspirations of the protesters, they feel it necessary to take power in order to throttle forces that threaten to speed the path of reform to the point of chaos.

Many observers liken the situation to that of the Roman Empire in the pretorian era. In Brazil and Argentina, for example, the Herodians are in full control, repressing the local populace for their own advantage and that of the imperialism of international capitalism. In Panama, Peru, and Bolivia, a nationalistically oriented army seeks to modify the structures in favor of a broader segment of society, while maintaining an unsteady equilibrium with the outside legions which forbid radical change and which they dare not challenge directly.

The Herodian process can be seen even in the countries not directly ruled by the armed forces. One obvious aspect is the manipulation of the voting process so as to limit the effective suffrage to a small minority. A study made of the hemispheric situation in 1966 showed that only 7 percent of the population had had an opportunity to vote for governments in power at that time, and that included countries like Haiti where the process had been openly rigged. Another aspect is the pressure, sometimes legal, sometimes extralegal, exerted on trade unions and other associations. In Argentina and Brazil, for example, the leadership is imposed on the trade unions by the government. The effect of all this has been to convince practically all those who seek to change the system that the only way open is violence.

The mood has been described by *Mensaje,* published by Chilean Jesuits, one of the most important and serious opinion magazines in Latin America. "Desired or feared, approved or resisted, revolution is present in every mind. And when we say revolution, we are not thinking of traditional garrison revolts or palace coups, but of something new and quite different. Almost without wanting to, we think of Russia, China, and Cuba. There is no doubt that revolutionary winds are blowing. A big and steadily growing majority is becoming aware of its power, of its misery, and of the injustice of the political, juridic, social and economic 'order' to which it is subjected; and this majority is not prepared to wait. It demands change—a rapid, profound and total change of structures. If violence is necessary, it is ready to use violence. It is the mass of the people that seeks to acquire power in order to bring into being an authentic 'common good.' Logically, this mass which wants 'revolution' takes its inspiration from the only revolutionary ideology within its reach—Marxism. To deny that 'fact' is to close one's eyes to a very obvious reality. Year by year, the population of Latin America grows by millions, but who are these millions? They are millions of men who suffer from malnutrition, who lack all education, who shelter in disgraceful shacks. These millions simply mean that each year brings an additional quota of desperation and an accompanying strengthening of determination to 'change,' come what may. This, and nothing else, is what 'Revolution in Latin America' means. It is the desperation which, by constant addition, acquires the force of a tidal wave and threatens to put an end to the 'order' which is order for few and disorder for many."[4]

This statement, published in 1962, remains unsurpassed as a description of the mood of contemporary Latin America. The only modification that the passage of time might demand would be in the suggestion that the tidal wave of desperation was approaching uncontrollable dimensions. In Latin America's evolutionary process, Brazil is the country which has moved farthest toward confrontation. As the previous chapter explained in detail, when popular pressures mounted to a danger level in the early 1960s, the grand strategy developed by the United States for the maintenance of order in Latin America was put to the test. The entire governmental system was made over. Political parties were suppressed; the courts were purged; the press was placed under censorship and multiple manipulative controls. All intermediate structures, including trade unions and student organizations, were destroyed or put under government appointed leaders. All authority was vested in the military government, including the legislative function. Army officers still subject to military jurisdiction were named to key posts in federal and state government and in state controlled industry. Popular leaders and uncooperative university professors, newsmen, and other professionals were jailed, stripped of their civil rights or exiled. A police regime equipped with advanced techniques of torture reached into every home. Short of the withdrawal of United States support—and there were no indications of such a possibility in spite of the revulsion of world opinion—the military dictatorship seems unshakable for ten to twenty years.

The success of the United States strategy in Brazil means that it will undoubtedly be applied wherever similar threats to stability arise. The process is already clearly visible in Argentina and Uruguay. When the Argentine military in 1966 ousted Arturo Illia, who had been elected president in 1963, and named General Juan Carlos Onganía to replace him, they immediately dissolved Congress and all political parties and they also closed the universities in order to purge potential opponents. As in Brazil, a quick return to "constitutional government" was promised, but instead—as in Brazil—each year has brought more repression. New controls were introduced in 1968 on all political activity, on the press, universities, and trade unions. Student riots in Cordoba, supported by the workers, were harshly suppressed. The universities suffered new purges, losing nearly a thousand professors, many of them in the exact sciences. When these professors left the country, they took with them a whole sector of technological capability which will require a generation to replace. Trade union leaders were ousted and replaced by government nominees. An army officer was named administrative head of the province of Cordoba, and heads of most other provinces were also replaced. And, as mentioned above, a start has been made on moving slum dwellers into camps where they will be more easily controlled by the police and military.

Uruguay, which used to pride itself on being the Switzerland of the Americas—democratic, egalitarian and progressive—no longer even pretends to be any of these things. During the 1960s, its neocolonial dependence on the export of raw materials (wool, meat, hides) changed its former prosperity into economic bankruptcy and social demoralization. By 1970, soldiers in battledress, with automatic weapons at the ready, guarded all public buildings and many private ones in Montevideo. Government officials and diplomats went in constant fear of assassination or kidnapping at the hands of guerrillas. Relations between the authorities and the public had deteriorated to the point that, in the already quoted words of a committee of the Uruguayan Senate, torture was "a normal, frequent, and habitual occurence," many of the victims being students and labor leaders.

The Rockefeller Report recognized one potential danger in the policy of building up Latin American armies to the point where they are the sole arbiters of vice and virtue, subversion and patriotism, in their respective countries. Having taken control of the apparatus of power in order to guarantee internal security, they may become impatient with corruption, inefficiency, and stagnation. In their eagerness to speed up economic development, they will then be tempted to use their power to enforce sacrifices on the public, and the Marxist theories which are in the air will be advanced as a justification. What Rockefeller fears is the hope of many Latin Americans. They see the military regimes in Panama, Peru, and Bolivia committed to resist United States economic and political control of their respective countries and pledged to policies which broaden the patterns of distribution of the national wealth, as the vanguard of liberation.

The success of the military regimes in Peru and Bolivia in their moves against United States interests, especially the oil companies, made a deep impression on the military in Brazil and Argentina. Argentina officers chafing under the Pentagon decision to make Brazil the kingpin of its continental security and reduce Argentina to the status of a subsatellite were particularly pleased. In the war colleges and among the junior officers of both countries, the alternatives are openly discussed. The corruption at the top levels, which has resulted from uncontrolled power, particularly on the part of officers put in charge of licence-granting departments and business activities, is known and deplored by the subordinates. Nevertheless, there are no indications of organized opposition within the armed forces. Instead, each year makes the process more difficult. Sharing collectively the odium of the public for mounting repression and torture, the military will have no choice but to stick together for self-protection.

It is premature to draw definitive conclusions from the experience of the nationalistically oriented military governments in Panama, Peru, and Bolivia, the first two dating from 1968, the third from 1969. For extrinsic reasons, one can conclude that the Panama experiment will not radically alter either the political or the socioeconomic situation. With a population of less than a million and a half, Panama is totally dependent for its existence on the Canal and the United States military and naval bases. If basic change comes, it will result less from its own efforts than from a regrouping of world lines of force. The same is probably true of Peru and Bolivia, with populations of 13 million and 5 million respectively. Both have classical colonial economies. They are totally dependent on raw materials exported to international markets over which they have no control, importing in return manufactured goods and part of their food supply. Theoretically, they might follow the Cuban model, escaping the United States orbit to be captured by Russia. The Soviet Union's prompt response to Peru's appeal to the world for aid after the disastrous earthquakes in 1970 shows that it would like everyone to think that this option exists. Its difficulties, however, in organizing an airlift halfway round the world, and its inadequate delivery on its promises, leave the question open. It is also doubtful whether the Soviet Union would count the propaganda and prestige value of such satellites worth the cost. And it is quite certain that the United States would go to extreme lengths, even to a second nuclear confrontation, to prevent another Cuba in Latin America.

So we end up in Peru and Bolivia with a stalemate. The Peruvians nationalized an oil company and some efficiently operated plantations. But they diverted the proceeds into an industrial development that will leave the country as vulnerable as ever to the international companies who dominate Peru's industry. And they continue to seek and accept foreign aid, with its multiple ties and obligations. The Bolivians also nationalized an oil company, only to find themselves stuck with the oil and compelled to make a deal that leaves them as dependent as ever on their foreign clients. Like the Peruvians, they continue to take foreign aid. Their leverage is ultimately reduced to the difference between the interests of the United States government, whose primary concern is tranquility, and those of international business, whose primary concern is profits. Time and again the distance between these viewpoints has been shown not to be very great. Meanwhile, the stalemate works in favor of the business interests. The Bolivian revolution of 1952 produced a political and social transformation far more profound than anything envisaged by the present military regime. But diplomacy, patronage, and bribery gradually undid all that had been accomplished. In May, 1965, in the presence of the United States ambassador, the Bolivian government signed decrees which denationalized the mines and ended the state monopoly on marketing of minerals. When the miners protested, Bolivian soldiers shot them down. The same process of erosion of the social gains achieved by the present military regimes of Bolivia and Peru has already started. In addition to the intrinsic inequality between the contending forces, a military regime is deeply handicapped. The generals make poor politicians. Their recipe for a country is the same as for an army—discipline, obedience, a puritanical inability to live with human weaknesses and compromises. They equate criticism with insubordination. In consequence, they curb public opinion, destroy intermediate structures in society such as trade unions and political parties, and alienate the people without whom they cannot survive. In this respect, the whole of world history is reinforced by the repeated experience of Latin America. A military regime often achieves short-term gains, but in the end the nation pays dearly for them.

Unattractive as military dictatorship is for all these reasons, it is the only transitional process which Latin American progressives see as capable of getting them out of their current satellite condition within the neocolonial system of Western capitalism. Although most would agree, for the reasons set out above, that countries like Peru or Bolivia cannot hope to make it alone, they believe that Latin America as a whole, or one of several subregions, could withdraw successfully from the system and achieve a China-type autarchy. Of the subregions, the most promising would be the southern cone, comprising Argentina, Brazil, and Chile as essential elements, to which would logically be attached Paraguay, Bolivia, and Peru. The relatively high level of industrial development of Argentina and Brazil would provide the economic basis on which to build. The distance from the United States would cause that country to feel less threatened and consequently to react more moderately than if a powerful socialist state were to emerge nearer its borders; for it is accepted as a first principle that such a state would be organized along socialist principles, and with a harsh curtailment of individual liberties during the long process of development, or as they now prefer to say, of liberation.

These conclusions emerge clearly from the profound analyses Latin Americans have been making of the root causes for the failure of all attempts to develop their countries within the existing politico-economic system. The element they single out as the most distorting is the ethos of American advertising. It converts man into a consuming machine, measuring his success by his ability to consume without regard to the quality of what he consumes or the contribution that consumption makes to his development as a man. The decision-making process is usurped by techno-crats who concentrate on the manipulation of emotions and the destruction of imagination in order to ensure that there will be purchasers for the things the society in fact produces most efficiently, thereby maximizing profits.

The assumption of the technocrats, according to Brazil-ian theologian Rubem Alves, perhaps the most brilliant Latin American analyst of this issue, is that the problem of a more human society is solved by know-how. "What we need to know, in their view, is simply how to solve certain practical problems. They take for granted that the 'what' question is already answered, and that consequently the only possible utopia for all societies is the production-con-sumption model. The ideal society is one in which everyone is transformed into a consumer: consumption is happiness." While on the surface, this attitude may seem to be purely technical, Dr. Alves shows that it is profoundly philosophi-cal in its effects. "To be a consumer, man has to wish to consume precisely what this society can produce. Man's imagination must, in consequence, be kept under strict control, so that it will always find in the goods that are offered the fulfillment of its desires. Otherwise, the system breaks down. What we have here thus seems to be a secularized form of the Augustinian theology in which man said to God: 'Command what thou wilt, and grant that which thou commandest.' It limits man to seeking detailed solutions within a system whose structural elements are unchallengeable. He may not, for example, ask what is wrong with a system which destroys the ecological balance in the world by its functioning, but only how he can slow down the ecological destruction without significant damage to the functioning of the system."[5]

In practice, the Latin American country is offered the model of the United States. This allows private enterprise, that is, the producer-distributor complex, to monopolize the media of communications and persuade the consumer reached by these media to consume those products which its technology has provided for the United States consumer —movies, bikinis, hair spray, deodorants, wigs, pornog-raphy, key clubs, and the entire range of useful, harmless and harmful goods and services, complete with tailfins and pollutants. The motivational process operates within the narrow swathe of the population which is in the market economy. It increases "needs" faster than the low wages can supply them, not only preventing savings, but encouraging debt. Capital is not accumulated at the rate needed to maintain the buoyancy of even this limited economy, demanding progressive reliance on capital from outside and an intensification of the vicious circle of dependency. That vicious circle cannot be broken until the judgmental processes are transferred from the business community to a body or bodies motivated exclusively by the public interest. They would fix the priorities for capital accumulation and investment, as also the priorities for production of the different consumer goods according to the level of needs of the different strata of society. Theoretically, this system could operate within the framework of the personal freedoms which one associates with the democratic way of life. In practice, however, no country has yet found the way to combine the two. And while today's proponents of change in Latin America insist that they are not bound by the model of China or Russia, or even of Cuba, most of them are ready to sacrifice as much freedom as may prove necessary to achieve the objective. Besides, as they quickly add, for the vast majority of us, there's nowhere to go but up. Even Cuba, in spite of the artificial difficulties deliberately created by the United States boycott, has from the outset provided a significantly higher level of goods and services for most of its people than they ever had before.

Latin Americans, accordingly, interpret liberation to mean their escape from the values of American society no less than from political and economic manipulation. It is understandable, therefore, that they should give major emphasis to the movements within the United States which challenge or seem to challenge those values—the revolt of students against the war in Vietnam (and more widely against the values of their parents), the radicalization of black movements and the confrontation of extremists with the police and the courts, the emergence of a sense of identity and group power among Puerto Ricans and

Chicanos, these last being groups with which they identify historically and linguistically. Nevertheless, while most would admit that the current challenge to the American Way of Life is stronger than ever before, few are yet prophesying its proximate demise. The challenging groups are far from a community of interest. Withdrawal from Vietnam, or even an end to the draft, would take much of the steam out of the student protests—unless, of course, we get into a similar morass in Latin America or the Middle East, an eventuality that cannot be automatically excluded. Blacks identify little with bourgeois students, and—in spite of Martin Luther King's warning and appeals—not at all with Latin Americans. Wedged between whites and blacks, Chicanos are more conscious of abrasion from the side of the blacks with whom they have more daily contact and competition. Cesar Chavez keeps insisting that this is a fight of all the poor for dignity, but nobody listens.

No matter in what direction one probes, the answer that comes back remains the same. The deterioration of the human condition in Latin America is going to continue for the foreseeable future. Each year, there will be more people, a few of whom will be better off than their parents, but most of them worse off, denied the level of food, clothing and shelter without which a man can hardly perform a human act. The mind boggles at the projections, but they are projections based on precise statistics. Under the present system, the proportion of the population of Latin America employed in industry grew from 13.7 to 14.3 percent between 1925 and 1960, while the proportion employed in agriculture fell by 50 percent. The proportion in industry is projected to reach only 17 percent by the year 2000, the needs of agriculture continuing meanwhile to fall. Between 1925 and 1960, the population doubled, from 100 million to 200 million. In 2000, it will be 600 million. The slow expansion of industrial employment coupled with the steep decline in agricultural employment forces more and more into a false tertiary sector of fictitious services. Almost half of the 600 million people in the year 2000 will be surplus to the society's labor needs and absorptive capacity.

Logic tells us something has to give. But where and

how? So far, all that shows is that each increase of pressure brings an equal and opposite application of counterpressure. Logically, that process also has an end. The time comes when so much of the system's productivity must be invested in maintaining it—in this case, in pacification and counterterror—that the policy ceases to be profitable, even to the oligarchs. While there is no indication of such a crisis as yet, this issue of terror and counterterror may prove decisive. It is the point of dynamic escalation in a generally static field of battle.

Guerrilla movements are as endemic as enteritis in Latin America.[6] Fidel Castro did not invent them. It may well have been the other way around. He is credibly stated to have been in Bogotá in August, 1949, when the assassination of a popular politician provoked an outburst of destruction and killing that gave the Spanish language a new word, the *bogotazo*. Before it spent itself, a hundred thousand Colombians had died violently over a period of several years. United States counterinsurgency experts and equipment have brought guerrilla activities under control in Colombia and elsewhere, but have not wiped them out. The "independent republics" in Colombia have been reincorporated into the nation, but the pattern is being repeated in squatter suburbs of cities in various countries. The guerrillas represent many elements. They include army officers, professional men, university students, office workers, peasants, and Indians, often with several of these categories in the same group. They get some help from Cuba, though not much, and they would continue if Cuba were at the bottom of the sea. Some are idealists, but most are driven principally by frustration and despair at the inability of their people to find any way out of their misery. Like the slave revolts in the United States during the centuries before the Civil War, the guerrilla outbreaks have been numerous and often bloody. But also like the slave revolts, they have lacked a broad strategy, a clear plan, and a power base. In consequence, they are nowhere a military threat—which is not to say that they lack importance as a symbol.

It is perhaps significant that the four men whom Latin Americans today revere as contemporary heroes and saints were all cut down in the prime of life by a bullet; two in the United States and two as members of guerrilla bands in the Andes. We cannot simply exploit their canonization by the masses; we must begin to speak to long-patient neighbors whose dreams and needs can be understood in terms of a composite of the four: John F. Kennedy, Martin Luther King, Jr., Che Guevara and Camilo Torres.

NOTES

1. A DECADE OF DEVELOPMENT

1. *Latin America: The Eleventh Hour* (New York: Kenedy, 1962 and revised edition, 1963), p. 8. Also published in German, French, and Italian editions.
2. *Colombia and Venezuela and the Guianas* (New York: Life World Library, 1965 and revised edition, 1971).
3. Ruiz is a pseudonym. "I must insist on anonymity in order not to jeopardize my work," he said. For reasons which will become clear in the course of the book, many of my informants imposed the same conditions. I have changed names and shaded identities to protect them, but without altering substantive facts.
4. Dana S. Green, ed., *Chasms in the Americas* (New York: Friendship Press, 1970), p. 62.
5. *The Challenge of World Poverty* (New York: Pantheon Books, 1970), p. 152.
6. *Abortion: Law, Choice and Morality* (New York: Macmillan, 1970), pp. 290, 163, 174.
7. *The Challenge of World Poverty* (New York: Pantheon Books, 1970), p. 161.
8. "In Latin America an egregious presence of United States economic and, occasionally, military power, and the common awareness of American subterfuge activities by the CIA and other agencies, undoubtedly tends to make even parts of the broad masses more alert and politically conscious. Such a movement then becomes anti-American and tends to take on a radical taint." Gunnar Myrdal, *The Challenge of World Poverty* (New York: Pantheon Books, 1970), p. 69.
9. *Requiem para una república* (La Paz, Bolivia: Universidad Mayor de San Andrés, 1969), p. 27.
10. Gustavo Gutiérrez and others, *Liberación* (Bogota, Colombia: Editorial Presencia, 1970), p. 10.

11. *La dependencia político-económica de América Latina* (Mexico City: Siglo Veintiuno, 1969), p. 81.
12. George C. Lodge, *Engines of Change* (New York: Knopf, 1970), p. 207.
13. Carlos Guzmán Böckler and Jean-Loup Herbert, *Guatemala: una interpretación histórico-social* (Mexico City: Siglo Veintiuno, 1970), p. 91.
14. Several such testimonies are cited in the course of this book.
15. Original poem in Spanish from which this extract is taken appeared in *Spes,* Montevideo, January, 1970. Translation by Gary MacEoin.
16. *Celebration of Awareness* (New York: Doubleday, 1970), p. 153.

2. THE PEOPLE

1. Carlos Guzmán Böckler and Jean-Loup Herbert, *Guatemala: una interpretación histórico-social* (Mexico City: Siglo Veintiuno, 1970), p. 24.
2. *Ibid.,* p. 108.
3. Gunnar Myrdal has made a similar comment about the "naïveté among conventional economists" and its impact on their work. "There is danger in economists carrying on their research while remaining ignorant of how they are conditioned by the surrounding society—and also, of course, by tradition and their personal inclinations. . . . Research, when not purged from bias, becomes opportunistic in the service of the interests of the power collectivity as commonly understood by those making up that collectivity and determining its policy choices. . . . A purge of bias from economic research will lead to policy conclusions demanding radical reforms in underdeveloped countries." *The Challenge of World Poverty* (New York: Pantheon Books, 1970), p. 441.
4. Told by Miguel Cardozo in *Vispera,* Montevideo, III, 10, May, 1969, p. 34.
5. Jean Toulat, *Espérance en Amérique du Sud* (Paris: Librairie Académique Perrin, 1965), p. 290.
6. Henry A. Landsberger, ed., *The Church and Social Change in Latin America* (Notre Dame, Ind.: University of Notre Dame Press, 1970), p. 200.
7. *Catholic Radicals in Brazil* (New York: Oxford University Press, 1970).

3. Neocolonialism

1. Carl Oglesby and Richard Shaull, *Containment and Change* (New York: Macmillan, 1967), p. 244.
2. Address to Latin American Council of Social Sciences (CLASCO), Santiago, Chile, as reported in *Mensaje,* Santiago de Chile, December, 1969, p. 633.
3. Irving L. Horowitz, ed., *Latin American Radicalism* (New York: Random House, 1969), p. 238.
4. *Ibid.*
5. *Ibid.,* p. 108.
6. See, for example, Helio Jaguaribe and others, *La dependencia político-económica de América Latina* (Mexico City: Siglo Veintiuno, 1969), p. 199.
7. Neal D. Houghton, ed., *Struggle Against History* (New York: Washington Square Press, 1968), p. 175.
8. "Una etapa conflictiva en la Reforma Agraria," in *Mensaje,* Santiago de Chile, Nos. 183–184. November–December, 1969.
9. Edmund Stillman and William Pfaff, *Power and Impotence* (New York: Random House, 1966), p. 149.
10. *La sociedad justa según Marx* (Caracas, Venezuela: Monte Avila Editores, 1968), p. 71.
11. Jordan Bishop, professor of history in Bolivia, indicates the semantic difficulty of all such summations. "The somewhat ambiguous term 'Third World' becomes less applicable than ever to Latin America: drawn ever more tightly into the spider's web, Latin America becomes simply an appendix to North American capitalism. It is not a part of the Third World, but a subordinate part of the first: the relationship of Latin American economy with that of United States capitalism is one of dependent integration." *Commonweal,* New York, XCI, 11, December 12, 1969, p. 335.

4. Indian Givers

1. Irving L. Horowitz, ed., *Latin American Radicalism* (New York: Random House, 1969), p. 240. According to John Gerassi, 86 percent of Alliance for Progress outlays are tied to purchase of United States products (Neal Houghton, ed., *Struggle Against History,* New York: Washington Square Press, 1968, p. 172). Michael Hudson, formerly a balance-of-payments analyst for Chase Manhattan Bank and now a pro-

fessor at the New School for Social Research, New York, has analyzed official figures to show that every year since 1963 the United States has recouped in the form of interest and repayment of principal more dollars than it sent abroad for Foreign Aid nonmilitary grants and loans. In 1968, repayments totaled $1.5 billion against new grants and capital outflows of $641 million, giving a net inflow of $903 million. The net inflow is growing substantially each year. (*The Bulletin,* Institute of Finance, New York University, Nos. 61–63, March 1970, p. 26.)

2. *Commonweal,* New York, XCI, 11, December 12, 1969, p. 335.
3. *Cristianismo y Sociedad,* Montevideo, 20, 1969, p. 29.
4. Senate Committee on Foreign Relations, *Colombia—A Case History of U.S. Aid* (Washington, D.C.: U.S. Government Printing Office, 1969).
5. *Le Monde,* Paris, Sélection Hebdomadaire, No. 1079, June 26–July 2, 1969.
6. Nelson A. Rockefeller, *Quality of Life in the Americas: Report of a U.S. Presidential Mission for the Western Hemisphere* (Washington, D.C.: U.S. Government Printing Office, 1969).
7. Dwight D. Eisenhower, *Mandate for Change* (New York: Doubleday, 1963), p. 422.
8. Francine du Plessix Gray, *Divine Disobedience* (New York: Knopf, 1970), p. 180.
9. See Juan A. Casasco, "The Social Function of the Slum in Latin America," in Louis M. Colonnese, ed., *Human Rights and the Liberation of Man in the Americas* (Notre Dame, Ind.: University of Notre Dame Press, 1970), p. 92. An additional detail about Pedro Mineiro's relocation can be found in *Trans-action,* September, 1969, p. 8: "Because the Brazilian government thinks Pedro doesn't know what's good for him, they brought him from his shack overlooking beautiful Botofogo Bay to Villa Alliance in handcuffs."
10. Herbert K. May, *The Effects of United States and Other Foreign Investment in Latin America* (New York: Council for Latin America, 1970).
11. *The Role of Private Investment in Latin American Economic Development,* CLA Report, V, 9, October, 1969. (New York: Council for Latin America.) It does not seem possible to reconcile the May figures with those from other sources. The Inter-American Development Bank's annual report for 1969, p. 38, says that total profits remitted for the previous year

were $3.7 billion. When one adds local taxes and profits re-
invested, this indicates a rate of profit several times higher
than the $1.3 billion average given by May.
12. *The Challenge of World Poverty* (New York: Pantheon
    Books, 1970), p. 455.
13. Leo Model, "The Politics of Private Foreign Investment,"
    Foreign Affairs, July, 1967, pp. 639–651.
14. *Correio da Manha*, Rio de Janeiro, May 3, 1970.
15. Irving L. Horowitz, ed., *Latin American Radicalism* (New
    York: Random House, 1969), p. 72.
16. Dana S. Green, ed., *Chasms in the Americas* (New York:
    Friendship Press, 1970), p. 53.

5. THE CHURCH

1. Nelson A. Rockefeller, *Quality of Life in the Americas: Report of a U.S. Presidential Mission for the Western Hemisphere*, 1969.
2. *Engines of Change* (New York: Knopf, 1969).
3. Seymour Martin Lipset and Aldo Solari, eds., *Elites in Latin
   America* (New York: Oxford University Press, 1967).
4. *Social Research*, Vol. 36, No. 2, Summer, 1969.
5. For details, see Alain Gheerbrant, *L'Eglise rebelle d'Amérique
   Latine* (Paris: Editions du Seuil, 1969), p. 191 ff.
6. David Abalos, "The Medellín Conference," *Cross Currents*,
   XIX, 2, Spring, 1969, p. 116.
7. *Documentos finales de Medellin* (Buenos Aires: Ediciones
   Paulinas, 1969), p. 50.
8. *Une Eglise en état de péché mortal* (Paris: Grasset, 1969).
9. *Documentos finales, loc. cit.*, p. 31.
10. *The Critic* (Chicago: Thomas More Association, 1967). Re-
    printed in Ivan D. Illich, *Celebration of Awareness* (New
    York: Doubleday, 1970).
11. *National Catholic Reporter*, Kansas City, Missouri, January
    31, 1968.

6. THE ARMED FORCES

1. Westmoreland speech at 8th Conference of American Armies,
   Rio, September, 1968. Spanish text in *Cristianismo y Sociedad*,
   Montevideo, VII, 19, 1969, p. 31.
2. Carlos Guzmán Böckler and Jean-Loup Herbert, *Guatemala:*

una interpretación histórico-social (Mexico City: Siglo Veintiuno, 1970), p. 180.

3. Helio Jaguaribe and others, *La dependencia político-económica de América Latina,* (Mexico City: Siglo Veintiuno, 1969), p. 17.
4. *Army Digest,* September, 1968.
5. *Washington Post,* March 13, 1970.
6. *Commentary,* New York, January, 1970.
7. Paul E. Sigmund, ed., *Models of Political Change in Latin America* (New York: Praeger, 1970), p. 139.
8. Neal D. Houghton, ed., *Struggle Against History* (New York: Washington Square Press, 1968), p. 171.
9. *Cristianismo y Revolución,* Buenos Aires, IV, 23, April, 1970, p. 37. Originally published in *Marcha,* Montevideo, December 19, 1969.

7. La Cía

1. Richard J. Barnet, *Intervention and Revolution* (New York: World Publishing Co., 1968), p. 225.
2. *New York Times,* June 8, 1970.
3. Dwight D. Eisenhower, *Mandate for Change* (New York: Doubleday, 1963).
4. *Ibid.,* p. 425. An extended account of the CIA operations in Guatemala, as well as of similar operations in Iran, Indonesia, British Guiana (now Guyana) and the Congo can be found in Barnet, p. 244 ff.
5. Dwight D. Eisenhower, *Waging Peace* (New York: Doubleday, 1965).
6. *Ibid.,* p. 613.
7. *Le Monde,* Paris, Sélection Hebdomadaire, No. 1109, January 22–28, 1970, p. 5.
8. *Requiem para una república* (La Paz, Bolivia: Universidad Mayor de San Andrés, 1969).
9. *The Lamp* (New York: Standard Oil Co. of New Jersey, Spring, 1967).
10. Louis Horowitz, ed., *Latin American Radicalism* (New York: Random House, 1969), p. 107.
11. Helio Jaguaribe and others, *La dependencia político-económica de América Latina* (Mexico City: Siglo Veintiuno, 1969), p. 196.

12. Alice Embree, in *NACLA Newsletter,* New York, Vol. 1, No. 9, December, 1967.

8. THE FUTURE PRESENT

1. American Committee for Information on Brazil, *Terror in Brazil: A Dossier* (New York, 1970).
2. *Le Monde,* Paris, Sélection Hebdomadaire, No. 1115, March, 5–11, 1970.
3. *New York Times,* July 23, 1970.
4. *Informations Catholiques Internationales,* Paris, June 15, 1970.
5. *America,* New York, June 20, 1970, p. 646.

9. AFTERTHOUGHTS

1. *Celebration of Awareness* (New York: Doubleday, 1970), p. 138.
2. *Ibid.,* p. 144.
3. The text was written before I read Gunnar Myrdal's almost identical observations. "Is there a limit to the misery human beings can bear without revolting? Or is there no such limit? The utterly miserable living conditions quietly endured by many in the rural and urban slums today would suggest that there is no such limit.

   "But would such a development stir up factions in the upper class, in the first place students and intellectuals in general? Would they be moved to raise more determined demands for radical reform? Would they back these demands by going out among the poor masses to try to educate and organize them? What success would they have? I do not know." (*The Challenge of World Poverty,* New York: Pantheon Books, 1970, p. 432).
4. *Mensaje,* Santiago de Chile, No. 115, December, 1962.
5. From an unpublished lecture delivered at Union Theological Seminary, New York, February 20, 1970. Dr. Alves has developed his ideas more fully in *A Theology of Human Hope* (Washington, D.C.: Corpus Books, 1969).
6. Luis Mercier Vega has made a documented study of guerrilla activity and effectiveness in Latin America, especially Venezuela, Argentina, Colombia, Bolivia, Guatemala, Brazil, Paraguay, and Peru, in *Guerrillas in Latin America* (New

York: Praeger, 1969). He concludes that guerrillas played a marginal part in Castro's success, that they have achieved no significant objectives elsewhere, and that the likelihood that they can play a worthwhile part in the liberation of Latin America is remote.

Selected Annotated Bibliography

Alba, Victor. *The Latin Americans.* New York: Praeger, 1969.
Immensely knowledgeable and highly readable survey, but author's interpretations are limited by his old-style "liberal" perspective.

Alexander, Robert J. *Today's Latin America,* rev. ed. New York: Praeger, 1968.
Quick and balanced introduction, in textbook style, to the complexities of the continent.

Almaraz Paz, Sergio. *Requiem para una república.* La Paz, Bolivia: Universidad de San Andrés, 1969.
Moving and illuminating account of the undoing by international business of Bolivia's 1953 social revolution.

Alves, Rubem A. *A Theology of Human Hope.* Washington, D.C.: Corpus Books, 1969.
A leading Latin American Protestant theologian shows destructive impact of the U.S. "society of consumption" on the Third World.

Arciniegas, Germán. *Latin America.* New York: Knopf, 1967.
Scholarly survey of arts, customs and the influence of ideas, providing a perspective for judging the present.

Bailey, Helen, and **Nasatir, Abraham.** *Latin America, the Development of its Civilization,* 2d ed. New York: Prentice-Hall, 1966.
Authoritative college-review survey of history, culture, economics and politics.

Colonnese, Louis M., ed. *Conscientization for Liberation.* Washington, D.C.: Division for Latin America, U.S. Catholic Conference, 1970.
Paulo Freire and other experts offer program to arouse the masses in this seventh annual volume of the series, which collectively traces progressive radicalization of church in Latin America.

De Broucker, José. *The Violence of a Peacemaker.* Maryknoll, N.Y.: Orbis Books, 1970.
First biography of the recognized leader of the progressive church movements in Latin America, Archbishop Helder Camara of Recife, Brazil.

De Castro, Josué. *Death in the North-East.* New York: Random House, 1966.
Must reading for everyone who really wants to understand what it means to be a poor Latin American by one who grew up with poverty in Brazil's Northeast.

De Madariaga, Salvador. *Latin America Between the Eagle and the Bear.* New York: Praeger, 1962.
An early analysis of the distorting impact of the Cold War on Latin America's development by one of Spain's greatest scholars.
Fagen, Richard R. *The Transformation of Political Culture in Cuba.* Stanford: Stanford University Press, 1969.
A study, both sympathetic and scholarly, of what the author calls "the most profound social transformation ever seen in the Americas."
Fals Borda, Orlando. *Subversion and Social Change in Colombia.* New York: Columbia University Press, 1969.
Scholarly, left-of-center sociologist evaluates the constructive contribution of subversion in past and present to Colombia.
Foreign Areas Studies Division, American University. *Area Handbooks.* Washington, D.C.: U.S. Government Printing Office.
Social, political and economic information, in a separate volume for each country of Latin America, updated periodically: excellent reference sources.
Galeano, Eduardo. *Guatemala: Occupied Country.* New York: Monthly Review, 1967.
An insight into motivations of guerrillas from a sensitive Argentine newsman who lived with them.
Geyer, Georgie Anne. *The New Latins.* New York: Doubleday, 1970.
Firsthand overview of contemporary scene by journalist who combines superior knowledge with sound value judgments.
Gheerbrant, Alain, ed. *La Iglesia rebelde de América Latina.* Mexico City: Siglo Veintiuno Editores, 1970.
Excellent collection of manifestos and other statements of Latin America's progressive religious leaders and movements.
Gonzáles, Luis J., and **Sánchez Salazar, Gustavo A.** *The Great Rebel: Che Guevara in Bolivia.* New York: Grove Press, 1969.
New firsthand material in this candid, authentic, well-written and sympathetic account of two Bolivian journalists.
Gunther, John. *Inside South America.* New York: Harper & Row, 1966. A quick introduction to ten republics for the nonspecialist. Tends to take official handouts seriously.
Guzmán, Germán. *Camilo Torres.* New York: Sheed and Ward, 1969.
Pedestrian but authoritative story of life and death of the priest turned guerrilla, by a close friend.
Guzmán Böckler, Carlos, and **Herbert, Jean-Loup.** *Guatemala: una interpretación histórico-social.* Mexico City: Siglo Veintiuno Editores, 1970.

Brings new and profound perspectives to the problems of Latin America's underdevelopment.

Hilton, Ronald, ed. *Movement Toward Latin American Unity.* New York: Praeger, 1969.
Symposium on all aspects and problems of integration prepared in cooperation with the California Institute of International Studies.

Horowitz, Irving Louis, ed. *Latin American Radicalism.* New York: Random House, 1969.
Excellent selections from works of continent's leading social scientists and politicians.

Ianni, Octavio. *Crisis in Brazil.* New York: Columbia University Press, 1970.
Review of political causes and results of 1964 coup reveals a fascist system depending on foreigners for survival, foresees evolution to a socialist state.

Illich, Ivan D. *Celebration of Awareness.* New York: Doubleday, 1970.
Radical critique of conventional state and church policies for Latin America by a profound thinker and scholar.

Inter-American Development Bank. *Socio-Economic Progress in Latin America.* Washington, D.C., 1970.
IADB's 1969 annual report gives a continental overview of economic and social trends, followed by brief survey of each country including latest statistics.

Jaguaribe, Helio, and others. *Le dependencia político-económica de América Latina.* Mexico City: Siglo Veintiuno Editores, 1969.
Latin American economists examine critically the developmental approaches offered by the rich nations.

Landsberger, Henry A., ed. *Latin American Peasant Movements.* Ithaca: Cornell University Press, 1969.
Well-documented accounts by recognized authorities of peasant movements in Bolivia, Brazil, Chile, Guatemala, Mexico, Peru and Venezuela.

Landsberger, Henry A., ed. *The Church and Social Change in Latin America.* Notre Dame, Ind.: University of Notre Dame Press, 1970.
Progress report by leading scholars on updating of Roman Catholic Church.

Léon, Pierre. *Economies et sociétés de l'Amérique Latine.* Paris: Société d'Edition d'Enseignement Supérieur, 1969.
A French professor summarizes 150 years of complex social, political and economic development.

Lieuwen, Edwin. *U.S. Policy in Latin America.* New York: Praeger, 1965.
A military expert documents historical and continuing pattern of U.S. interventionism in internal affairs of neighbors.

Lipset, Seymour Martin, and Solari, Aldo, eds. *Elites in Latin America.* New York: Oxford University Press, 1967.
Incisive analysis of the value patterns of various power groups in politics, the military, religion, culture, labor and peasant movements.

Lodge, George C. *Engines of Change.* New York: Knopf, 1969.
Highly optimistic evaluation of internal forces in Latin American society encouraging peaceful evolution.

Mercier Vega, Luis. *Guerrillas in Latin America.* New York: Praeger, 1969.
Documented study of continent-wide guerrilla activity, stressing its marginal impact in process of revolutionary change.

Myrdal, Gunnar. *The Challenge of World Poverty.* New York: Pantheon Books, 1970.
General evaluation of the problems of development with a specific application to Latin America.

Nehemkis, Peter. *Latin America: Myth and Reality.* New York: Knopf, 1964.
An informed and enlightened U.S. businessman believes capitalism can be made to work in Latin America.

Stillman, Edmund, and Pfaff, William. *Power and Impotence.* New York: Random House, 1966.
Shows danger of applying in Latin America tomorrow U.S. policies that have failed in Vietnam.

Szulc, Tad. *Latin America.* New York: Atheneum, 1966.
Quick but superficial once-over of Latin America, past and present.

Tully, Andrew. *CIA, the Inside Story.* New York: William Morrow, 1962.
Includes several episodes in Latin America.

Urquidi, Victor. *Challenge of Development in Latin America.* New York: Praeger, 1964.
A critique of the conventional formulas for Latin American development by a leading Mexican economist.

Veliz, Claudio, ed. *Politics of Conformity in Latin America.* New York: Oxford University Press, 1967.
An evaluation of the gap between the professed intentions and the real objectives of power structures in Latin America.

Yglesias, José. *Down There.* New York: World, 1970.
Impassioned plea to U.S. to avoid Vietnams in Latin America, based on reporting in depth from Cuba, Brazil, Chile and Peru.

INDEX

Abernathy, Ralph David, 190
AFL-CIO, 11, 172
Agency for International Development (AID): promotes contraception, 8–9; in Bolivia, 84ff.; loans untied, 86; not a Marshall Plan, 87; in Brazil, 94; benefits wealthy, 97; counterinsurgency training by, 140; CIA infiltration of, 161; political use of, in Brazil, 166. *See also* Alliance for Progress
Albrook Air Force base, 141
Alessandri, Jorge, 75
Allende, Salvador, 75
Alliance for Progress, 3, 88; housing projects, 4; failure of, 17. *See also* AID
Almaraz Paz, Sergio, 12, 171
Alves, Rubem, 220
American Institute for Free Labor Development (AIFLD), 172
Amnesty International, 192
Antonio, Julio A., 191
Arbenz Guzmán, Jacobo, 96, 164
Argentina: slums in, 4, 208; Third World priests in, 117; colonial fascism in, 146; repression grows in, 215

Army Jungle Warfare School, 141
Army School of the Americas, 140
Arroyo, Gonzalo, 76
Ayoroa, Juan, 171

Barreiro, Julio, 82
Belaunde Terry, 95
Bennett, John, 190
Bezerra, Almery, 48, 52
Bishop, Jordan, 87
Black Berets, in Chile, 168
Bolatti, Guillermo, 118
Bolivia: Indians in, 27, 30; credit unions in, 44; impact of foreign aid on, 84ff.; military regime in, 156; CIA in, 171; outlook for, 217
Brain drain, 181
Brazil, 183ff.; torture in, 14, 190; peasant leagues in, 44ff.; Movement of Basic Education in, 46; youth movements in, 48ff., 187; exile of intellectuals in, 51; impact of AID in, 94; foreign capital's penetration of, 105; repression in, 117, 187; AID's "public safety" programs in, 141; colonial fascism in, 146, 196; cost of armed forces